Contents

Foreword .... *viii*

Chapter 1   Extreme MINDSTORMS *3*

The Hackers Step In *4*
MINDSTORMS Expands *6*
RIS 2.0 .... *8*
An Extreme Future *8*

Chapter 2   The RCX *11*

Architecture *11*
Hardware *14*
Output Ports *16*
Sensor Ports *18*
LCD *25*
Sound *26*
Standard Firmware *27*
Programming the RCX *29*

Chapter 3   Seeker: A Light-Seeking Robot *31*

Construction *31*
Using the Bumper *36*
Seeking a Light *41*
Bumping and Seeking *44*
More Explorations *51*

Chapter 4   RCX 2.0 Firmware *53*

Getting Started *53*
Local Variables *56*
Display *57*
Arrays *60*
Access Control *64*
Events *68*
Bits and Pieces *76*

Chapter 5   Introduction to pbForth 79

pbForth Is Interactive 79
pbForth Is Interpreted 80
pbForth Is Extensible 80
Why Learn pbForth? 80
Why Learn about RCX Details? 81
Installing pbForth 83
pbForth Fundamentals 85
RCX Basics and Generating Output 89
Numbers and Expressions 95
Defining New Words for pbForth 101
Conditionals and Bitwise Operators in pbForth 104
Basic RCX Sensors and Motors 107
Looping in pbForth 110
Using the Pushbuttons 111
Summary 117

Chapter 6   Programming Seeker in pbForth 119

Making Seeker Move 120
Displaying Motor States 122
Making Seeker See and Feel 130
Using the Timers 138
The Light Sensor and Thresholds 141
Summary 148

Chapter 7   Introduction to LegOS 151

So Why LegOS? 151
So What's the Catch? 152
So, How Does it Work? 152
Basic LegOS Functions 156
The LegOS Seeker 170
Conclusion 180

Chapter 8   Advanced LegOS 181

Rotation Sensors 181
Sound 183
Math in LegOS 186
LegOS Network Protocol (LNP) 187
LegOS Debugging 188

Extreme MINDSTORMS™: An Advanced Guide to LEGO® MINDSTORMS™

DAVE BAUM, MICHAEL GASPERI, RALPH HEMPEL, AND LUIS VILLA

Extreme MINDSTORMS™: An Advanced Guide to LEGO® MINDSTORMS™
Copyright ©2000 by Dave Baum, Michael Gasperi, Ralph Hempel, and Luis Villa

ISBN (pbk): 1-893115-84-4

Printed and bound in the United States of America 12345678910

Trademarked names may appear in this book. Rather than use a trademark symbol with every occurrence of a trademarked name, we use the names only in an editorial fashion and to the benefit of the trademark owner, with no intention of infringement of the trademark.

Editorial Directors: Dan Appleman, Gary Cornell, Karen Watterson

Technical Reviewers: Dave Baum, Rodd Zurcher

Projects Manager: Grace Wong

Developmental Editor and Indexer: Valerie Perry

Copy Editor: Kiersten Burke

Production Editor: Janet Vail

Page Composition and water braiding: Susan Glinert

Artist and Cover and Part Opener Designer: Karl Miyajima

Distributed to the book trade in the United States by Springer-Verlag New York, Inc.,175 Fifth Avenue, New York, NY, 10010

and outside the United States by Springer-Verlag GmbH & Co. KG, Tiergartenstr. 17, 69112 Heidelberg, Germany

In the United States, phone 1-800-SPRINGER; orders@springer-ny.com; http://www.springer-ny.com

Outside the United States, contact orders@springer.de; http://www.springer.de; fax +49 6221 345229

For information on translations, please contact Apress directly at 901 Grayson Street, Suite 204, Berkeley, CA, 94710

Phone: 510-549-5931; Fax: 510-549-5939; info@apress.com; http://www.apress.com

The information in this book is distributed on an "as is" basis, without warranty. Although every precaution has been taken in the preparation of this work, neither the authors nor Apress shall have any liability to any person or entity with respect to any loss or damage caused or alleged to be caused directly or indirectly by the information contained in this work.

Trailerbot 189
Going Further with LegOS—"Use the Source, Luke!" 213

Chapter 9   Homebrew Passive Sensors 219

Getting Parts 219
Alligator Clip Quickie 220
Coin Detector 222
Cut Wire Connector 223
Stick-In-Ring Switch 224
Terminal Block Temperature Sensor 225
RCX Input 227
More Accurate Temperature Sensors 228
Waterproof Temperature Sensor 231
A Relative Humidity Sensor 232
50K Ohm Potentiometer Angle Sensor 234
Cut Electric Plate Connector 237
CdS Photocell Sensor 238
Galvanic Skin Response 240
Voltage Input Sensor 242
Battery Tester 243
A Tachometer 244
A Potpourri of Passive Sensors 245
Part Cross-reference List 246
Conclusion 247

Chapter 10 Homebrew Powered Sensors 249

Getting Parts and Tools 249
Getting Started 249
RCX Powered Interface 250
Sensor Power Circuit 250
Sensor Measurement Circuit 254
Optointerrupter Sensor 256
Buffer Circuit 258
Buffered Voltage Input 261
Amplifier Circuit 261
Amplified Voltage Input 263
Differential Light Sensor 263
Sound Sensor 266
Printed Circuit Board 271
Soldering 272
Packaging 277

Going Further *279*
Bill of Materials for Powered Sensors *279*
Conclusion *282*

Appendix A Internet Resources *283*

General Information *283*
NQC *283*
pbForth *284*
LegOS *284*
Homebrew Sensors *284*
Suppliers *284*

Appendix B NQC API Reference *287*

Sensors *287*
Outputs *289*
Sound *290*
Display *291*
Communication *291*
Timers and Counters *292*
Access Control *293*
Events *294*
Miscellaneous *296*
Special Features–RCX *296*
Special Features–Scout *297*
Special Features–CyberMaster *298*

Appendix C Frequently Used Forth Words *299*

Stack Words *300*
Math Words *301*
Logical Words *302*
Conditional Words *303*
Compiler and Memory Words *303*
Control Structure Words *306*
Input and Output Formatting Words *307*
RCX Extension Words *308*

Appendix D LegOS API Reference *317*

LCD Functions *317*
Motor Functions *318*

Sensor Functions 318
Math Functions 319
Program Control 320
Time Control 320
Hardware Control 321
Music 321
Buttons 322
Semaphores 322
LNP functions 323
Standard C Library Functions 323

Appendix E Installing LegOS 325

LegOS Installation for Debian Linux 326
LegOS Installation for Red Hat Linux 327
LegOS Installation for Windows 329

Index 333

Foreword

THIS BOOK COVERS a diverse set of topics. Consequently, it was written by a diverse set of authors. Rather than a single homogenized foreword to the book, we felt it was appropriate for each author to introduce the book from his own perspective.

Dave Baum

About midway through writing Dave Baum's Definitive Guide to LEGO® MIND-STORMS*TM*, it became clear that there just wasn't enough time and space to do justice to all of the different ways of working with MINDSTORMS. Besides, I was hardly an expert on legOS, pbForth, or sensor design. My editor, Gary Cornell, and I decided that we'd keep the first book focused on mechanical design, RCX Code, and NQC. The other topics would be postponed for a future work, possibly a collection of papers from various Mindstormers.

Following the publication of my first book, this second idea—a "topics" book—was brought to life. It was not something I could write alone, so I sought out key contributors in the MINDSTORMS community to lend their expertise: Ralph Hempel for pbForth, Luis Villa for legOS, and Michael Gasperi for custom sensors.

I led a dual role in the development of the book. As an author, I wrote the first four chapters, which covered the basic history of LEGO MINDSTORMS, general information on the RCX, and the latest developments in the RCX 2.0 Firmware. My second role was that of a coordinator/reviewer. There's a saying about being a good manager: "hire good people, then get out of the way." That was my philosophy in putting this book together. Mike, Luis, and Ralph are experts in their fields—I just had to stir the pot on occasion.

I'd like to thank my wife, Cheryl, for her seemingly endless patience. Putting this book together took a lot of time and energy, and I couldn't have managed without her support. I'd also like to thank Rodd Zurcher for reviewing early drafts of my chapters with his usual thoroughness and for making excellent suggestions for the book's improvement. Rodd also created the original 3D models for my first book, which I reused as the basis for this book's illustrations. As usual, Apress has been wonderful to work with—I can't imagine a better publisher. My deepest thanks go to Mike, Ralph, and Luis—this book was a team effort from a great team. Last, I'd like to thank my parents for not thinking I'm crazy to still be playing with LEGO.

Ralph Hempel

The story of pbForth began weeks before I actually got the RCX. I had been reading all about it on LUGNET, where other members of our online community gathered around the virtual water cooler to discuss this new product. Like many, I had been involved in discussions about making controllers for our TECHNIC creations. My opinion was that buying a controller off the shelf was probably cheaper than anything we could come up with. Most importantly, the controller should be available to all members of the community so we could share our creations. LEGO's announcement of the RCX put the discussion to an end for me—I had to get one.

Now there was the anticipation of hearing the first reports. The graphical language, while useful for almost any practical robot, did not lend itself well to more advanced applications. As an embedded systems engineer, my immediate goal was to stretch the RCX beyond its limits.

Once Kekoa Proudfoot announced that he had "cracked" the firmware in the RCX, I decided to buy one and see how much more we could do. Not long afterward, Dave Baum announced he had figured out the firmware download procedure, and it wasn't long before Kekoa had the first bit of custom firmware in the RCX. As I recall, all it did was turn on the LCD segments and beep. Then Markus Noga posted that he was working on an operating system for the RCX based on the GNU C toolchain. Finally, a real programming environment for the LEGO RCX brick was taking shape. About the same time, Dave was busy with the first versions of NQC. Of course, Mike Gasperi was busy taking apart sensors and sharing his knowledge with us.

While all of this was going on, I had fond recollections of my early days in embedded systems design. I used a little single board computer with a 68HC11 running Forth to help me understand how embedded systems worked. Before that, I had a Commodore PET and an HP41C calculator to program. I thought it might be fun to take an established Forth kernel and port it to the RCX. Forth is especially suited to embedded systems in that it has a very small memory footprint and it is relatively easy to get running on a new piece of hardware. I settled on hForth, an ANSI-compliant kernel that had all the core functions required in the standard, and the source code was available in 8086 assembler. Now all I had to do was port it to the H8 microcontroller in the RCX. In all, it took about forty hours over the Christmas holidays to get it running and posted on the Internet.

Support from the community was immediate and several individuals contributed suggestions for improvement. Over the last two years, I've had email from around the world, from young students to old-time programmers like myself. Almost all tell me that the RCX and its different software tools have rekindled the spirit of imagination that goes along with designing something that actually thinks for itself. Without the support of the LUGNET pbForth community and the regular visits and comments on my own Web site, there is no way that I would have continued to invest my time in this project. I can't imagine getting this done without the Internet and all the good things that come from sharing knowledge with others.

Speaking of time, there is no way I would have been able to write this book without the patience and tolerance of my wife Christine, and my three sons: Eric, Owen, and Graham. I've often read acknowledgements like this and glossed over them without realizing the tremendous load that writing even a few chapters in a book puts on the people surrounding the author. Now I know better.

I would also like to thank Gary Cornell at Apress and Dave Baum, our fearless coordinator, for giving me the opportunity to contribute to this book. After meeting Kekoa, Dave, Mike, Markus, and other LUGNET members at the MIT Mindfest in 1999, my suspicions regarding online communities were confirmed. They are all first-class individuals and fun to be with. Dave also suffered gracefully through my inability to get things done on time, prodding me along when I got stuck and giving me encouragement whenever it was needed. Thanks again, Dave.

Michael Gasperi

I work as a research engineer for Rockwell Automation, a company that makes, among other things, industrial computers like the RCX, called programmable controllers. I was looking through a Business Week magazine in early October of 1998 when I noticed a little article about the LEGO MINDSTORMS kit. I thought it would be great to use this kit to show my daughter Audrey, who was seven at the time, the kind of stuff I do at work. So I bought one on the way home that day.

Everything went fine for a couple of nights while we watched the little video and went through the tutorials. However, when we got to the Challenges section or tried to think up a new robot design, I realized she didn't have the patience for the tinkering process of making something like that. I began to look around on the Web to see what other people were doing with the kit and I quickly realized that many were trying to reverse engineer the RCX. Just about everybody had piled in on hacking software and a few were disassembling hardware. People were figuring out bits and pieces daily. Their spirit of discovery was very addictive.

I set the RCX down on my workbench at home and started to make measurements and reverse engineer the sensor inputs. After a while, I figured how they worked and began to contribute to the flow of emails. My problem was that the language of hardware was schematics and diagrams, but I didn't want to attach images to emails. So I started to publish simple Web pages to share the schematics.

Early on, I attached a Web page hit counter. Now, I don't know much about Web publishing, but I saw that every time I loaded the page, the counter went up by one. Funny thing is, sometimes the counter went up by two or three. If I didn't touch it for an hour it went up by twenty, and over a day it went up by almost one hundred! I realized that a lot of people were looking at this stuff. As of this writing, the Web page has had tens of thousands of hits. I know this is tiny compared to a commercial site but it is thousands more than I could have ever dreamed.

One of the most amazing things that happened to me because of this site was being asked to speak and give tutorials at Mindfest. I was billed as an Extreme

Mindstormer! The truth is, practically everyone who attended the conference was an Extreme Mindstormer in some way or another. This book is an attempt to document some of the extremes more thoroughly than can be provided in a simple Web page or during a short tutorial.

It is impossible to recognize all of the people who have contributed to my sensor chapters. Certainly my dad is responsible for my interest in electronics and my curiosity for how things work. Russ Nelson and Todd Lehman deserve recognition for creating the forums through which the original discoveries were shared. Finally, I want to thank Forrest Mims and W. Grey Walter for inspiring me to tinker seriously. I hope that in some way this book inspires you to tinker seriously as well.

Luis Villa

Since I'm still a year short of graduating from college, my focus on legOS has been a strongly educational one. When I first started using it, the point was to find a way to make the RCX easy for fellow Duke CS students who already knew C and wanted to do "serious" programming, which really couldn't be done at that point in anything other than legOS. I quickly discovered that it wasn't that simple: with an unintuitive API, the only way to learn it quickly was for someone to document it, which hadn't yet been done. In tackling that, I was in the right place at the right time. What started as simple notes for my independent study turned into success beyond my wildest dreams (50K+ hits): The legOS HOWTO Web page. The opportunity to contribute to Extreme MINDSTORMS was the last logical step in that educational process: when Dave asked me to write a couple chapters of the book, it took all of thirty seconds to say yes. Hopefully, what I've collected here will help a new group discover the power of legOS and spread it to a wider audience.

Of course, I'd be lying if I said that the educational aspect of this was entirely one way: I've learned a ton too. I've learned a great deal about why CS majors hate documentation, though I know that the experience of having to think through the code of others (and lots of it) will make me a better programmer. Of course, it is also a pretty safe bet that when I finally take an Operating Systems class in the fall, I'll be the only one in class who will have already coordinated the release of an OS. More important (to me) in the long run, is that through legOS, I've had wonderful working relationships with Italians, a German, Colombians, a British colleague, a Belgian, and of course, the other authors of this book. That kind of interchange of ideas has been a unique and invaluable experience to me. When my children ask me what it was like in the early days of the Internet, I will answer by telling them the story of legOS. Then, of course, they'll laugh because I'll have mentioned keyboards, robots that didn't teach themselves English, and other such anachronistic things.

I'd like to thank a bunch of people who contributed in many different ways to my experience with this book: My parents and grandparents, because the dedication just isn't enough. My brother, because he's a good guy (despite me arguing otherwise for his first sixteen years.) Krissa, for loving me despite (heck, maybe because of) the growing evidence that I really don't want to grow up. Besides my loved ones, I must also thank Professor Michael Littman who was the first to allow me to fulfill a childhood dream to get paid to play with LEGO. It's not just that he scraped up some money to pay me, but that he allowed me to teach others what I had learned. I truly appreciate that opportunity. I can't mention Prof. Littman without thanking the kids in Duke CPS 196 who could have (and should have) killed me for saying, "I don't know why the robot does that" at three in the morning, six hours before an assignment was due. I also thank Dave, who somehow saw through the broken links and bad style of the HOWTO and believed I could pull this off. His faith (and his occasional, "I need this chapter NOW!") was important in convincing me I could do this. Finally, of course, I owe the entire legOS community, especially Markus, a huge debt of thanks. There are (as of this writing) nineteen different names in the CONTRIBUTORS file in legOS. Without their unique contributions, legOS, as I know it, (and as you will soon) would be impossible.

MINDSTORMS

Dave Baum

Part One

CHAPTER 1
Extreme MINDSTORMS

IN 1949, GODTFRED KIRK CHRISTIANSEN began producing the early forerunners of LEGO bricks—Automatic Binding Bricks. A few years later they became known as "LEGO bricks," and in 1958 they took on the stud-and-tube design that has remained to this day. Throughout the 1960s and 1970s the bricks started appearing in new sizes and shapes, along with some decidedly non-bricklike pieces, such as hinges and wheels.

In 1977, LEGO launched the Expert Builder series of sets (later renamed to TECHNIC). Featuring gears, axles, beams, bushings, and even universal joints, these sets could create models that actually *worked*. Helicopters had adjustable rotors, cars had rack-and-pinion steering, and engines had pistons that moved. These sets brought a new level of engineering sophistication to the LEGO universe. Over the years, new elements continued to be introduced: spring-loaded shock absorbers, pneumatic pistons and valves, and numerous structural and connector pieces. All of these pieces interlocked with one another making LEGO the most versatile construction system in the world.

In the fall of 1998, LEGO released the first MINDSTORMS set—the Robotics Invention System (RIS 1.0). To some, this was just another step in a journey that had started nearly 50 years earlier. To others, however, this was a revolution. There were still all of those familiar beams, bricks, and gears. But there was also the RCX— LEGO's programmable brick that allowed models not just to move, but to sense and respond to their environment. RIS 1.0 became an instant hit and was one of the hottest selling toys for the 1998 Christmas season. More surprisingly, a significant portion of the "kids" playing with MINDSTORMS were adults.

It seemed to be a long-overdue merging of construction toy and computer. Actually, the idea of merging LEGO with computers wasn't new. For years, researchers at the MIT Media Lab (http://www.media.mit.edu/), sponsored in part by LEGO, had been experimenting with programmable toys and the educational opportunities they presented. In the course of this work, several different *programmable bricks* were developed. LEGO decided to make a commercial product based on the research and the RCX was redesigned from the ground up. Even so, the early programmable bricks from MIT could certainly be considered ancestors of today's MINDSTORMS sets.

The Hackers Step In

LEGO's software was intended to provide an intuitive introduction to programming. However, many of the MINDSTORMS users were experienced programmers who felt that LEGO's simple drag-and-drop environment was too limiting. LEGO was tight-lipped about the details of the RCX, but that didn't prevent me and others from taking matters into our own hands.

Several of us endeavored to unravel the secrets of the RCX and expand its capabilities. Our independent efforts may never have amounted to much if Russell Nelson had not created the LEGO-robotics mailing list. Russell also culled through all of the postings and collected the most interesting tidbits into his *LEGO MINDSTORMS Internals* Web site (http://www.crynwr.com/lego-robotics/). These two resources, the mailing list and the Web site, greatly facilitated our sharing of knowledge and allowed newcomers to also join in the adventure. Eventually, the LEGO-robotics mailing list was merged with the robotics forum at LUGNET (http://www.lugnet.com/robotics/), run by Todd Lehman. LUGNET is the unofficial repository for all things LEGO and the robotics discussions can be particularly valuable to MINDSTORMS users.

Kekoa Proudfoot was the first pioneer into RCX hacking and did a substantial amount of reverse engineering. He revealed many details about the hardware, published a list of bytecodes for the interpreter, and documented the System ROM (see Chapter 2 for more information). His *RCX Internals* Web site (http://graphics.stanford.edu/~kekoa/rcx/) contains a wealth of valuable information about the inner workings of the RCX.

At about the same time, I was working towards creating a more "traditional" way of programming the RCX. Starting with old source code to a C preprocessor and a rudimentary understanding of the RCX bytecodes, NQC—the first unofficial programming language for MINDSTORMS—was born. Looking back, it was pretty crude. No local variables. No expressions. No functions. Just a preprocessor, tons of macros, and some code to send the resulting bytecodes over to the RCX. It was, however, a way to write an RCX program with text rather than with graphics; furthermore, it had a very C-like syntax. What started life as an interesting little hack so I could program the RCX from my PowerBook became a popular way for "advanced" users to play with MINDSTORMS. Features were gradually added to NQC to make it more powerful. However, since it relied on LEGO's standard firmware, there were always some fundamental limitations, such as a very small amount of storage for variables and no recursive functions.

Other people were striving to break through those limitations by replacing the standard firmware. Starting with Kekoa's documentation for the inner workings of the RCX, Markus L. Noga created legOS (http://www.noga.de/legOS/), the first replacement firmware for the RCX. This was no small task—writing embedded software is always a difficult business, and writing an operating system without complete documentation of the hardware or System ROM borders on masochism. Fortunately for us, Markus succeeded and legOS now lets programmers use a *real* C-compiler to program the RCX. Early on, the legOS environment and tools were notoriously difficult for people to install and use. However, with the contributions of Luis Villa and many others, this entire process has become significantly easier and better documented.

Ralph Hempel also created a replacement for the standard firmware, but took a very different approach from Markus by creating a Forth interpreter for the RCX. Forth is a very old computer language, and although it hasn't captured mainstream interest the way that C or Java has, it has never quite disappeared either. This is because Forth is exceptionally well suited for certain situations, such as running in very small spaces and providing a high degree of interactivity. Unlike compiled languages such as C, Forth programs are executed immediately as they are typed. To Ralph, Forth sounded like the perfect way to program the RCX, thus pbForth was born (http://www.hempeldesigngroup.com/lego/pbForth/).

While Ralph, Markus, and I were working on new ways of creating software for the RCX, Michael Gasperi was busy figuring out how to make new hardware. Specifically, Michael wanted to attach things other than LEGO sensors to the RCX. Delving into the details of the RCX's sensor ports, he published information on how to make homebrew sensors. Some of these projects simply provided less expensive alternatives to the official LEGO sensors. Others, like the Galvanic Skin Response sensor, gave the RCX new senses. Perhaps most importantly, Michael's work laid the foundation for others to create even more new sensors—some of which are featured on his Web site (http://www.plazaearth.com/usr/gasperi/lego.htm).

Those early days of unraveling the RCX's secrets were exciting times. If you read through Russell's excerpts from the LEGO-robotics mailing list, you can feel the sense of discovery as the technology progressed. I've mentioned several of the key individuals and developments above, but there were countless other contributors as well.

Personally, I think there's a lesson here about how the Internet can change the way we work and interact. Somehow, in a completely ad-hoc manner, we managed to produce significant results in an extremely short time. In addition, we created a strong sense of community. There were no conference calls, committee meetings, or hidden agendas. Just a large group of people who collectively wanted to make MINDSTORMS do more and the Internet served as an ideal communication medium. Some of us eventually did meet face to face. The setting was Mindfest— a conference sponsored by the MIT Media Lab. Educators, tinkerers, parents, and children gathered from around the world to spend a couple of days talking about and playing with MINDSTORMS. Kekoa, Markus, Ralph, Michael, and I were invited to participate in one of the discussion panels at Mindfest, entitled "Extreme MIND-STORMS." I like that name—not because I think of myself (or any of the others, for that matter) to be extreme. I just think the title captures the spirit of what we were doing: taking MINDSTORMS further than its creators originally intended. The title isn't an exclusive club either—anyone who is pushing the boundaries of what MINDSTORMS can do is an Extreme MINDSTORMER.

LEGO was very quiet about these developments. They never publicly approved of our efforts, but they weren't suing any of us either. I think that demonstrated an admirable amount of restraint on their part. There we were, ripping apart our RCX's, telling people what we found, publishing software and information (for free!) that in some ways competed against LEGO's own software. A narrow-minded company would have acted out of fear and paranoia and tried to quell this activity.

On the other hand, the only way to take advantage of any of the information or software that was published was to actually own an RCX, which basically meant spending about $200 for a MINDSTORMS set. And once you got started, you would want more motors, beams, and gears, thus spending even more money on LEGO pieces. I like to think that in some small way we helped MINDSTORMS become a success. Why? Because I want LEGO to make many more of these fantastic toys.

MINDSTORMS Expands

In the fall of 1999, LEGO updated the RIS to version 1.5. Significant improvements were made to the drag-and-drop programming environment (called RCX Code) that resulted in it being both easier to use and more powerful than the 1.0 version. The set itself contained a slightly different mix of pieces, dropping some standard bricks in favor of specialty pieces, such as the clutch gear. The RCX itself still used the same ROM and firmware as 1.0, so existing tools, such as NQC, legOS, and pbForth continued to work without a hitch. The only down side to RIS 1.5 was that the RCX no longer featured an external power connector (in 1.0 the RCX could be powered from an optional AC adapter). Overall RIS 1.5 was a nice incremental improvement to an already excellent set.

LEGO was also busy creating new flavors of MINDSTORMS. Two smaller beginners' sets—the Robotics Discovery System (RDS) and Droid Developer Kit (DDK)—were released with their own versions of programmable bricks.

The Robotics Discovery System (RDS)

The RDS used a programmable brick called the *Scout*, which is sort of the RCX's little brother. On the surface the two look quite similar—same overall size and shape, same connectors for sensors and motors, and four colorful pushbuttons. A closer look, however, reveals some major differences. Like the RCX, the Scout can handle three sensors, but one is a built-in light sensor, and the two external ones must be passive sensors—external rotation or light sensors are not supported. The Scout only supports two motors directly (compared to three for the RCX). However, it does have the capability of communicating with other LEGO products, such as the *Code Pilot* or *Micro Scout* which could then be used to provide a third motor.

The biggest difference, however, is in programming the Scout. Rather than being dependent on an external computer for programming, the Scout can be programmed using its four push buttons and oversized LCD display. Actually, calling this process "programming" is, perhaps, stretching things. The Scout comes with a number of built-in behaviors, such as driving in a zigzag pattern or seeking a light. By selecting the appropriate behaviors, you can make the Scout do some interesting things, but of course, its vocabulary is still limited to these basic behaviors. Even so, the Scout provides a nice introduction to robotics without some of the complexities of using the RCX.

LEGO later released a Software Development Kit (SDK) which revealed that the Scout contained a bytecode interpreter remarkably similar to the RCX and could be programmed from a computer using the same InfraRed (IR) interface that the RCX used. In fact, some of the new Scout capabilities improved upon the RCX. The tools in the SDK (specifically the bytecode assembler – known as LASM) were also more advanced than the previous RCX-based offerings from LEGO. NQC was updated to allow it to be used with the Scout. For pbForth and legOS, however, the Scout was not a suitable platform. This is because the Scout contains its entire operating system in ROM, therefore, there is no way to download custom firmware and give the device a new personality. Due to its various hardware limitations, the Scout remained largely ignored by Extreme MINDSTORMERS. Quite simply, the RCX provided a lot more flexibility for only slightly more money.

The Droid Developer Kit (DDK)

The Droid Developer Kit used a programmable brick even simpler than the Scout— the *Micro Scout*. The Micro Scout contains its own motor and light sensor but has no external connectors. It contains several built-in programs, which pretty much cover all the basic things you can do with one sensor and one motor. It is also possible to create small custom programs for the Micro Scout, but not with the IR interface used by the RCX and Scout. Instead, it uses what LEGO calls Visible Light Link (VLL) for communication. The Scout contains built-in support for VLL, so it can be used to control or program the Micro Scout. Although not supported by LEGO, others have figured out how to get the RCX to send VLL commands when running NQC or legOS. Although it is possible to use a Micro Scout as an extra motor for the RCX or Scout, it is rarely practical. Compared to a regular motor, a Micro Scout often requires more programming to use and there is no way to control its power level (it always runs at full power).

With the Scout and the Micro Scout, LEGO was making MINDSTORMS easier and less expensive to get started with, but at the cost of flexibility and functionality. Advanced users were still waiting for a successor to the RCX—perhaps one that included some of those cool new features embedded in the Scout.

RIS 2.0

LEGO is busy at work on RIS 2.0. Due to the delays inherent in the publishing business, RIS 2.0 may very well be in stores by the time you read this, but as of this writing, most of RIS 2.0 remains a mystery. However, LEGO has already made the SDK for RIS 2.0 publicly available available for beta testing. This is a big move on LEGO's part—previous SDK's (such as for RIS 1.0 and Scout) didn't appear until some time after the products themselves. In the case of RIS 2.0, we get a sneak peek at what's coming, and can even start using it today. One of the key components of the RIS 2.0 SDK is a new version of firmware, officially known as the *RCX 2.0 Firmware*. This adds significant new capabilities while still remaining compatible with the RCX 1.0 bytecodes. Best of all, the new firmware runs perfectly well on existing RCX's. It's like getting a brand new RCX for free.

Perhaps most importantly (at least for us Extreme MINDSTORMERS), the SDK also includes complete technical documentation for the bytecodes used by the firmware. The original RIS 1.0 SDK only documented the operation of the SDK itself (specifically, the SPIRIT.OCX component). The Scout SDK took matters a step further by providing a bytecode assembler (LASM) along with descriptions of all the assembler mnemonics. However, low-level details, such as the actual encoding of the bytecodes, weren't published and we had to work them out for ourselves. With the new SDK, complete documentation is provided, allowing tools such as NQC to take immediate advantage of the new features.

These recent developments are encouraging for several reasons. First, the early public release of the SDK demonstrates that LEGO is thinking more like a modern software company and sees leading-edge users as an asset to be tapped, rather than a potential customer-support problem. Second, with both the Scout and RIS 2.0 SDK's, LEGO is moving towards more sophisticated tools, such as LASM. Third, the improvements made in the RCX 2.0 Firmware address some long-standing gripes among NQC users—Chapter 4 discusses these features at length. Lastly, LEGO's documentation of the RCX internals is a sign that they embrace Extreme MIND-STORMERS rather than fear them.

An Extreme Future

More extreme developments are on the way. We have only begun working with the RCX 2.0 Firmware and discovering what we can do with it. NQC, legOS, and pbForth continue to be enhanced and improved. New options are being developed as well—a tiny version of the Java Virtual Machine has recently been ported to the RCX. On the hardware front, I've seen some pretty amazing custom accessories for the RCX, ranging from simple sensors to controls for servo motors (a special kind of motor often used in robotics) to interfaces that provide additional input and output ports. Some of these developments aren't ready for primetime yet, but they are a glimpse of what may be ahead. LEGO is also likely to be developing more sophisticated software and hardware for future MINDSTORMS products.

Hopefully, by now you want to try some of these ideas out and become an Extreme MINDSTORMER yourself. That's where this book comes in. There's a lot of ground to cover and there's no single individual who is an expert in all of the fields. That's why this book has four authors—I wanted to ensure that you as a reader were getting firsthand information from the best possible sources.

Chapters 2 and 3 present an overview of the RCX, then show you how to build a sample robot and program it using RCX Code and NQC. These chapters aren't comprehensive guides to robot building, RCX Code, or NQC. They are merely a foundation for the remaining chapters. Chapter 4 dives into the special features of the RCX 2.0 Firmware and how it can be used from within NQC. In chapters 5 and 6, Ralph Hempel will guide you through pbForth, which provides significantly more capability than NQC, yet is very interactive and easy to learn. Luis Villa will get you started with legOS in chapters 7 and 8. Although the learning curve for legOS can be a bit steeper than for the other environments, you'll be rewarded with significantly more programming power. For the final two chapters, we switch gears from software to hardware as Michael Gasperi illustrates how to build homebrew sensors for the RCX.

Most importantly, don't constrain yourself to the examples given in the book. Take time to experiment and play with what you learn in each chapter. Often there are many ways to do the same thing and none of them are "best." If you don't like the old way, invent a new way. Who knows? Perhaps you'll contribute to tomorrow's *Extreme MINDSTORMS*.

CHAPTER 2

The RCX

LEGO HAS ALWAYS BEEN a versatile construction toy that allows almost limitless creativity. MINDSTORMS sets add a new dimension to the LEGO universe. LEGO models can be more than just a collection of beams, bricks, gears, and motors. They can sense and respond to their environment and can be programmed to accomplish nearly anything, from picking up and stacking blocks to playing "tag" with one another. This amazing capability comes from one very special LEGO brick—the RCX. Although there are many different ways to program the RCX, they all share certain common capabilities—namely the features of the RCX itself.

This chapter describes the basic architecture of the RCX and provides some details about the hardware. We present generic features of the RCX, such as output ports and sensor ports. Finally, we offer a brief description of some features that the standard firmware provides.

Because the following pages deal with the generic capabilities of the RCX rather than the details of using them from a given programming environment, the discussion is a bit abstract and may be somewhat confusing at times. Once you begin programming the RCX, however, the concepts should become clearer.

Architecture

The RCX may look and feel like a LEGO brick (which it is), but it is also a small computer system, complete with a CPU, display, memory, and peripherals. When discussing the RCX, it is convenient to view it as having several different layers of functionality—each layer building upon the capabilities of the layers below.

The Hardware Layer

The bottom-most layer is the *hardware* itself: the microcontroller (CPU), the LCD, the memory, and other electronic components. At the most primitive level, the hardware determines what the RCX can and cannot do.

The System ROM Layer

In addition to the CPU and various peripherals, the microcontroller also contains a ROM (Read Only Memory), which comes preprogrammed with some low-level software. This software will be referred to as the "System ROM." In general, the System ROM provides convenient interfaces to the hardware, making it a lot easier for other software to utilize the RCX's hardware, including showing a number on the LCD or playing a sound out of the speaker.

The most important feature of the System ROM is that it allows a second piece of software, often called the *firmware*, to be downloaded into the RCX's memory. In many cases, the firmware will still use features from the System ROM, but, if desired, the firmware can assume total control of the RCX and bypass the System ROM completely. Unlike the System ROM, which is always present, the firmware will be erased if power is removed from the RCX for any significant amount of time. The LEGO Company provides its own firmware—referred to as the *standard firmware*—but custom versions of firmware also exist and can open up new programming possibilities (such as pbForth and legOS).

> **NOTE** *Firmware is a generic term for software that is built into a device. The term is intended to convey the fact that such software is something in between hardware and the common notion of software. Technically, the System ROM in the RCX is also firmware, but when discussing the RCX, the term firmware is typically reserved for the portion of the system that is kept in RAM.*

Standard Firmware

The standard firmware is used when writing RCX programs using any of the official environments (RCX Code, Robolab, or SPIRIT.OCX) as well as NQC. Figure 2-1 shows how RCX Code and NQC programs are run on the RCX. Special tools (called compilers) on the *host computer* translate the program into *bytecodes*. These bytecodes are then downloaded to the RCX and stored as user programs. The CPU in the RCX cannot execute the bytecodes directly—the standard firmware interprets each bytecode when a user program is executed. Using the standard firmware is convenient (many of the tools download it automatically as needed), but it also comes with some limitations.

NOTE *Recently, LEGO released its own replacement for the standard firmware. This new firmware, known as RCX 2.0 Firmware, is compatible with the existing standard firmware bytecodes, but also provides significant new features. The RCX 2.0 Firmware will be explored in Chapter 4.*

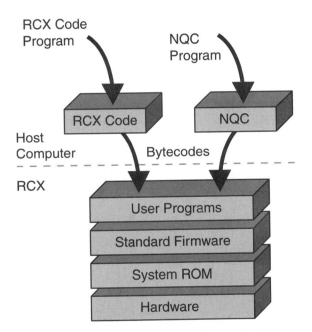

Figure 2-1. RCX architecture with standard firmware

pbForth Custom Firmware

One example of custom firmware is pbForth, which allows the RCX to be programmed using the Forth computer language. Like the standard firmware, pbForth provides an interpreter for a user's programs, but instead of using the LEGO bytecodes, it executes compiled Forth code. Another important distinction is that most other programming tools translate the user's program on the host computer, then download the translated version (also called the compiled version) to the RCX. With pbForth, this translation takes place on the RCX itself. This has some interesting benefits, which are explored in the pbForth chapters in Part Two of this book. Figure 2-2 illustrates this operation.

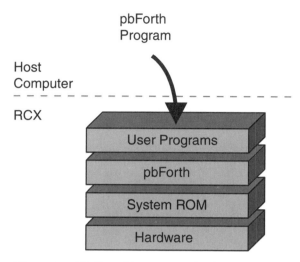

Figure 2-2. RCX architecture with pbForth

LegOS Custom Firmware

LegOS is another replacement for the standard firmware. Just as pbForth relies on the Forth language, legOS uses the C language. As shown in Figure 2-3, the host computer compiles a legOS program (written in C) and generates binary code that can be executed natively on the RCX. This binary is then downloaded to the robot, where the legOS operating system executes the program and provides an interface to the RCX's hardware. Because C is one of the most commonly used computer languages, legOS allows an RCX programmer to draw upon a large body of experience and code that has already been written.

Hardware

The RCX is based on a Hitachi H8 series microcontroller. This 8-bit CPU provides most of the control logic for the RCX, including serial I/O, ADC (Analog to Digital Converter), and built-in timers. It even contains 16KB of internal ROM, which is preprogrammed with the System ROM. The RCX also contains 32KB of static RAM. This memory is used to hold the firmware, user programs, and any data required by those programs.

Compared to a desktop computer, 32KB sounds too small to be of any practical value. However, within the RCX, programs are typically measured in a few

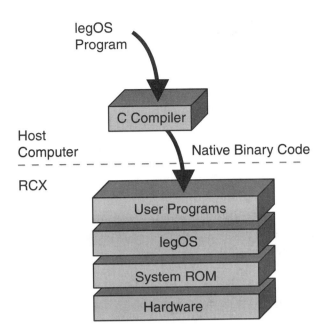

Figure 2-3. RCX Architecture with legOS

hundreds or thousands of bytes—not the millions of bytes used by desktop computer programs. Rest assured there are plenty of interesting things that can be done within 32KB.

The RCX also contains special circuitry to interface with the real world. An LCD, four pushbuttons, and a small speaker are provided for user interaction. Special driver chips allow the RCX to control motors or other electric devices attached to the output ports, and the internal ADC allows the RCX to read its three sensor ports and check the condition of the batteries.

IR (InfraRed) Interface

The RCX uses IR (InfraRed) light to communicate with a desktop computer or another RCX. IR communication for the desktop computer is provided by an IR interface (included in the Robotics Invention System) that attaches to a standard 9-pin serial port. Many laptop computers (and palmtop devices) already have their own IR port. All IR devices use infrared light for communication, but the protocols they use to communicate can differ widely. Most laptops and other computing devices use a set of standards known as IrDA for communication, while the RCX uses a simpler proprietary protocol. Because of this, a laptop's IR port will not automatically be able to communicate with the RCX. Of course, anything is possible with the right amount of hacking, but as of this writing I know of no general-purpose solution to making a laptop IR port communicate with the RCX.

Battery Power

Six AA batteries typically power the RCX. How long the batteries last is highly dependent on how the RCX is being used. The biggest drain on the batteries comes from the motors that the RCX must power. When running, motors can consume considerable power, and this power increases when the motor is under great strain. Needless to say, heavy use of the RCX will result in many battery changes— using rechargeable alkaline batteries is a good idea. Some versions of the RCX (such as those found in the original Robotics Invention System 1.0) can also be powered with an external AC adapter.

Some versions of firmware (such as the standard firmware and legOS) allow the RCX to be turned off using the **On–Off** button. In this case, the firmware and any programs that have been downloaded are retained. If the batteries are removed for any significant amount of time, however, this memory will be erased. When you need to change batteries, make sure the RCX is turned off, then quickly remove the old batteries and insert new batteries. As long as you work reasonably fast the memory will be retained and you will not need to reload the firmware.

Output Ports

The RCX has three output ports (A, B, and C), each of which can be operated in one of three modes: *on, off,* or *floating*. The on mode is just what it sounds like—any motor attached to the output will be running. In the off mode, the RCX turns off the output and the motor will be forced to stop. The floating mode is somewhat unusual. In this mode, the RCX is no longer powering the output, but a motor is still allowed to spin freely. In some cases, this will have a much different effect than off. For example, in terms of a car, off is like applying the brakes, while floating is more like coasting in neutral.

Output Directions

When turned on, an output can be run in either of two directions: *forward* or *reverse*. The actual direction of a motor's rotation (clockwise or counter-clockwise) depends upon how the wires are attached between it and the RCX. When using the standard firmware, an output's direction is remembered when the output is turned off or floating, and can even be changed. However, any changes won't take effect until the output is turned on again.

Adjusting the Power Level

The *power level* of an output may also be adjusted. The standard firmware and pbForth provide eight different power levels, while legOS provides 255 (plus, "off"). Like the direction, the power level only has effect when the output is turned on. The RCX is primarily a digital device, and digital devices like things to be either on or off, not "half on" or "three-quarters on." Hence, the RCX needs some way to create these intermediate power levels from a digital signal.

One way of doing this is with Pulse Width Modulation (PWM), as shown in Figure 2-4. Instead of turning a signal on and leaving it on, PWM rapidly switches back and forth between on and off. The time that is spent on is called a *pulse,* and the duration of this pulse is called its *width.* The percentage of time that the signal is on is called its *duty-cycle.* When using PWM, varying the pulse width to generate the appropriate duty-cycle creates intermediate levels of power. At low power levels, the pulse is very brief, while at full power the pulse never stops.

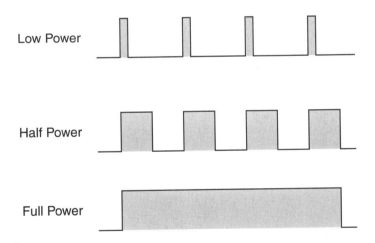

Figure 2-4. Pulse Width Modulation

One of the problems with PWM is that instead of continuously supplying partial power, it will instead supply full power part of the time. In many cases, this subtle difference has little overall effect. The LEGO MINDSTORMS motor, however, is an exception. This motor was designed to be very power efficient and it has an internal flywheel, which acts as a sort of energy storage tank. The flywheel is most effective when the motor has very little physical resistance (called *load*). Starting the motor consumes a lot of energy since the flywheel must also be spun up to speed. Once running, however, a lightly loaded motor (perhaps a motor that is turning a gear that isn't connected to anything else) can maintain its speed with very little external power. In this case, PWM does not affect the motor very much since the short pulses keep the flywheel spinning, and the flywheel itself keeps the motor spinning when the pulses stop. Under a heavy load (e.g., propelling a vehicle across a carpeted surface), the flywheel is less effective and changing power levels will have a more noticeable effect on speed.

Note that it is possible with custom firmware to change the timings used for output ports. This is done by legOS to provide finer control over power levels. This can also be useful for controlling devices such as servo motors, which require special waveforms. When using the standard firmware, however, the outputs must always be used in accordance with the timing previously described.

Sensor Ports

The RCX has three sensor ports, each of which can accommodate one of four different LEGO sensors (touch sensor, light sensor, rotation sensor, and temperature sensor), as well as the custom sensors described in Chapters 9 and 10 of this book. Sensors are connected to the RCX using the same type of wiring used to connect motors to the RCX output ports.

Passive and Active Sensors

There are two different classes of sensors: *passive* and *active*. Passive sensors operate as simple resistances and require no power from the RCX in order to function. The LEGO touch and temperature sensors are examples of passive sensors. Active sensors (also called *powered* sensors) require power from the RCX and involve slightly more sophisticated electronics. The LEGO light and rotation sensors are active sensors. The RCX has no way of knowing what kind of sensor has been hooked up, so at some point a program must tell the RCX what kind of sensor is attached and how to read it. It is possible to intentionally fool the RCX. For example, the light sensor is an active sensor containing an LED and a phototransistor. During normal use, the LED is turned on and the phototransistor measures the amount of light reflected back from nearby objects. If the RCX is configured to use a light sensor as a passive sensor, the LED will remain off, but the phototransistor will still respond to incoming light. As a result, the light sensor can then be used to sense ambient light levels rather than reflected light.

Using Sensors

The specifics of configuring and reading sensors vary greatly depending upon the programming environment used. For example, in legOS the programmer indicates whether a sensor is active or passive, then calls a function to read the sensor value whenever desired. There is minimal processing of the sensor values—they are generally just the raw values read from the ADC and scaled to a useful range. Rotation sensors are a special case because they must be continuously monitored. There are several functions to assist with this.

The standard firmware and pbForth allow the programmer more options for configuring the sensors. The following information on sensors applies only to those two environments—legOS users may wish to skip to the next section on the LCD.

There are two different settings that get configured for each sensor: the *sensor type* and the *sensor mode*. The sensor type determines how the RCX interacts with the sensor. For example, the RCX will passively read a touch sensor but must supply power to a light sensor. For LEGO sensors, the sensor type generally should match the actual type of sensor attached (touch, light, rotation, or temperature).

The sensor mode tells the RCX how to interpret a sensor's values. Some programming languages, such as RCX Code, automatically set the sensor mode based on the sensor type. Other languages, such as NQC, provide the additional flexibility of using any sensor mode with any sensor type (although some combinations are of little practical value).

Every sensor has three separate values associated with it: the *raw value, boolean value*, and *processed value*. The raw value is the actual ADC reading, which represents the voltage of the sensor and ranges from 0 (0 volts) to 1023 (5 volts). *Sampling* a sensor consists of reading the raw value from the sensor itself, then converting this value to both a boolean value and a processed value. The boolean value is always either 0 or 1 and is often useful in cases where a simple yes/no decision needs to be made. The range (and meaning) of a processed value is dependent on the sensor's mode. For example, in percentage mode, the processed value ranges from 0 to 100.

All three values (raw, processed, and boolean) are stored so that a program can read them later on. The standard firmware automatically samples each sensor every 3 milliseconds (ms). With pbForth, the programmer is responsible for sampling the sensors within the application itself.

Sensor Types

There are four sensor types that correspond to the standard LEGO sensors:

- Touch

- Temperature

- Light

- Rotation

There is also a fifth type, "None," which is a default setting for the sensor ports. Although this fifth type does not correspond to a particular sensor, it can be useful for reading generic passive sensors. The sensor type determines whether the RCX treats the sensor as an active or passive sensor. It also determines the default mode used when reading the sensor. The System ROM uses the codes listed in Table 2-1 for sensor types (for convenience, NQC defines symbolic names as well).

Table 2-1. Sensor Types

SENSOR TYPE	CODE	CLASS	DEFAULT MODE	NQC NAME
None	0	Passive	Raw	SENSOR_TYPE_NONE
Touch	1	Passive	Boolean	SENSOR_TYPE_TOUCH
Temperature	2	Passive	Celsius	SENSOR_TYPE_TEMPERATURE
Light	3	Active	Percentage	SENSOR_TYPE_LIGHT
Rotation	4	Active	Rotation	SENSOR_TYPE_ROTATION

Boolean Values

A sensor's boolean value can have one of two values: 0 or 1. Boolean values have their most obvious uses with a touch sensor, but occasionally other sensors can make use of boolean values as well.

The sensor mode includes a special parameter, called the *sensor slope*, which can range from 0 to 31 and determines how the raw value is converted into a boolean value. When the slope is zero, the RCX uses the conversion shown in Table 2-2.

Table 2-2. Default Boolean Conversion

CONDITION	BOOLEAN VALUE
raw > 562	0
raw < 460	1
$460 \leq raw \leq 562$	unchanged

Note that a high raw value results in boolean value of 0, while a low raw value is a boolean value of 1.

The cutoff points (460 and 562) represent approximately 45% and 55% of the sensor's maximum value. It is not unusual for the raw values to bounce around by a few points, thus if a single cutoff was used, the boolean value would be susceptible to a lot of jitter if the raw value were hovering near the cutoff. This method of reducing the amount of jitter in a boolean conversion is called *hysteresis*.

When the slope parameter is non-zero, a different boolean conversion is used. Each time the sensor is read, its raw value is compared to the previous raw value. If the absolute value of this difference is less than the slope parameter, the boolean value remains unchanged. If this difference exceeds the slope parameter, the boolean value will be set to indicate whether the raw value increased (boolean value of 0) or decreased (boolean value of 1). Special cases exist at the extremes of the raw value range. This conversion is summarized in Table 2-3.

Table 2-3. Boolean Conversion with Slope Parameter

CONDITION	BOOLEAN VALUE
change > slope	0
change < –slope	1
current > (1023-slope)	0
current < slope	1
change = current value minus previous value	
slope = the value of the slope parameter	
current = current raw value	

For example, consider the case where the slope is 10, and the initial raw value is 1020. This will result in a boolean value of 0. Let's say the raw value slowly decreases until it is 300. Even though a value of 300 is below the 45% threshold normally used for boolean values, the slope parameter causes the cutoff to be ignored and the boolean value will remain 0. If the raw value suddenly decreases, perhaps to 280 in a single reading, the boolean value will then become 1.

When set properly, the slope parameter can be used to configure a light sensor to ignore moderate variations and detect only abrupt changes. For example, the following NQC program configures sensor 2 to be a light sensor in boolean mode with a slope of 10 (more information about sensor modes appears later in this chapter). The program plays a high pitched tone whenever the sensor changes rapidly from dark to light (sensor value equals 1), and a low pitched tone during a rapid transition from light to dark (sensor value equals 0).

> **NOTE** *The following NQC program along with all the other sample programs in the book may be downloaded from the book's page on the Apress Web site at* `http://www.apress.com.`

```
// slope.nqc

task main()
{
    SetSensorType(SENSOR_2, SENSOR_TYPE_LIGHT);
    SetSensorMode(SENSOR_2, SENSOR_MODE_BOOL + 10);

    while(true)
    {
        until(SENSOR_2 == 1);
        PlayTone(880, 10);
        until(SENSOR_2 == 0);
        PlayTone(440, 10);
    }
}
```

If you are using NQC and feel like experimenting with the slope parameter, download this program to the RCX, attach a light sensor to sensor port 2, and run the program. Aim the sensor directly into a bright light, then try blocking and unblocking the light by covering the sensor with your finger. Rapid changes from light to dark (or vice versa) will cause the sensor's boolean value to change and the program will play a tone. Gradual changes, such as slowly turning the sensor away from the light, will not result in a change to the sensor's boolean value.

Small triangles on the RCX's display (below the sensor ports) indicate when a sensor's boolean value is 1.

Sensor Modes

There are eight different sensor modes (see Table 2-4), some of which only make sense for certain sensor types. The sensor mode actually consists of two separate values—a code that specifies the type of measurement to be made, and the slope parameter, which defines how to convert raw values into boolean values (as discussed in the previous section). The codes used by the System ROM are shown in Table 2-4 (in hexadecimal), along with the NQC names for each mode. The slope parameter must be between 0 and 31 inclusive and is simply added to the code. For example, mode 0x45 specifies edge counting with a slope parameter of 5.

Table 2-4. Sensor Modes

SENSOR MODE	CODE	NQC NAME
Raw	0x00	SENSOR_MODE_RAW
Boolean	0x20	SENSOR_MODE_BOOL
Edge Count	0x40	SENSOR_MODE_EDGE
Pulse Count	0x60	SENSOR_MODE_PULSE
Percentage	0x80	SENSOR_MODE_PERCENT
Celsius	0xa0	SENSOR_MODE_CELSIUS
Fahrenheit	0xc0	SENSOR_MODE_FAHRENHEIT
Rotation	0xe0	SENSOR_MODE_ROTATION

Several of the modes (Edge Count, Pulse Count, and Rotation) use a cumulative value. For example, when using Edge Count mode, each time the sensor's boolean value changes, the processed value will be incremented by one. A program may reset the sensor's value to 0 at any time—this is known as *clearing* the sensor.

For each mode, a brief description follows that explains how it converts raw values into processed values. The default modes (those automatically selected by the standard firmware) for each sensor type are also indicated.

Raw Mode

Raw mode is the simplest mode of all. In this mode the processed value of a sensor is always equal to its raw value (an integer between 0 and 1023).

Boolean Mode

When boolean mode is selected, the sensor's processed value is set to the boolean value determined by the conversion described previously. For sensors other than the touch sensor, a proper slope parameter is often essential for meaningful boolean values. This is the default mode for a touch sensor.

Edge Count Mode

When edge count mode is selected, the RCX counts how many times the boolean value changes value. This count is initially 0, and increments by 1 each time the boolean value changed from 0 to 1 or from 1 to 0. This mode is only useful when the boolean value is meaningful.

Mechanical switches (such as the touch sensor) tend to chatter a bit; that is, they will rapidly turn on and off several times in the process of being pressed or released. The RCX uses a *de-bouncing* process to filter out the chatter, which causes the RCX to ignore edges for 300ms after a transition occurs. This increases the reliability of edge counting for most purposes, but also limits it to detecting edges that are at least 300ms apart.

Pulse Count Mode

The pulse count mode is similar to the edge count mode, except that the counter is only incremented when a boolean value goes from 1 to 0. Like edge counting, the boolean value is debounced to eliminate chatter. This mode is ideal for counting the number of times a button is pressed, for example.

Percentage Mode

In percentage mode, the raw value is converted into a value between 0 and 100 (higher raw values correspond to a lower percentage value). This is the default mode for a light sensor.

Celsius and Fahrenheit Modes

Celsius mode uses a special function to convert the raw value into a temperature reading. This function compensates for the specific characteristics of the temperature sensor. Fahrenheit mode uses the same function as Celsius mode to convert a raw value into a temperature, but then converts the temperature from Celsius to Fahrenheit.

Internally the RCX multiplies temperature values by 10, so that a value of 22.5 degrees is represented as 225. The LCD, however, will still display the actual temperature (such as 22.5). The default mode for a temperature sensor is Celsius, although when using RCX Code, a user preference determines whether Celsius or Fahrenheit mode is used.

Rotation Mode

Rotation mode uses an algorithm that decodes the special output of the rotation sensor. This mode is the default for the rotation sensor and is meaningless when combined with any other sensor type. The resulting value from rotation mode is a cumulative rotation in increments of 22.5 degrees (a value of 16 represents a full revolution).

LCD

The LCD can display a four-digit signed number and a single-digit unsigned number, as well as various special indicators (see Figure 2-5). Actual use of the display depends on what software is used to program the RCX (standard firmware, pbForth, and so on).

When the standard firmware is used, all of the indicators are managed by the firmware. For example, the "sensor active" indicators reflect the current boolean value of each sensor, and the "output" indicators show which state each of the outputs is in. The four-digit numeric display normally shows the system clock—that is, the number of hours and minutes counted since

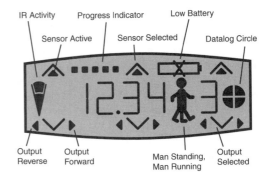

Figure 2-5. The LCD display

the RCX was turned on. However, the numeric display can also be used to monitor the current value of any sensor or the current state of any output. The display mode may be switched manually using the **View** button, or within an NQC program by calling SelectDisplay().

> **NOTE**   *When using the RCX 2.0 Firmware, programs have more control over the numeric display. See Chapter 4 for more information.*

When pbForth is used, programs have complete low-level control over the LCD. Segments may be individually turned on or off, and arbitrary numeric values can be shown on the display. This level of control is a mixed blessing: programs may use the display however they wish, but they also have the responsibility to update it. The details of how to control the display within pbForth are discussed in Chapter 5.

LegOS also provides complete low-level control over the LCD. In addition, it allows alphabetic characters to be displayed. Since the letters are formed from the segments in the digits, they are rather crude, but can still be quite useful within a legOS program. The details of how to control the display within legOS are discussed in Chapter 7.

Sound

The System ROM provides a special function that can play one of six predefined system sounds. The standard firmware provides access to this routine, as does pbForth, while legOS implements its own sound capability. The system sounds are listed in Table 2-5.

Table 2-5. System Sounds

SOUND	NUMBER	NQC NAME
Click	0	SOUND_CLICK
Beep Beep	1	SOUND_DOUBLE_BEEP
Downward Tones	2	SOUND_DOWN
Upward Tones	3	SOUND_UP
Low Beep	4	SOUND_LOW_BEEP
Fast Upward Tones	5	SOUND_FAST_UPP

The System ROM allows sounds to be *queued*. This means that a program can request the System ROM to play a new sound while a previous sound is still being played. Rather than interrupt the first sound, ignore the second sound, or force the program to wait for the first sound to complete, the System ROM will simply add the second sound to the queue of pending sounds. Once the first sound completes, the second sound will begin to play immediately. Of course, the RCX has limited resources, so the System ROM cannot queue an unlimited number of sounds—it only provides room to queue eight sounds, in addition to the one currently being played. This means that nine sounds can be requested and played, but if a tenth sound is requested before the first one finishes, the tenth request will be ignored.

Standard Firmware

The standard firmware is common to a number of programming environments. It is used by the official LEGO Company software (RCX Code and Robolab), as well as NQC. It is also the basis of the LEGO Software Development Kit (SDK) for the RCX. The capabilities and limitations of these environments are all shaped in some degree by the capabilities of the standard firmware. The following section discusses some of the highlights of the standard firmware.

The standard firmware (and its data) occupies much of the 32KB RAM provided by the RCX, leaving about 6KB free for user programs. Fortunately, the bytecodes used by the firmware are reasonably compact, so 6KB of program space is more than adequate for most programming tasks.

Bytecode Interpreter

The heart of the standard firmware is the bytecode interpreter. As mentioned previously, user programs (in RCX Code, NQC, and so on) are translated into bytecodes and then downloaded to the RCX. The bytecode interpreter is the piece of software within the RCX that runs these bytecodes. Using an interpreter has both advantages and disadvantages.

One significant advantage of using an interpreter is that it can enforce strict rules and behaviors to ensure that programs cannot crash the RCX, corrupt other programs, or perform any other undesirable actions on the RCX's hardware or System ROM. Of course, this can also be a disadvantage because the same rules that prevent crashes may also prevent the programmer from doing something desirable. Not all interpreters take the same approach to safety—some give the programmer plenty of rope to play (and hang) with, while others (such as the LEGO bytecode interpreter) take a safer (and more limiting) route.

Another advantage of creating a system that uses bytecodes and an interpreter is that completely different hardware can run the same user programs, provided a similar interpreter is implemented on the new hardware. This is one of the selling points for Java, which defines its own set of bytecodes that can then be run on a wide variety of computers and operating systems. LEGO has also taken advantage of this with their Scout product—a programmable brick that is the "little brother" to the RCX and uses a similar set of bytecodes.

Keeping Time

The standard firmware provides a system clock, called the *watch,* which keeps track of the number of minutes that have passed since the RCX was turned on. In the default display mode, the LCD shows the current watch time in hours and minutes. Although the watch's current time is available to a running program, most programs require more accurate timing information than can be provided by the watch.

The standard firmware also provides four *timers* that measure time in increments of 100ms (1/10th a second). The timers are running whenever the RCX is turned on. A program may reset each timer independently at any time. The timers will return to zero after about 55 minutes.

Variables

The standard firmware provides thirty-two global storage locations that a program can use to store global variables. Each location can store a single 16-bit signed integer (an integer between -32,768 and 32,767). Since the variables are global across all of a program's tasks, care must be taken to ensure that a program with multiple tasks uses the variables in a consistent manner. The locations are shared across all of the programs and are not reset when changing programs. This makes it possible for one program to store information that will later be used by another program.

Variables can be assigned nearly any kind of value, including constants, timer values, sensor readings, or random numbers. The firmware also provides a set of basic math operations for variables: addition, subtraction, multiplication, division, bitwise AND, bitwise OR, sign, and absolute value.

The Datalog

The standard firmware provides a data logging capability. A program may create a datalog of a fixed size, then add data points to the log. The data points may be sensor readings, variables, timer values, or the system watch. The datalog may then be uploaded to a host computer for analysis or for some other function.

Both the datalog and user programs must share the same 6KB of user memory (6101 bytes, to be exact). Since each data point requires 3 bytes of memory, the largest possible datalog will hold 2033 points. However, a datalog this large would leave no room for any programs.

The RCX's display includes a datalog indicator that consists of a circle cut into four quadrants. If no datalog exists, the indicator remains off. When a datalog is in use, one or more of the quadrants is shown, indicating roughly how much of the datalog is currently filled up. One of the quadrants will be flashing as long as there is still room for additional data points. Once the datalog is full, all four quadrants will become solid.

Communication

The standard firmware provides a simple mechanism for RCX's to communicate with one another (or even with a host computer). An RCX can send a special *message* with a value between 1 and 255. The RCX also has a buffer that keeps track of the most recent message received. A program can query this buffer at any time (the value 0 indicates that no message has been received). In addition, a program may clear the message buffer, thus allowing it to detect when a new message arrives. Although somewhat primitive, this basic messaging capability allows for the coordination of multiple RCX's.

Programming the RCX

The preceding pages describe the basic capabilities of the RCX. However, even with all this power, the RCX is still little more than an inert LEGO brick until it has been programmed. The next six chapters introduce how to program the RCX using RCX Code and NQC, then quickly move on to describe the more advanced systems: pbForth and legOS.

Seeker:
A Light-Seeking Robot

SEEKER IS A SIMPLE ROBOT that can drive around and search for a bright light. Seeker also has a bumper so that it can detect and avoid obstacles during its search. Although this chapter contains sample programs in RCX Code (the standard LEGO MINDSTORMS development software) and NQC, it is not intended as a tutorial for either of these systems. Rather, the purpose of this chapter is to present the Seeker robot and to demonstrate some of its basic behaviors. Later chapters in Parts Two and Three will show how similar behaviors can be implemented and even enhanced using more advanced tools, such as pbForth and legOS.

Construction

Seeker's design and construction should be relatively familiar to anyone who has experimented with MINDSTORMS robots. It is based on a simple tanklike chassis that uses a pair of motors to power the left and right treads. A bumper and a light sensor are then added to this chassis. The construction of the chassis is displayed in Figures 3-1 through 3-4. Note that whenever an axle is used, its length is indicated in the step in which it is added. For example, in Figure 3-2, two axles—each 8 units long—are added.

Figure 3-1. Seeker step 1

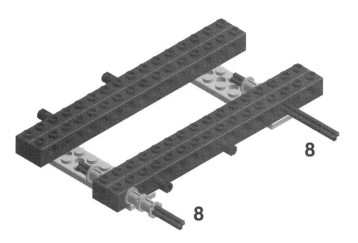

Figure 3-2. Seeker step 2

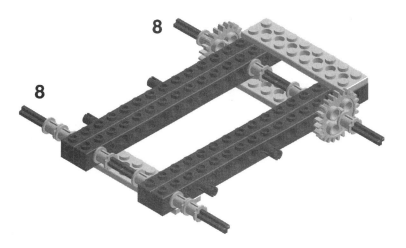

Figure 3-3. Seeker step 3

The motors, the RCX, and a number of wires are added in Figures 3-5 and 3-6. In the illustrations, the ends of each wire are labeled with a letter or number. In most cases, short wires should be used and the labels indicate the appropriate RCX port to use. For example, the wire added in step 5 is labeled "C," which indicates that it will eventually be attached to RCX port "C." An exception is made for devices that have built-in wires, such as the light sensor or the rotation sensor. In these cases, the wire is labeled with an "L" (light sensor) or "R" (rotation sensor) because you need to use the sensor's wire itself rather than a separate wire. For example, the light sensor itself won't be added to the robot until later, but its wire should be attached

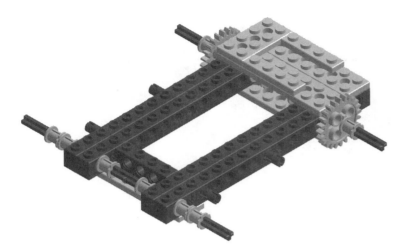

Figure 3-4. Seeker step 4

to RCX port 2 as shown in Figure 3-6. Pay particular attention to the orientation of the wires used to connect the motors. When connected as shown, programming a motor to run in the "forward" direction will propel the robot forward. If the orientation of either wire end is changed, the motor's direction may be reversed.

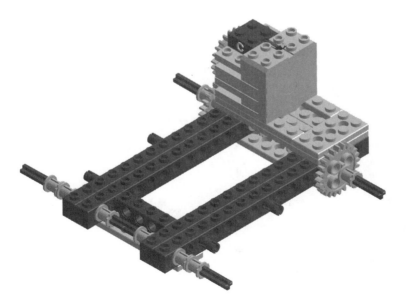

Figure 3-5. Seeker step 5

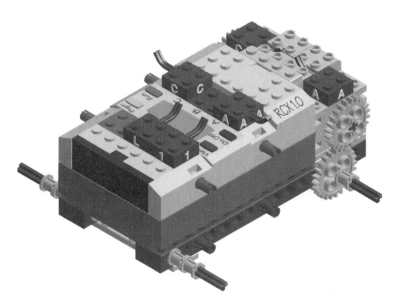

Figure 3-6. Seeker step 6

Figures 3-6 and 3-7 simply show initial support for the bumper. The rubber band you see in Figure 3-8 should wrap around the black peg added at this point, along with the #2 axle that has a bushing on the end of the bumper arm. Note the addition of a small black rubber band in Figure 3-9.

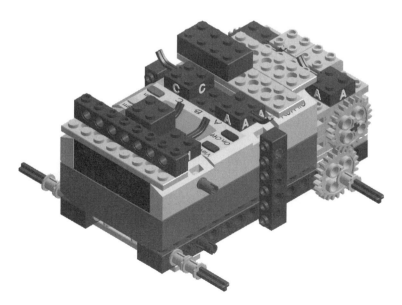

Figure 3-7. Seeker step 7

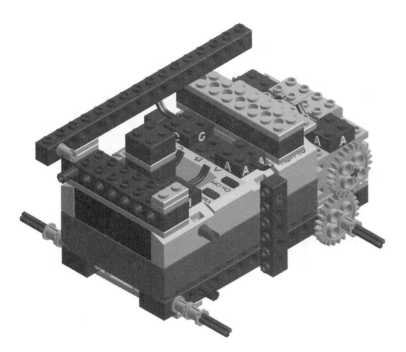

Figure 3-8. Seeker step 8

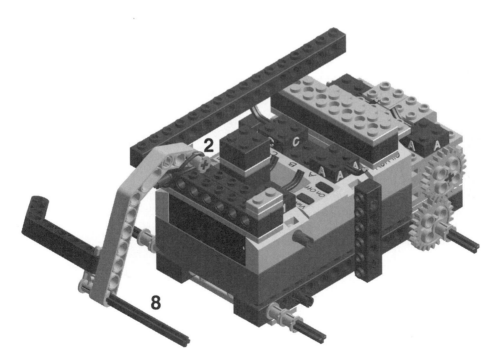

Figure 3-9. Seeker step 9

The bumper's touch sensor is added in Figure 3-10 and the bumper is completed in Figure 3-11. Note that as the rubber band holds the bumper in its forward position, the bumper arm will cause the touch sensor to be pressed. Hitting an obstacle will pivot the bumper, which will release the touch sensor.

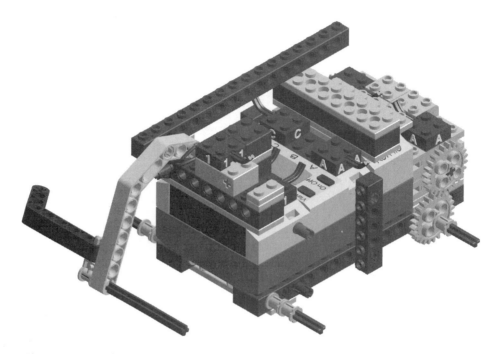

Figure 3-10. Seeker step 10

Seeker is completed in Figure 3-12 with the addition of several components. The light sensor (whose wire was attached to RCX port 2 in Figure 3-6) should point forward to allow Seeker to detect a bright light. The 1x10 vertical beams provide additional reinforcement by holding the top 1x16 beams, the RCX, and the bottom frame of the chassis all in place. When adding the treads, be sure to secure the rear hubs (near the motors) using 16-tooth gears. The hubs themselves spin freely on an axle; thus the gears are required to transfer power from the spinning axles to the hubs.

Using the Bumper

As a robot drives around it will inevitably run into an obstacle or two. There are numerous strategies for detecting and navigating around obstacles. In Seeker's case, a simple bumper at the front of the robot is used for obstacle detection. For this example, Seeker will steer around the obstacle using a very simple strategy: back up for 0.6 seconds, turn clockwise for 0.2 seconds, then resume driving.

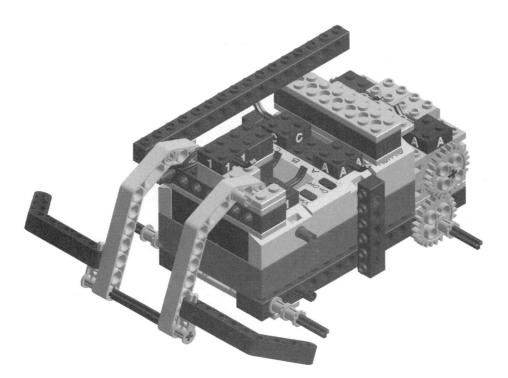

Figure 3-11. Seeker step 11

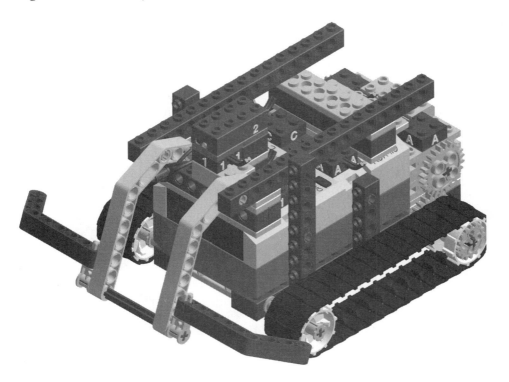

Figure 3-12. Seeker step 12

This strategy does a pretty good job of preventing Seeker from getting stuck, but it also has its drawbacks. Specifically, because Seeker always turns clockwise, it stands as good a chance of turning towards the obstacle as turning away from it. In practice, this means that after hitting something, Seeker will sometimes continue with only a minor course correction, but sometimes it will make several back-and-spin maneuvers and wind up heading in a completely new direction. In spite of this drawback, the back-and-spin strategy is reasonably effective and its overall simplicity makes it a good building block for more interesting programs.

Implementing this strategy in RCX Code is straightforward. A sensor watcher is used to monitor the bumper: when an obstacle is hit, the program backs up (both motors set to reverse), turns a little (one motor forward, the other still in reverse), and finally resumes travelling forward. Figure 3-13 shows the complete program.

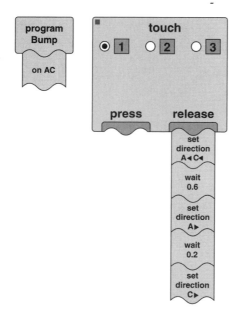

Figure 3-13. The bumper program in RCX code

A nearly identical program can be written in NQC, as shown in Listing 3-1. The program itself is actually quite short (only about ten lines of "real" code), but the listing uses #define to define symbolic constants and includes quite a few comments.

> **NOTE** *All of the sample programs used in the book can be downloaded from the book's page on the Apress Web site at* http://www.apress.com.

Listing 3-1. The bump.nqc program

```
/* bump.nqc
 *
 * Drive forward until hitting an obstacle, then back up,
 * turn right a little, and resume.
 */

// motors and sensors
#define LEFT     OUT_A
#define RIGHT    OUT_C
#define BUMPER   SENSOR_1

// timing
#define BUMP_BACK_TIME  60  // 0.6 seconds
#define BUMP_SPIN_TIME  20  // 0.2 seconds

task main()
{
    // setup sensor and start driving
    SetSensor(BUMPER, SENSOR_TOUCH);
    OnFwd(LEFT+RIGHT);

    while(true)
    {
        // wait for bumper to be activated
        until(BUMPER==0);

        // back up a bit
        OnRev(LEFT+RIGHT);
        Wait(BUMP_BACK_TIME);

        // spin a bit
        Fwd(LEFT);
        Wait(BUMP_SPIN_TIME);

        // resume
        Fwd(RIGHT);
    }
}
```

Defining items such as sensors, motors, and timing parameters as #define directives makes a program much easier to adjust, maintain, and re-use. For example, to re-use bump.nqc with a robot whose left motor was on output B (instead of output A), you would only need to change the #define line for LEFT. If #define was not used, then you'd have to replace every occurrence of OUT_A in the program with OUT_B. For small programs this is not much work, but in larger programs it can become troublesome and error prone. Thus it is a good habit to use #define up front for things that may be expected to change later on.

> **NOTE** *Adding comments or using #define for numerical constants may make a program's source code longer, but the actual code that runs on the RCX remains the same. The extra comments and #defines won't cause a program to take up more memory in the RCX or run less efficiently.*

Whichever version of the program you are using (RCX Code or NQC), it's time to test our robot. Download the program to Seeker from the PC to the RCX and run it. Seeker should immediately start driving forward. If it does something else, check to make sure the wires for motors A and C were placed properly. If they are turned a different way than shown in the instructions, the motor directions could be reversed. Another item to check is the bumper itself. Make sure that the rubber band is providing adequate tension and that in the "normal" state, the touch sensor is pressed. A good way to verify this is to look at the RCX's display. Below each sensor port a small triangle will appear if the corresponding sensor is pressed, as shown in Figure 3-14. If the triangle does not appear when the bumper is in its "normal" position, then you may need to adjust the #2 axle and bushing so that they press the button more firmly. If the rubber band is too loose, try wrapping it a second time around the black peg.

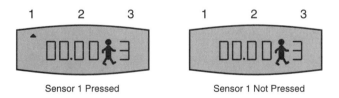

Figure 3-14. Sensor indicators

Now let Seeker wander around for a bit. Whenever it hits something, the bumper should pivot a bit, thus releasing the touch sensor. At this point, the program will cause Seeker to back up and spin a little. Experiment with various obstacles and different angles of attack. A limitation of Seeker's bumper is that it only returns one piece of information: that Seeker has hit an obstacle. A more advanced bumper design would be able to distinguish obstacles on the right from those on the left and allow Seeker to make more intelligent navigation decisions (for example, always turning away from the obstacle and never towards it). Even so, this simple bumper design and program are sufficient to keep Seeker moving around in most cases.

Seeking a Light

Wandering around bumping into things is a good start, but it is more interesting to get a robot to behave purposefully. Our next challenge will be to have Seeker locate and drive towards a bright light. If the light moves around, Seeker should adjust its course to head towards the new location. A flashlight works well as a bright light; you can then move about the room aiming the flashlight at Seeker and it will follow you.

Like obstacle navigation, there are numerous strategies for seeking out a light. We will use a simple and reasonably effective one: drive forward as long as the light sensor detects a bright light, otherwise spin around and look for a bright light. One particularly annoying problem with this strategy is that the robot always needs a "line of sight" to the bright light. If it ever wanders around a corner, it will get stuck spinning in circles forever. To remedy this, we'll add a small twist: when looking for the light, after three seconds of spinning, it will proceed forward for a second before resuming its spinning. In the absence of a light, the robot will thus be engaged in a *random walk*.

The resulting program is a little more complicated than our bumper example, but still well within the capabilities of RCX Code, as shown in Figure 3-15.

A similar program, like the one you see in Listing 3-2, can also be written in NQC (and, like before, the liberal use of #define and comments make the program look a bit more complicated than it really is).

Listing 3-2. The bump.nqc light-seeking program

```
/* seek.nqc
 *
 * Drive towards a bright light.  As long as the light
 * sensor sees a bright light, drive forward.  Otherwise
 * try to find the light first by spinning in place.
 * After 3 seconds of spinning, try driving forward
 * to a new location and then continue spinning.
 */

// motors and sensors
#define LEFT    OUT_A
#define RIGHT   OUT_C
#define EYE     SENSOR_2

// timing
```

```
#define SEEK_MAX_TIMER      30  // 3 seconds
#define SEEK_FWD_TIME       100 // 1 second

// threshold for light sensor
#define THRESHOLD    65

task main()
{
    // setup sensor and start driving
    SetSensor(EYE, SENSOR_LIGHT);
    OnFwd(LEFT+RIGHT);

    while(true)
    {
        // wait until too dark
        until(EYE < THRESHOLD);

        // start spinning and reset timer
        PlayTone(440, 10);
        Rev(LEFT);
        ClearTimer(0);

        while(EYE < THRESHOLD)
        {
            if (Timer(0) > SEEK_MAX_TIMER)
            {
                // spent too long spinning...
                // move forward a bit
                Fwd(LEFT);
                Wait(SEEK_FWD_TIME);

                // continue spinning and reset timer
                Rev(LEFT);
                ClearTimer(0);
            }
        }

        // found the light, resume
        PlayTone(880, 10);
        Fwd(LEFT);
    }
}
```

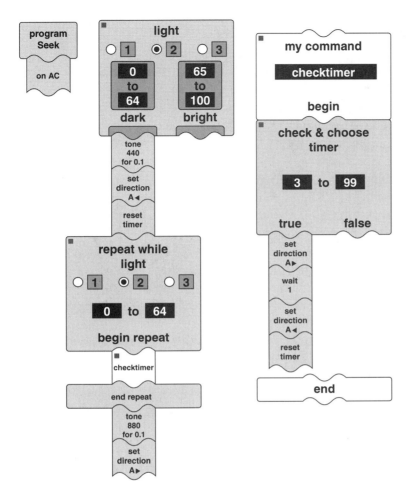

Figure 3-15. Finding a light in RCX code.

Both versions of the program must be able to look at the light sensor's value and decide if it represents the target (a bright light). Because the actual values read from the light sensor will vary depending on a variety of conditions (brightness of the light, amount of ambient light, and so on), you will need to adjust the value used for this decision. Both examples consider a value of 65 or above to be the target light. In the RCX Code program, this is reflected in the ranges used for the light sensor watcher and the "repeat while blocks." In the NQC program, this value is specified in the #define for THRESHOLD.

To determine the proper threshold value you can use the *view* mode of the RCX to show the current light sensor value on the LCD display. By default, the RCX displays the value of its internal clock. Pressing the **View** button cycles through each sensor and each output—an arrow appears in the LCD display pointing to the sensor or motor currently being viewed. Press the **View** button twice to switch from normal display mode to viewing sensor 2 (which is the light sensor). You will also need to run the program (just for a moment) so that it can tell the RCX that sensor 2 is a light sensor. Once this is done, the display should show the value of the light sensor (a number between 0 and 100). If you aim the light sensor at a bright light, this value will increase; if you cover it with your hand, you'll see a lower value. Move Seeker around the room and note the different values under normal conditions. Now aim Seeker at the target light (perhaps a flashlight) and note the value. Ideally, there will be a decent gap between the values in normal light and the values for the bright light. The threshold should be set to the middle of this gap. If there is no such gap, you will need to decrease the general amount of light in the room and/or use a brighter target light.

Both programs also incorporate sound for providing feedback about their operation. Two different tones are played—a lower tone (frequency 440 Hz) whenever Seeker no longer sees the target and must start looking for it, and a higher tone (frequency 880 Hz) when it has found the target again. These tones are purely to help in debugging the program. If Seeker is not behaving as expected, you can figure out which part of the program is currently running by paying attention to the most recent tone that was played.

Start running the program and observe Seeker's behavior. It should emit the low pitched tone, then alternate between spinning in place for three seconds and driving straight for one second. This is the random walk behavior that Seeker uses when it cannot find a bright light. If Seeker emits a high pitched tone and starts driving straight, the threshold value is probably set too low. Now aim a flashlight at Seeker—it should spin until it is facing the flashlight, and then emit a high pitched tone and start driving toward the light. If you move the flashlight, Seeker will again emit a low tone and begin searching for the light. If Seeker does not respond to the flashlight, the threshold may be set too high.

Seeker now does a pretty good job finding a bright light, but it has a problem—it doesn't know what to do if it bumps into anything. For this, we'll need to combine the original bump behavior with our new seek behavior.

Bumping and Seeking

Combining the bump and seek behaviors increases Seeker's versatility—it can then head towards a bright light and negotiate around any obstacles in its path. However, like many exercises in robotics, this is easier said than done.

A first attempt might be to simply merge both programs together. In the case of RCX Code, this would mean using both the touch sensor watcher from the bump program and the light sensor watcher from the seek program. In the case of NQC, the programs could be combined into a single program with two tasks—one watching the touch sensor and the other monitoring the light sensor. Unfortunately, this will lead to some unexpected side effects. Consider what would happen if Seeker actively headed towards a light source and then bumped into something. The *bump* behavior would begin backing up and spinning, but as Seeker started to spin, the *seek* behavior would notice that it could no longer sense the bright light and would send conflicting commands to the motors (spinning in the other direction, and so on). The result being that both behaviors would compete for control over the motors and the Seeker's consequent behavior would be very unstable.

What we need is a way to make the behaviors cooperate. First, consider the bump behavior: under normal circumstances (no obstacles) it drives straight, and when an obstacle is hit, it then takes some corrective action. The seek behavior is similar—under normal circumstances (bright light detected) it drives straight, otherwise it wanders around looking for the light. Clearly, if both behaviors are in normal mode, there is no conflict—Seeker should simply drive straight ahead. If one is normal and the other is not, then Seeker is still ok—it just has to take the corrective action prescribed by the appropriate behavior. What should Seeker do when *both* behaviors are active (for example, when it has hit an obstacle and cannot see the target light)? In this case, it is more important to back away from the obstacle than to spin around looking for the target, so the bump behavior should take precedence. In other words, the bump behavior should have a higher priority than the seek behavior.

It is often impossible (or at least convoluted and tedious) to implement this sort of cooperation in RCX Code. There just isn't an easy way to control which sensor watchers are active at any given time. NQC, however, provides much better control of tasks, so it is possible to make one task the *master* task, which allows it to start and stop the other task. In the case of Seeker, we want the bump behavior to be the main task, and relegate the seek behavior to a secondary task, which is only running when the bump behavior has not detected an obstacle. The body of the bump behavior would then look something like this:

```
while(true)
{
    // start seeking
    start seek;

    // wait for bumper to be activated
    until(BUMPER==0);

    // stop seeking
    stop seek;

    // do whatever necessary to avoid obstacle...
}
```

Because we're abandoning RCX Code, we can also solve the annoying problem of how to determine a correct threshold. Rather than manually setting a threshold, we'll let Seeker determine the value using a *calibration process*. The concept behind calibration is that Seeker will first take a light sensor reading of the normal ambient light. This value is called the *baseline*. Seeker will then wait for the level to become brighter and assume that this new level is the brightness of the target light. It can then set a threshold slightly lower than the target light's brightness. In order to prevent Seeker from triggering the calibration due to slight variation in background light, the bright value will have to exceed the baseline by a specified minimum amount, called the *margin*.

The complete program, including a calibration function, follows in Listing 3-3.

Listing 3-3. The seekbump.nqc program

```
/* seekbump.nqc
 *
 * Drive towards a bright light.  As long as the light
 * sensor sees a bright light, drive forward.  Otherwise
 * try to find the light first by spinning in place.
 * After 3 seconds of spinning, try driving forward
 * to a new location and then continue spinning.
 *
 * If an obstacle is encountered during seeking, back
 * up and spin a bit.
 *
 */


/*
 * The first section of source code defines the basic
 * building blocks of the program including function to
 * setup the robot, find a target, and avoid an obstacle.
 */

// motors and sensors
#define LEFT     OUT_A
#define RIGHT    OUT_C
#define BUMPER   SENSOR_1
#define EYE      SENSOR_2

// timing
#define BUMP_BACK_TIME  60   // 0.6 seconds
#define BUMP_SPIN_TIME  20   // 0.2 seconds
#define SEEK_MAX_TIMER  30   // 3 seconds
#define SEEK_FWD_TIME   100  // 1 second
#define SEEK_DELAY      40   // 0.4 seconds
```

```
// threshold for light detector
int threshold=0;

// margin used to determing threshold
#define MARGIN  4


// setup the sensors and start moving
void setup()
{
    // setup sensors and start driving
    SetSensor(BUMPER, SENSOR_TOUCH);
    SetSensor(EYE, SENSOR_LIGHT);

    // determine light sensor threshold
    calibrate();

    OnFwd(LEFT+RIGHT);
}


// determine proper threshold
void calibrate()
{
    int baseline = EYE;

    do
    {
        int delta = EYE - baseline;

        if (delta > MARGIN)
        {
            threshold = baseline + delta - MARGIN/2;
        }
    } while(threshold == 0);

    PlaySound(SOUND_UP);
    until(EYE < threshold);
    PlaySound(SOUND_DOWN);
}
```

```
// spin and move around looking for target
void find_target()
{
    // start spinning and reset timer
    PlayTone(440, 10);
    Rev(LEFT);
    ClearTimer(0);

    while(EYE < threshold)
    {
        if (Timer(0) > SEEK_MAX_TIMER)
        {
            // spent too long spinning...
            // move forward a bit
            Fwd(LEFT);
            Wait(SEEK_FWD_TIME);

            // continue spinning and reset timer
            Rev(LEFT);
            ClearTimer(0);
        }
    }

    // found the light, resume
    PlayTone(880, 10);
    Fwd(LEFT);
}


// back and spin to avoid obstacle
void avoid_obstacle()
{
    // back up a bit
    OnRev(LEFT+RIGHT);
    Wait(BUMP_BACK_TIME);

    // spin a bit
    Fwd(LEFT);
    Wait(BUMP_SPIN_TIME);

    // resume
    Fwd(RIGHT);
}
```

```
/*
 * The second section of the source code uses the
 * functions defined above in two tasks - the
 * main task avoids obstacles while the seek task
 * finds the target.
 */

task main()
{
    setup();

    while(true)
    {
        start seek;
        until(BUMPER==0);

        stop seek;
        avoid_obstacle();
    }
}


task seek()
{
    Wait(SEEK_DELAY);

    while(true)
    {
        until(EYE < threshold);
        find_target();
    }
}
```

The bump.nqc and seek.nqc programs shown in Listings 3-1 and 3-2, respectively, consist primarily of a single task that does all of the work. This approach works fine for simple programs, but as things get more complex, breaking a program into several smaller pieces can make it easier to write and understand. In seekbump.nqc several different functions, such as avoid_obstacle, are first defined, then combined into the bump and seek behaviors in the main and seek tasks. Breaking a complicated problem into several smaller pieces has another advantage—it increases the flexibility of the source code. In this specific case, the same basic functions will be recombined into new programs in the next chapter.

The calibration process expects a certain sequence of events when the program is started. First, position Seeker such that it is aimed at what could be considered the brightest light that should be considered "normal." For example, in a room with a window, you'll probably want to aim Seeker towards the window during calibration. Then run the program. At this point Seeker should remain motionless waiting for you to show it what a bright light looks like. Stand a few feet away and shine a flashlight on Seeker's light sensor. You should hear a series of ascending tones that indicate Seeker has detected the brighter light. If you don't hear these tones, the difference between the bright light and the normal light doesn't exceed the margin. Try working with a brighter target light or in a slightly darker room. After detecting the target light, Seeker waits for it to disappear before starting its seek and bump behaviors. Turn off the flashlight and observe Seeker as it begins seeking (using the same random walk from before).

Now that the bump behavior and seek behaviors are both running, Seeker should be able to handle bumping into obstacles during its random walk. Specifically, the bump behavior will take precedence over the seek behavior, and Seeker will back away from the obstacle and turn slightly. At that point, seeking will start again.

What happens if Seeker hits an obstacle en route to the target light? In this case, the bump behavior causes a back-and-spin, which will generally cause Seeker to no longer aim towards the target light. The seek behavior will then resume and Seeker will try to find the light. The bump behavior results in a small clockwise spin, and the seek behavior spins in a counterclockwise direction. If the seek behavior were to start spinning immediately after the bump behavior stopped spinning, Seeker would back up, turn slightly clockwise, turn back counterclockwise, and drive straight into the same obstacle again. However, by delaying the seek behavior slightly, we ensure that some forward progress is made in a new direction before the seek spin starts. This is the reason for the Wait(SEEK_DELAY) statement at the start of the seek task.

Often this works quite well. Consider the case where Seeker heads towards its target and runs into a small obstacle, such as a table leg. Seeker will back up and turn slightly to the right. It will then proceed ahead for a short distance, due to the SEEK_DELAY. Seeker will have probably moved far enough to the right to clear the obstacle by the time the seek task begins spinning. After spinning just a short rotation to the left, Seeker will once again find its target and resume travelling towards it, but will this time miss the obstacle completely.

The same situation holds for a larger obstacle that is only partially blocking Seeker on the left. On the other hand, if the obstacle is blocking the right-hand side of Seeker, Seeker's reaction of turning to the right just makes matters worse. In this case, a small turn to the left could have saved Seeker a lot of bumping and spinning. This is where a more informative bumper, which could discern right from left-hand impacts, would really start to pay off. Seeker could then always turn the correct way (right or left) to negotiate around the obstacle, and then make the corresponding spin (left or right) in the seek behavior to find the target again.

More Explorations

This chapter presented four different concepts:

- Construction of the Seeker robot

- Programming the bump behavior

- Programming the seek behavior

- Combining both behaviors into a single program

Mechanically speaking, Seeker is not a particularly complicated robot. Nor are the bump and seek behaviors very complicated from a software perspective. When combined together, however, some interesting behavior emerges. That is one of the keys to experimenting with MINDSTORMS—combining several simpler elements together into a robot that is greater than the sum of its parts.

One of these parts—the Seeker robot itself—will be used continually throughout this book. The next chapter explores certain new features available in the latest versions of LEGO's standard firmware. Some of these features will be demonstrated using the Seeker robot and the bump and seek behaviors. Later chapters in Parts Two and Three, which discuss pbForth and legOS, will also utilize Seeker and demonstrate some of the strengths of those two programming environments.

CHAPTER 4

RCX 2.0 Firmware

IN THE FALL OF 1998, LEGO released their first MINDSTORMS set: the Robotics Invention System (RIS) 1.0. The following year, a new version of the set (RIS 1.5) was released. This new version featured a number of improvements to the RCX Code software, to the documentation included with the set, and it included a few new pieces. The RCX itself was slightly different physically (it had no external power connector), but the firmware remained unchanged.

LEGO is planning another update to the RIS. As of this writing, LEGO has not announced an official release date, but an educated guess is that RIS 2.0 will be available early in 2001. Most of the specifics of RIS 2.0 are also unknown, but one thing is certain: the RCX will get new firmware. Furthermore, this new firmware can be used with existing RCX's, which is good news for owners of RIS 1.0 and RIS 1.5. As an added bonus, this new firmware is available today (albeit in pre-release form). In March of 1999, LEGO made an early version of this firmware available to the public as part of the RIS 2.0 pre-alpha SDK (Software Development Kit). Among other things, the SDK contains the RCX 2.0 Firmware, which can be easily downloaded to any RCX.

The RCX 2.0 Firmware adds a number of new capabilities to the RCX. Presumably, the programming environment for RIS 2.0 will utilize these new capabilities. However, you can get started today by using either the tools contained in the SDK or by using NQC. This chapter will explain some of the major new features and illustrate using them in NQC.

Getting Started

In order to start working with the RCX 2.0 Firmware you will need two things: the firmware itself, and a version of NQC that supports the new features (version 2.2 or higher).

The firmware was initially made available as part of the RIS 2.0 SDK, which can be downloaded from the MINDSTORMS Web site at http://www.legomindstorms.com. However, Web sites change much faster than books, so the specifics of getting this software from the MINDSTORMS site may change. Future MINDSTORMS products will also include the new firmware, so if you are an RIS 2.0 user you already have the new firmware and it has probably been downloaded to your RCX. The firmware is contained in a file named FIRM*xxxx*.LGO, where *xxxx* is the firmware's version number. For example, the original firmware was version 3.0.9 and thus named FIRM0309.LGO. As of this writing, the most recent version of the new firmware is FIRM0328.LGO (version 3.2.8).

The new firmware is compatible with the original firmware, so all of the existing tools and programs for the original firmware should also work with an RCX running the new firmware. However, to take advantage of the new features using NQC, you will need NQC 2.2 or higher. The latest version of NQC can be found at `http://www.enteract.com/~dbaum/nqc`. If you want to determine the version of NQC you are currently using, just type the following command:

```
nqc
```

In order to download firmware to the RCX you should use either the -firmfast or -firmware options for NQC. As its name implies, -firmfast will be faster, but it is also more susceptible to interference. In general, try firmfast. If that doesn't work, step back to -firmware. You will also need to specify the firmware file to be downloaded. For example, if the firmware file was named FIRM0328.LGO and located in your current directory, you can use either of the following commands to download it:

```
nqc -firmfast FIRM0328.LGO
nqc -firmware FIRM0328.LGO
```

After a successful firmware download, NQC will query the RCX and report the versions of the ROM and the firmware. For example, after downloading FIRM0328.LGO you may see something like this:

```
Current Version: 00030001/00030208
```

This indicates that the ROM version is 3.0.1 and the firmware version is 3.2.8. The features discussed in this chapter apply to firmware versions 3.2 and higher.

When compiling a program with NQC you need to tell it if you want to generate code for the original firmware or for the new RCX 2.0 Firmware. You can do this with the -T<*target*> option, where <*target*> is a name that specifies where you plan on running the program. NQC supports a number of different targets, but the most important ones (for RCX owners) are `rcx` and `rcx2`, which specify, respectively, an RCX running the original firmware and an RCX running the 2.0 firmware. If no target is specified, the default is the original RCX, although this may change in later versions of NQC.

> **NOTE**   *If you are using an IDE (such as RcxCC or MacNQC), you may be able to specify the target using preferences within the IDE itself. If the IDE doesn't support the rcx2 target, you may still be able to use the NQC_OPTIONS environment variable to set a default target for NQC to use. Whenever NQC is launched, it first reads the NQC_OPTIONS environment variable and acts as if the options specified in this variable were also typed on the command line. By setting NQC_OPTIONS to "-Trcx2," NQC will default to targeting the new firmware.*

Here is a simple program that uses a couple of the new firmware features. First, it uses the `SetUserDisplay` function to write a value to the LCD. Second, it uses `FirmwareVersion` to determine the current firmware version.

> **NOTE**   *All of the sample programs used in the book can be downloaded from the book's page on the Apress Web site at* `http://www.apress.com`.

```
// firmcheck.nqc

task main()
{
    SetUserDisplay(FirmwareVersion(), 2);
    while(true);
}
```

You can compile and download this program to the RCX using the following command:

```
nqc -Trcx2 -d firmcheck.nqc
```

If NQC reports an error during compilation, either you made a mistake typing in the program or you forgot to tell NQC to target the new firmware (-Trcx2). At this point, if you run the program you should see the firmware version displayed on the LCD. For example, when using firmware 3.2.8, the display shows "3.28.". Note that this program depends on new firmware features; if you try to run it on an RCX with the original firmware, the display will remain unchanged. We're now ready to explore some of the special features of the new firmware.

Local Variables

One of the most limiting aspects of the original firmware is that it only provides thirty-two storage locations that must be shared between all of the tasks in a program. The primary use for this storage is for variables in an NQC program, but they are also used whenever an NQC program needs a temporary variable to hold an intermediate result of a calculation. The new firmware provides sixteen additional storage locations, and unlike the initial thirty-two which are *global* (shared across all tasks), the sixteen new locations are *local* to a task. This means that each of the RCX's ten tasks has its own set of sixteen local locations (for a grand total of 32 + 16 x 10 = 192 storage locations).

The terms *global* and *local* have slightly different meanings when applied to RCX storage locations versus NQC variables. When discussing a storage location, the distinction between global and local locations is simply that global locations may be shared across multiple tasks, while local locations are private to each task. When discussing NQC variables, the meanings are somewhat different. Variables that are declared outside of a task, function, or subroutine are global variables, which means that they can be accessed from anywhere in the program. Variables declared within a task, function, or subroutine are local variables and can only be accessed within the block that declares them. The following code illustrates how global and local variables may be declared and where they can be accessed.

```
int g; // g is a global variable

task main()
{
    int x; // x is a local variable
    while(true)
    {
        int y; // y is another local variable
        // x, y, and g can all be accessed here
    }
    // x and g can be accessed here, y cannot
}

task foo()
{
    // only g can be accessed here
}
```

When NQC compiles a program it must assign each variable to a specific storage location. In general, global variables must be assigned to global locations, but local variables can use either global or local locations. It is important to note that NQC still enforces the restrictions for access to local variables even when they are assigned to global locations. In the previous example, task foo would not be able to use variables x and y even if they were placed in global locations.

Because the firmware's new locations are local to a task, NQC is able to re-use the locations more efficiently and can even generate code for certain cases that were impossible when using the original firmware. Using these new storage locations couldn't be easier; NQC automatically uses local storage locations, as appropriate, when compiling a program for the RCX2.

To realize the greatest benefit from the new storage locations, it is a good idea to use local variables instead of global ones whenever possible. This gives the NQC compiler the freedom to put the variable in either global or local storage. It can thus try to maximize the total number of variables available to your program. When assigning locations for local variables, NQC will generally attempt to use local locations first and resort to global locations only after the local ones have been exhausted for a given task. In the following code, variable g must be assigned to a global location, while variable x is declared such that the compiler can use what-ever storage space happens to be available (local or global).

```
int g; // g will have to use a global location

task main()
{
    int x; // x can use local or global location, NQC will pick
}
```

Display

With the original firmware, a program's control over the LCD was somewhat limited. The default mode was for the LCD to display the value of the RCX's watch (its internal clock). Other modes allowed the current value of a sensor or output to be displayed instead. However, the ability to display an arbitrary number or monitor a variable was missing.

The new firmware adds one more display mode: user display. In user display mode, the LCD can display the value of any RCX data source (for example, sensors, timers, and so on). The most obvious use for this mode is to display constant numbers. However, the mode can also be used to display the contents of dynamic sources, such as variables or timers. NQC supports this new feature with a single function: SetUserDisplay(source, decimal_point). The first argument is the data source to display; the second argument specifies where the decimal point (if any) should be drawn.

```
SetUserDisplay(123, 0);  // displays "123"
SetUserDisplay(123, 2);  // displays "1.23"
SetUserDisplay(Timer(0), 0); // display the value of timer 0
```

The behavior of displaying a timer may surprise you. At first glance, it looks like Timer(0) will be evaluated, and its current value will then be passed to SetUser-Display(), presumably to be written to the LCD. In NQC, however, things operate a little differently. The expression Timer(0) is passed by reference to SetUserDisplay(). When the display is in user mode, it continuously reads and displays the data source (in this case Timer(0)). Run the following program to see this effect in action.

```
// viewtimer.nqc

task main()
{
    ClearTimer(0);
    SetUserDisplay(Timer(0), 0);
    until(false);  // keep the program running
}
```

The RCX normally returns to the default display mode (the watch) whenever a program ends. In the preceding program, the until statement prevents the program from finishing, thus allowing the display to stay in user mode. Note that the RCX will only reset the display mode when a program ends normally—interrupting the program by pressing the Run button will leave the display mode unchanged. Thus the value of Timer(0) in this case would continue to be displayed even after the program was stopped.

The fact that the RCX will continuously update the display in user mode has some interesting consequences. First, it must be possible for the RCX to read the value to be displayed. Because the LCD does not belong to any specific task, local storage locations (which are only valid within their own task) cannot be used. If you want to display the value of a variable, you generally need to make the variable global (by declaring it outside a task, function, or subroutine).

Another consequence of displaying a variable is that you may occasionally see its value partway through a calculation because it is continuously being updated on the LCD. For example, the following program gives the impression that it will always be showing the value of 1 plus timer 0. However, if you run the program you will notice that although the timer continues to count upwards, every once in a while the value 1 is shown on the LCD. This is because sometimes the LCD grabs the value of x in the middle of the calculation x = 1 + Timer(0).

```
// display_bad.nqc

int x = 0;

task main()
{
    ClearTimer(0);
    SetUserDisplay(x, 0);
    while(true)
    {
        x = 1 + Timer(0);
    }
}
```

This problem can be fixed by latching the calculated value into a separate global variable that actually gets displayed, as shown in the code that follows. Even though the value of x moves around during the calculation of x = 1 + Timer(0), the LCD will always show the correct value since the update to displayValue happens in a single operation. Since x is no longer displayed directly, it can be moved to a local variable.

```
// display_ok.nqc

int displayValue = 0;

task main()
{
    int x;

    ClearTimer(0);
    SetUserDisplay(displayValue, 0);
    while(true)
    {
        x = 1 + Timer(0);
        displayValue = x;
    }
}
```

One of the best uses of the display is to assist in debugging a program. In cases where you want to inspect a variable's value, just insert the appropriate call to SetUserDisplay in your program. Another useful technique is to display constant values at various points in the program. Then by observing the value on the LCD you can tell what part of the program was last executed.

Arrays

Not only does the new firmware provide more variable storage, but it also provides a new way to access the storage: *arrays*. An array is a set of storage locations that share a common name. The individual locations are then accessed by their position—called the *index*—within the array. In NQC, arrays must be of a fixed size. In theory, the maximum size for an array is thirty-two. However, such a large array would use up all of the global storage locations, leaving no room for additional global variables. In general, arrays should be kept as small as possible because storage locations are such a precious resource. Declaring an array is similar to declaring a normal variable except that you must also specify the size of the array. For example, the following statement declares an array named my_array that can hold four values:

```
int my_array[4];
```

The size of the array can involve a calculation, but must be constant at compile time, as shown by the two declarations (one legal, the other an error) that follow.

```
int my_array[2 * 3]; // ok - compiler knows that 2 * 3 = 6
int x;
int bad_array[x]; // error - x is not constant!
```

The values inside an array are called *elements* and are accessed by specifying the array name and the index of the element. In NQC, the first element has an index of 0. At first, this may seem a bit strange—shouldn't the first item be number 1? However, arrays in C are zero-based (first element has an index of 0), and NQC uses this same model. Don't worry, after a while you'll get used to asking for element 0. The following code illustrates setting and reading elements of an array.

```
my_array[0] = 123; // set first element to 123
my_array[1] = my_array[2]; // copy third element into second
```

Unlike the size of an array, which must be constant, indexes do not have to be constant. This is where the true power of an array comes in because it allows a set of statements to operate on any (or all) elements in the array. For example, the following code declares an array of five elements and sets them all to 0:

```
int my_array[5];
int i;
for(i=0; i<5; ++i)
    my_array[i] = 0;
```

Note that NQC does not check to see if an index is within the bounds of the array. In the previous example, if the array were declared with a size of 4, the code would still compile without any errors. The result of running the program, however, would be undefined since it would be attempting to set element 5 of an array that only contained 4 elements.

The for loop that sets the elements to 0 is certainly more compact than writing five separate assignment statements. At first arrays may just seem like a fancy way to save a little typing, but they also allow functionality that would be impossible (or at least difficult and obscure) with ordinary variables.

As a more complex example we'll write a program that starts by taking several readings from a light sensor and then computes their average. Then as new samples are taken, the oldest one will be discarded and a new average will be computed. The key to this entire program is to store the samples in an array. The complete program is shown in Listing 4-1.

Listing 4-1. average.nqc

```
// average.nqc

// sensors
#define BUTTON      SENSOR_1
#define EYE         SENSOR_2

// number of samples
#define N      3

// average needs to be global for display
int average = 0;



// this function waits for a press and
// release of the touch sensor

void wait_for_touch()
{
    until(BUTTON == 1);
    until(BUTTON == 0);
    PlaySound(SOUND_CLICK);
}
```

```
task main()
{
    int index;
    int current;
    int samples[N];
    int total = 0;

    // setup sensors and display
    SetSensor(BUTTON, SENSOR_TOUCH);
    SetSensor(EYE, SENSOR_LIGHT);
    SetUserDisplay(average, 1);

    // start with N samples
    for(index=0; index<N; ++index)
    {
        wait_for_touch();

        current = EYE;
        samples[index] = current;
        total += current;
    }

    PlaySound(SOUND_UP);

    index = 0;
    while(true)
    {
        // compute the average
        average = total * 10 / N;

        // get new sample
        wait_for_touch();
        current = EYE;

        // replace sample
        total -= samples[index];
        total += current;
        samples[index] = current;

        // adjust index
        ++index;
        if (index==N) index = 0;
    }

}
```

The program assumes that a touch sensor is attached to port 1 and a light sensor is attached to port 2 (the same sensor configuration used in Seeker, discussed in Chapter 3). The `wait_for_touch` function waits for the touch sensor to be pressed and released, then emits a brief sound. The main task starts by declaring its variables and configuring the sensors and display. Note that the variable `average` was intentionally kept as a global variable so that it could be displayed.

The program gets the initial N readings and stores them in the `samples` array. It also keeps a running `total` of the readings. After the initial samples have been read the `SOUND_UP` sound will be played and the program will be ready to update its samples.

The update process is a little more complicated than reading in the initial samples. That's because each time a new sample is read, the oldest sample must be discarded. The `index` variable is used to keep track of the oldest sample, which, initially, is element 0.

The `while` loop is where most of the work gets done. First, it computes the average from the current total. Normally, an average would be computed by dividing the total by the number of samples, but in this case we are also multiplying by ten. By doing this, `average` will actually contain a value that is ten times the actual average. However, the display was configured to display values in tenths, so the overall result is that the LCD will display the real average including a single decimal digit of precision (for example, "45.3" instead of just "45").

Next, the program waits for the touch sensor to be activated, then it reads the light sensor. Replacing the old sample with a new one requires three operations—subtracting the old sample from `total`, adding the new sample to `total`, and saving the current sample in the `samples` array. Now that the oldest sample has been replaced with the newest, `index` must be adjusted to point to the next oldest sample. In most cases, this will be the next higher index, but we also have to take into account the case where `index` needs to *wrap-around* to the start of the array.

Download the program to the RCX and give it a try. When you first run the program it should display "0.0.". Now press and release the touch sensor three times (if you are using Seeker, then just hit the bumper three times). You should hear the SOUND_UP sound and the display will now show the average of those first three light sensor readings. Aim the sensor at a bright light or into a dark corner and take more samples (press the touch sensor or bumper). If you move the RCX from a light environment to a dark one and then take several samples, you should see the average gradually change from the old value to a new one during the first three samples. It will then tend to stabilize (at least until the lighting changes again). This method of averaging is called *finite response* because any given sample (such as the initial bright sample) will only affect the average for a finite number of new samples before the given sample is discarded. Finite response can be a very useful way to keep a running average and is just one example of the many things you can do with arrays.

Access Control

At times, a situation will arise where two separate tasks would like control over the same resource, and without some degree of coordination, the resulting behavior is likely to be surprising. For example, in the last chapter the bump and seek behaviors both needed control over the motors at certain times. Coordination was implemented in the main task (bump behavior) by having it explicitly stop and later restart the seek task. In some situations, this approach of starting and stopping tasks is a bit too severe.

The new firmware provides another option: *access control*. In general terms, access control allows a task to request ownership of a *resource*. If the resource is not owned by any task, the request is successful. If the resource is owned by a task with higher priority than the requestor, then the request fails. If, however, the resource is owned by a task with the same or lower priority than the requestor, then the request succeeds with the added consequence that the original owner loses their access to the resource. Besides requesting ownership, a task may also release ownership of resources when it is finished with them.

These basic abilities—requesting and releasing ownership—can be used to implement a kind of if/then logic for resources:

> if ownership request succeeds then
>
> > do something with the resource
> >
> > release resource
>
> else
>
> > do something to recover from failure or loss

Note that the RCX treats losing a resource the same as a failed request. In other words, any recovery code must be able to deal with two situations: the initial request failed, or the initial request succeeded, but the task later lost ownership (to an equal or higher priority task) before releasing the resource.

So far the discussion has been a bit abstract—it's time for some details. The firmware defines four physical resources:

- Motor A

- Motor B

- Motor C

- Sound

In NQC, these are represented by the constants ACQUIRE_OUT_A, ACQUIRE_OUT_B, ACQUIRE_OUT_C, and ACQUIRE_SOUND. There are also four user-defined resources that can be used:

- ACQUIRE_USER_1

- ACQUIRE_USER_2

- ACQUIRE_USER_3

- ACQUIRE_USER_4

The only difference between physical and user-defined resources is that when ownership of a physical resource is lost from one task to another, the firmware takes some default action (in addition to any recovery defined by the task that lost the resource). The default action for outputs is to turn them off, and the default action for the sound resource is to stop the currently playing sound and remove any pending sounds from the sound queue.

Each task has a priority, which ranges from 0 to 255 with 0 being the highest priority. This can be a bit counter-intuitive because lower numbers are actually higher in priority. I find it convenient to think of priority 1 as the first priority, 2 as the second priority, and so on. In NQC, a task can set its own priority with the SetPriority function:

```
SetPriority(0); // the highest priority
SetPriority(255); // the lowest priority
```

NOTE   *It is imperative that any task using access control set its priority, otherwise, the initial priority of a task will be undefined and the results may be surprising.*

An NQC task may request a resource using the acquire statement, whose syntax contains the following :

```
acquire(resources) body [catch handler]
```

In this statement, acquire and catch are keywords, resources is a list of resources to acquire, and *body* and *handler* are statements. The catch and handler portion is optional. The acquire statement requests access to the resources, then executes the body, then implicitly releases the resources. If the request fails or if the resources are lost to another task, the handler (if present) is executed. For example, the following code acquires outputs A and C and then waits 10 seconds.

```
acquire(ACQUIRE_OUT_A + ACQUIRE_OUT_C)
{
    Wait(1000);
}
ClearTimer(0);
```

In the preceding example, ClearTimer will always get called, regardless of whether the request fails, succeeds, or if ownership is lost during Wait. If the program needs to differentiate between normal completion of the acquire and a failure/loss, then a handler should be used as shown in the following example.

```
acquire(ACQUIRE_OUT_A + ACQUIRE_OUT_C)
{
    Wait(1000);
}
catch
{
    PlaySound(SOUND_CLICK);
}
ClearTimer(0);
```

At this point, if the request fails or ownership is lost, control will transfer to the handler and PlaySound will be called. In all cases, control will still eventually drop through to the ClearTimer call.

Access control provides a convenient way to coordinate Seeker's bump and seek behaviors from the previous chapter. Using the same functions and definitions from the original seekbump.nqc program, new main and seek tasks can be written that use access control rather than starting/stopping a task to coordinate the behaviors. These tasks are shown in Listing 4-2.

Listing 4-2. Tasks in seekbump_access.nqc

```
task main()
{
    setup();
    SetPriority(1);
    start seek;

    while(true)
    {
        until(BUMPER==0);
```

```
        acquire(ACQUIRE_USER_1)
        {
            avoid_obstacle();
        }
    }
}


task seek()
{
    SetPriority(2);

    while(true)
    {
        acquire(ACQUIRE_USER_1)
        {
            Wait(SEEK_DELAY);
            while(true)
            {
                until(EYE < threshold);
                find_target();
            }
        }
    }
}
```

NOTE   *The program in its entirety is contained in the file seekbump_access.nqc,*
which you can download from the book's Web site at `http://www.apress.com.`

Overall, the structure of both tasks is the same as before—the main task sets things up, then enters an infinite loop waiting for the bumper to be activated and then avoiding an obstacle. The seek task waits for the light sensor to drop below the threshold, then tries to find the target. Most of the time, the seek task owns the ACQUIRE_USER_1 resource. However, once the bumper is hit, the main task requests ownership and because it is a higher priority task, the seek task loses ownership. The main task is then free to avoid the obstacle. Once the seek task loses ownership, it will continue in its while loop—each time requesting access of the resource. Only after the main task is finished avoiding the obstacle will it release the resource, thus letting the seek task re-acquire it and resume checking the light sensor and finding the target.

Events

All of the programs so far have explicitly checked their sensors using conditional statements such as if, while, or until. This is a relatively easy and straightforward way to construct a program, but it does have some limitations. For example, conditional statements begin to get unwieldy if the program needs to accommodate multiple stimuli (such as both a touch sensor and a light sensor). In the case of Seeker, introducing a second task so that each task would only have to watch a single sensor solved this problem. However, this approach had its own drawback since it added the complexity of coordinating the two tasks.

Conditional statements are also limited to testing the immediate state of a sensor (for example, "is the sensor pressed?"). In order to respond to more complicated stimuli (for instance, "has the sensor been held less than one second?" or "has the sensor been pressed twice?"), additional code would have to monitor the sensor and keep track of characteristics such as how long it was held or how many times it was pressed.

The new firmware provides another mechanism to react to stimuli: *events*. As their name implies, events represent something that can happen that is of interest to the program. For example, a light sensor that detects darkness, a touch sensor pressed for longer than one second, or a timer that exceeds the preset limit are all examples of potential events. The firmware can monitor up to 16 independent events. Each event is referred to by its *event number*, which is simply a number from 0 to 15. There is no implicit difference between any of the event numbers— a program may decide to use event 0 to watch a light sensor or event 7 to monitor a timer. The program is thus responsible for configuring the events—telling the firmware what condition should result in the triggering of the event.

Event Monitoring

Before digging into the details of how events are configured, it will be helpful to understand how they can be monitored from within a program. In many ways, event monitoring is similar to access control, but rather than requesting access to a specific resource, a task indicates that it wishes to have a certain set of events monitored. This request always succeeds. However, if a monitored event later becomes triggered, the program can have special handler code executed—this is similar to the handler code that executed when ownership of a resource was lost. In fact, event monitoring and access control are so similar that their syntax in NQC is nearly identical. The major difference is that instead of the keyword acquire, event monitoring uses the keyword monitor, and instead of a list of resources, it takes a list of events:

```
monitor(MY_EVENTS)
{
    // normal code to execute
}
catch
{
    // code that handles the events
}
```

Events are numbered 0 to 15, and are each represented by a single bit in the event list (also called an event mask). The EVENT_MASK macro creates the appropriate mask from a single event number, and these masks can be added together in order to monitor multiple events. For example, to monitor events 2 and 5 the following line could be used:

```
monitor(EVENT_MASK(2) + EVENT_MASK(5))
```

Event Configuration

Each event has a number of parameters that determine how and when it will be triggered. The first parameter is the *event source*, which determines which stimulus the event should be monitoring. The source can be a sensor, timer, counter, or the message buffer (SENSOR_2, Timer(1), and so on).

The second parameter is the *event type*, which defines what condition the event should be looking for. There are eleven different event types as shown in Table 4-1.

Table 4-1. Event Types

EVENT TYPE	CONDITION	EVENT SOURCE
EVENT_TYPE_PRESSED	value becomes *on*	sensors only
EVENT_TYPE_RELEASED	value becomes *off*	sensors only
EVENT_TYPE_PULSE	value goes from *off* to *on* to *off*	sensors only
EVENT_TYPE_EDGE	value goes from *on* to *off* or vice versa	sensors only
EVENT_TYPE_FASTCHANGE	value changes rapidly	sensors only
EVENT_TYPE_LOW	value becomes *low*	any
EVENT_TYPE_NORMAL	value becomes *normal*	any
EVENT_TYPE_HIGH	value becomes *high*	any
EVENT_TYPE_CLICK	value from *low* to *high* back to *low*	any
EVENT_TYPE_DOUBLECLICK	two clicks within a certain time	any
EVENT_TYPE_MESSAGE	new message received	Message() only

Boolean Value Events

The first four event types (pressed, released, pulse, and edge) are most useful with touch sensors because the sensors have obvious *on* and *off* conditions. However, these event types can also be used with other sensors provided that the default boolean conversion (described in Chapter 2) is acceptable.

The program you see in Listing 4-3 illustrates how to use the EVENT_TYPE_PRESSED event with a touch sensor on port 1. Whenever the touch sensor is pressed the program will emit a short beep.

Listing 4-3. event_pressed.nqc

```
// event_pressed.nqc

#define MY_EVENT 0  // we'll use event #0

task main()
{
    SetSensor(SENSOR_1, SENSOR_TOUCH);
    SetEvent(MY_EVENT, SENSOR_1, EVENT_TYPE_PRESSED);

    while(true)
    {
        monitor(EVENT_MASK(MY_EVENT))
        {
            until(false);
        }
        catch
        {
            PlaySound(SOUND_CLICK);
        }
    }
}
```

The SetEvent function configures an event with the specified source and type. The event can then be used in a monitor statement (after computing its EVENT_MASK).

If the default boolean conversion is not acceptable, then a slope parameter may be used (see Chapter 2). In this case, an EVENT_TYPE_FASTCHANGE will be triggered whenever the sensor's value changes more rapidly than the slope parameter.

Range Events

Many event sources don't have such well-defined boolean values. Sensors other than the touch sensor generally work better as a range of values, and sources such as timers and counters have no boolean equivalent. For these cases, the firmware provides the *range event* types. Two additional parameters—the *lower limit* and *upper limit* are used to decide which range a sensor's value falls into. If the value is less than the lower limit, then it is considered to be *low.* If the value is greater than the upper limit, then it is *high.* When the value is between the lower and upper limits (or equal to either limit) it is considered *normal.* The low, normal, and high event types are triggered whenever the event source first enters that range. For example, if a source goes from normal to low then a low event will be triggered, but while it remains low no additional low events will be triggered.

There's another wrinkle in the conversion from a source's value to the low/normal/high ranges. In the real world, sensors don't instantly change value from one extreme to another—sometimes they may waver a bit. If they waver near one of the limit values, this can cause many events to happen, even though the value isn't changing in a significant way. For example, consider a light sensor (values from 0 to 100) where the range 0–59 is considered "dark" and 81–100 is "bright". To use events with this sensor it would make sense to set the lower limit to 60 and the upper limit to 80. Now consider what would happen if the sensor's value was wavering between 80 and 81. Each move to 80 would cause it trigger a normal event, and each move to 81 would trigger a high event. This is probably not very helpful to the program—it would be much better if the program considered this wavering value to be either normal or high and not continue to generate new events.

One way to overcome this problem is to use a slightly lower cutoff for exiting the high range than was used to enter it. For example, the cutoffs 75 and 80 could be used so that a value of 75 or below would be in the normal range and anything above 80 would be in the high range. Values from 76 to 80 would leave the range unchanged. Let's say the initial value starts at 50 (normal state) and begins to increase. As soon as the value reaches 81 or above it would be considered high and an appropriate event would be generated. Now if the value wavers a bit—perhaps decreasing to 78 then back up to 81—the value would still be considered in the high range. The value would have to drop all the way to 75 or lower before the range would transition back to normal. This difference between the two cutoffs is called hysteresis and is a very effective way of minimizing the jittery effects of real world sensors. An event's hysteresis parameter affects both the lower limit and upper limit as shown in Figure 4-1.

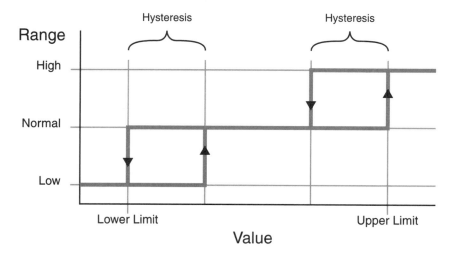

Figure 4-1. Hysteresis

By default, the lower limit and upper limit are set to the minimum and maximum values of the source, and hysteresis is set to 0. The current values of these parameters can be read with LowerLimit(event), UpperLimit(event), and Hysteresis(event), where event is the event number. The values can be set with SetLowerLimit(event, value), SetUpperLimit(event, value), and SetHysteresis(event, value), where event is the event number and value is the desired setting. The program shown in Listing 4-4 monitors the light sensor using an EVENT_TYPE_HIGH event. For completeness the lower limit is also set, although this isn't strictly necessary because the program is only concerned with the normal and high ranges.

Listing 4-4. event_high.nqc

```
// event_high.nqc

#define MY_EVENT 0  // we'll use event #0

task main()
{
    SetSensor(SENSOR_2, SENSOR_LIGHT);
    SetUserDisplay(SENSOR_2, 0);

    SetEvent(MY_EVENT, SENSOR_2, EVENT_TYPE_HIGH);
    SetUpperLimit(MY_EVENT, 80);
    SetLowerLimit(MY_EVENT, 50);
    SetHysteresis(MY_EVENT, 5);
```

```
    while(true)
    {
        monitor(EVENT_MASK(MY_EVENT))
        {
            until(false);
        }
        catch
        {
            PlaySound(SOUND_CLICK);
        }
    }
}
```

The program displays the current value of the light sensor (which is assumed to be on sensor port 2) on the LCD. By slowly turning the light sensor towards a bright light you should be able to gradually increase the sensor value. As soon as the value exceeds 80, the event will be triggered and a sound will be played. The sensor's value may then be lowered all the way to 76, then back above 80 without triggering an additional event. This difference of cutoff values (above 80 to enter the high level, but less than or equal to 75 to remain) is due to the hysteresis parameter.

NOTE *In the previous example, it will sometimes appear that the event is being triggered at 80 rather than 81. This is because event monitoring is a bit faster than the display and a momentary value of 81 may be enough to trigger the event, even though the display may still register a value of 80.*

Click Events

The firmware also has the ability to watch for a transition from low to high and back to low. If both transitions happen within a certain time—called the *click time*—then the entire sequence will trigger an EVENT_TYPE_CLICK event. If a second click occurs, and the time between the end of the first click and the start of the second is also less than the click time, then an EVENT_TYPE_DOUBLECLICK event will also be triggered. The click time is specified in units of 10 milliseconds (ms). It defaults to 15, which is equivalent to 150 ms. It can be read using ClickTime(event) and set with SetClickTime(event, value).

The program you see in Listing 4-5 watches for the touch sensor on port 1 to be clicked. Note that the upper limit and lower limit are set to 0 and 1 respectively so that when the sensor is pressed (value of 1) it will be high and when it is released (value of 0) it will be low. The click time has been set to half a second (500 ms). If the touch sensor (attached to sensor port 1) is pressed then released within a half second, the event will be triggered and a sound will be played. Pressing and holding the sensor for longer than a half second will not trigger an event.

Listing 4-5. event_click.nqc

```
// event_click.nqc

#define MY_EVENT 0  // we'll use event #0

task main()
{
    SetSensor(SENSOR_1, SENSOR_TOUCH);
    SetEvent(MY_EVENT, SENSOR_1, EVENT_TYPE_CLICK);

    SetUpperLimit(MY_EVENT, 0);
    SetLowerLimit(MY_EVENT, 1);
    SetClickTime(MY_EVENT, 50);

    while(true)
    {
        monitor(EVENT_MASK(MY_EVENT))
        {
            until(false);
        }
        catch
        {
            PlaySound(SOUND_CLICK);
        }
    }
}
```

Message Event

The last event type, EVENT_TYPE_MESSAGE, only applies to events using Message() as their event source. This event type is triggered whenever a new message arrives, regardless of whether the value of Message() itself changes.

Using Events with Seeker

Now that the basics of event monitoring have been presented, we can look at how events can help with the bump and seek program. As discussed before, the robot will normally be engaged in seeking. Whenever a bump occurs, however, seeking must be interrupted while the robot attempts to avoid the obstacle. Previous approaches used two separate tasks for the seek and bump behaviors and then sought to coordinate those tasks. With events, however, both the seek and bump actions can be implemented within a single task. We'll accomplish this by using an event to detect bumping. Because monitored events interrupt normal program flow, bumping into an obstacle can then interrupt seeking and the obstacle can be avoided. Using the functions defined in the original seekbump.nqc, the main task shown in Listing 4-6 both seeks and bumps (no seek task is required).

Listing 4-6. Main task for seekbump_event.nqc

```
#define BUMP_EVENT 0

task main()
{
    setup();

    SetEvent(BUMP_EVENT, BUMPER, EVENT_TYPE_RELEASED);

    while(true)
    {
        monitor(EVENT_MASK(BUMP_EVENT))
        {
            // seek
            Wait(SEEK_DELAY);
            while(true)
            {
                until(EYE < threshold);
                find_target();
            }
        }
        catch
        {
            // bump
            avoid_obstacle();
        }
    }
}
```

NOTE *The program in its entirety is contained in the file seekbump_event.nqc, which can be downloaded from the book's page on the Apress Web site at* http://www.apress.com.

This is perhaps the most elegant of the Seeker programs and is an excellent example of how event monitoring can be used to simplify a problem.

Bits and Pieces

Although this chapter explored some of the major new features of the RCX 2.0 Firmware, it is not by any means a comprehensive guide to its capabilities. Several of the features have additional calls or options that weren't discussed. There are numerous other features that are smaller in scope but can be just as important if they solve a specific problem you are having. Here is a partial list of some of these improvements:

- The capabilities for playing sounds have been enhanced to allow a program to mute and unmute sound, clear pending sounds, and play a note whose frequency is determined by a variable (previously the frequency had to be a constant).

- The timers have been enhanced to provide 10 ms measurement in addition to the original 100 ms resolution timers.

- Programs can now cause the RCX to switch to another program and start it.

- Programs now have direct access to the IR port. They can send arbitrary bytes of data rather than just the simple message capability previously available.

- Programs can read the present battery level.

For more information about this firmware, your first stop should be the official documentation provided by LEGO. The RIS 2.0 SDK contains a PDF document titled "LEGO MINDSTORMS RCX 2.0 Firmware Command Overview," which describes all of the commands and bytecodes supported by the firmware.

The documentation for NQC also contains some pertinent information about the new firmware, although, in general, its focus is more on how the features are called from within NQC rather than the internal workings of those features.

Bear in mind that this is a relatively new field—NQC only recently added support for the new firmware, and programmers are just starting to understand how the features can be used to build better programs. Hopefully this chapter has piqued your interest—perhaps you will even help contribute to our knowledge of how to use the RCX 2.0 Firmware effectively!

pbForth

Ralph Hempel

Part Two

Introduction to pbForth

WITH SO MANY TOOLS to choose from when programming the RCX, it's natural to ask why anyone would use a dowdy old language like Forth. The answer is the reason Forth was created in the first place. It's a low-level, interactive language, designed specifically to interact with computers with few resources. In fact, the original version of Forth was designed to run a radio telescope from a minicomputer not much more powerful than the RCX itself! Back in the early 1970s, a machine with 32KB of RAM and a typical instruction time of 500 nanoseconds was hot stuff—but you could forget about holding it in your hand.

You might want to use pbForth over some of the alternatives for the following reasons:

- Interactivity

- Interpreted language

- Extensibility

Each of these strengths is discussed in the following sections.

> **NOTE** *Forth is a computer language that has been implemented on a wide variety of systems. One such implementation is pbForth—a version of Forth for the RCX. When discussing generic concepts or programming features that apply to all Forth versions, the term Forth will be used, while the term pbForth will be used when discussing features of that specific implementation.*

pbForth Is Interactive

Most modern computer languages are not interactive. You can't just type something in at the keyboard and expect your computer to perform any work. You have to write the code and submit it for compilation before you can run your program. You generally change how the program works by running it with different command-line options, or by interacting with the user interface.

That's not how you write programs for the RCX using pbForth. Once the replacement firmware is loaded into the RCX you can type in commands and programs and see your results right away. You receive feedback either from values that the RCX sends back to your host machine, or by some action of the RCX itself, such as a sound being played.

pbForth Is Interpreted

Although pbForth is interpreted, but don't get the idea that it is slow like some of the early dialects of BASIC. The pbForth kernel translates your source code into compact bytecodes, which are then interpreted by a highly optimized virtual machine.

The neat thing about an interpreter is that it is always running. You can query or change the state of any variable or memory location in the RCX. This is very powerful when you need to figure out why something is not working, or if you want to experiment with how something might work.

pbForth Is Extensible

The most powerful feature of pbForth is that it is extensible. You will be able to write almost all the code you need for your first projects using only standard Forth words. Eventually, you may want to manipulate advanced data structures, or write a word that uses different types of data in an unusual way. You can extend the Forth interpreter and compiler to customize the way it handles data.

You simply send ASCII text to the compiler, which is located on the RCX itself. Instead of having on your host machine a compiler that must be rewritten for every platform, the entire process is on the RCX. By extending the compiler, you finally have complete control of the RCX.

Why Learn pbForth?

After deciding that pbForth might be fun to try, the next hurdle you need surpass is learning pbForth. One look at the source code might be enough to send you screaming, but if you understand the philosophy of Forth, it will be easier to embrace. By learning another computer language, especially one that asks you to think differently about problems, you will deepen your bag of programming tricks. Even if you don't write software for a living, learning a language like Forth can be fun mental exercise.

Learning any programming language is pretty much the same no matter which one you choose. After reading the background material on why the language was written in the first place and how it applies to your problem, you need to be able to perform several tasks to be effective:

- Enter numbers, calculate expressions, and generate output.

- Set and query variables.

- Create and execute new functions or subroutines.

- Use control structures to make decisions within your program.

The basics of pbForth are easy to master. I will teach you a bit about each of the aforementioned topics, then you'll apply what you learn directly to the RCX. Learning to write programs is fun if you can get immediate feedback.

Why Learn about RCX Details?

Before exploring pbForth firsthand, you should know the fundamentals of the LEGO RCX brick. The RCX is a great platform for bringing together the three disciplines that make up mechatronics:

- Mechanics

- Electronics

- Software to connect the mechanics and electronics

This little brick can be the brains of many different kinds of creations and under your complete control. If you invest time in understanding how the routines built into the RCX work, you can get more functionality out of the RCX. You can manipulate many of the most interesting routines with pbForth. The routines give you direct access to the LCD, timers, motors, sensors, sounds, and pushbuttons. There are even extensions that let you control servo motors and custom sensors, which are beyond the scope of this book. You can find out about them at www.hempeldesigngroup.com/lego/pbForth. Chapter 2 of this book gives a detailed description of each of the RCX hardware systems. Here, we'll explore how pbForth is used to control them.

As you delve further into RCX programming, it will become clear that there are many different systems working cooperatively to help you build interesting robots. This section describes these systems. Figure 5-1 illustrates how the systems fit together.

> **NOTE** *Learning how the RCX works can give you insight into the fascinating world of embedded systems design. These are systems that you use every day without even thinking about them—from the front panel of your microwave oven to the engine controller in your car, embedded systems are all around you. The RCX can be used to learn more about how these systems work, and to try your hand at developing embedded systems of your own.*

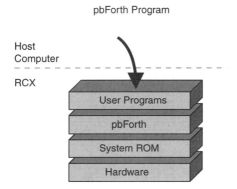

Figure 5-1. Using pbForth on the RCX

System Hardware

The hardware is the brick itself. This includes the motor drivers, passive/active sensor inputs, the LCD, the piezo sounder (often called the speaker), the buttons, the IR link, and so on. These systems are used to interface the brick to the robot and to the host computer. The hardware also includes the RAM that stores your software and system firmware. On a desktop computer, you don't really have to think too much about RAM because the applications and operating system you use manage it for you. On the RCX, writing a value into the wrong memory location can crash your application, rendering the RCX unresponsive. Don't worry, you can't actually break the RCX—but you might have to remove the batteries to regain control.

User Programs

The software is the code you write to run on the RCX. When you use RCX Code, NQC, legOS, or any other development tool, you are writing software for your RCX. This is where you develop your skills in designing algorithms to get your robot to do useful things. It is also an opportunity to expand your debugging skills when the robot doesn't do what it is supposed to. By the end of this section on pbForth, you should be able to write simple programs and debug them—even if you have never programmed before.

System Firmware

Somewhere in the middle lies the firmware, which is really just special code that acts as an interface between your software and the RCX hardware. Actually, there are two kinds of firmware on the RCX. There is *non-volatile* firmware (called System ROM in this book), which is permanently stored on the microprocessor inside the RCX. This is the code that runs when you first power up the RCX. Its job is to manage all of the hardware, as well as to prepare the RCX for communication with the IR tower.

As you might guess, the other kind of firmware is *volatile*, and it goes into the RAM in the system. This is the firmware that gives the RCX its different programming environments. If the power is removed from the RCX, the RAM contents are lost. Before you start programming in pbForth, you need to load its *kernel* (another word for firmware) into RAM. Then you can load your software into whatever RAM is left over. There is about 28KB of free RAM in the system. After pbForth is loaded, you will have about 14KB left. This doesn't sound like much, but it's more than enough for any practical RCX application.

Installing pbForth

The requirements for running pbForth are small. I designed the system to be programmable from a dumb terminal once the firmware is loaded. You can load it using the GUI provided with the pbForth distribution, NQC, firmdl, or any other tool you like. The dumb terminal can be any program that runs on your computer and allows it talk to a serial device, like a modem. To take advantage of the ability to save your work from the RCX to your computer for subsequent download, your terminal program should support XMODEM transfers.

You can get pbForth from my Web site at `www.hempeldesigngroup.com/lego/ pbForth`. Follow the links to the latest version and download it to your computer. As part of the distribution, you'll get a firmware downloader and terminal emulator written in Tcl—another free scripting language. The system works on Windows and Linux/Unix computers. The Macintosh version will be released as soon as I can find a stable serial driver for Tcl. If you use the GUI, you'll need a current version of Tcl. Please read the installation notes on the Web site or in the distribution for more detailed instructions on getting Tcl and installing pbForth as they will have the most current information.

There are three standard pbForth images that come with the distribution:

- `pbforth.srec`: The minimal pbForth kernel.

- `pbedu.srec`: A pbForth kernel with some extra words for younger students.

- `pbmax.srec`: A full-blown pbForth kernel with multi-tasking and XMODEM support.

All of the examples in this book assume you are loading the minimal pbForth kernel. You can customize your own kernel with the features and words you use most. You can find more details on the pbForth Web site at `www.hempeldesigngroup.com/lego/pbForth`.

Aside from the installation notes on the official pbForth Web site, there is an online community where everyone can share their experiences with pbForth. The LUGNET Web site, `http://www.lugnet.com`, is the Grand Central Station for all things Lego. It is a fan-supported Web site and is in no way affiliated with The LEGO Company. There is a public newsfeed/email section for pbForth support at `http://www.lugnet.com/robotics/rcx/pbforth/`. This is where I prefer questions and answers to be posted so that everyone gets the most benefit.

To get started, make sure you have fresh batteries in your tower and your RCX, then download pbforth.srec to the RCX. Users of firmdl and NQC downloaders will get a "No response from RCX" error at the end because the pbForth firmware does not reply to the last bytes properly. The upload worked if LCD on the RCX has a stylized "4th" onscreen. Now fire up your terminal emulator and you are ready to go to the first step in learning to program in pbForth. The default settings for the terminal emulator are 2400 baud, no parity, 8 data bits, and 1 stop bit.

Battery Consumption and pbForth

The standard RCX firmware powers itself off to conserve batteries if it has been idle for some time. The pbForth firmware is always running, which means that your batteries will run down if you leave it on all night. On the other hand, reloading the firmware is cumbersome too. Running the following script will prepare your RCX for a manual shutdown:

```
POWER_INIT POWER_OFF
```

It will wake up again exactly where you left off when you press the **On–Off** key.

If you don't see the "4th" in the LCD, the upload failed. This may be due to IR interference from other IR sources such as cameras, remote controls, security systems, or even other RCX towers. You can reduce the effects of other IR sources by throwing a towel over the RCX and the tower, or even by covering them with a box.

pbForth Fundamentals

The Forth language is not new. In fact, its roots can be traced back almost thirty years to Charles Moore. The `http://www.forth.com` Web site has a good history of how and why Forth evolved the way it has. The `http://www.forth.org` Web site is put together by the Forth Interest Group and should be your first stopping point when looking for general Forth resources.

Furthermore, this small section of the book is not an in-depth tutorial on how to use Forth, it's really just an overview. Entire books have been written on Forth, including Tim Hendtlass' *Real Time Forth*, which is available by FTP from `ftp://ftp.taygeta.com/pub/Forth/Literature/rtfv5.pdf`. His book is a good resource if you want to explore some of the finer points of the Forth language.

If you have programmed in other languages, Forth will seem a bit unusual. There are no braces to delimit blocks of code like loops; you generally don't need to declare variables; and the expressions are written in *postfix* notation. More on this in "Numbers and Expressions," later in this chapter. You need to get your arms around two important concepts to understand the elegance of Forth as a programming environment—the *stack* and the *dictionary*.

The Forth Stack

In most programming languages, the stack is invisible. Almost all programming languages use a single stack for parameter passing and control flow operations. The compiler for the language will take care of all the stack operations for you. However, the Forth system uses separate stacks and gives you complete access to them as well. Think of a stack of blocks with numbers or values on their faces. The last block you put on the stack is the first one you take off. You can do simple operations like swapping the top two blocks, adding a new block, removing a block, and so on. Later on you will discover that there are ways to manipulate blocks further down the stack, but for now keep the "last in, first out" idea in your mind. Figure 5-2 shows how the stack works.

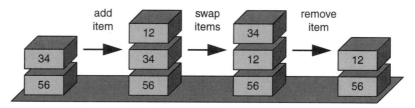

Figure 5-2. Using the stack

The Forth Dictionary

The dictionary is where you store your *words*, which is just another way of saying subroutine. Think of the dictionary as, well, a dictionary. Every time you define a word, the name of the word and what it does gets stored in a new entry in the dictionary. The entries go in chronological order, which means that if you define the same word twice, the *newer* definition gets used in subsequent calls. This is discussed in "Defining New Forth Words," later in this chapter.

As you type or send text to the RCX, an interpreter intercepts the characters. Its job is to look up the words you typed in the dictionary. If the interpreter can't find the word, it tries to make a number out of it. If that fails, the interpreter simply gives up with an error message like "ASDF? undefined word." You can tell the interpreter to pass your text to the compiler if you want to save a definition instead of executing it. This is also discussed in "Defining New Forth Words," later in this chapter.

Over the years, a notation has been developed to help programmers describe how the words affect the stack. The notation also provides a pronunciation for many Forth words because they are often abbreviated or even look like punctuation. Figure 5-2 shows a vertically oriented stack, but the stack notation is horizontal. Converting between the two modes is easy. Recall the stack of blocks discussed under "The Forth Stack" earlier in this chapter, then turn it clockwise so the top element is on the right. This is what the stack notation looks like in a *stack diagram*:

SWAP   (n1 n2 -- n2 n1)   "swap"

Exchanges the top two elements on the stack.

This example exchanges the top two elements on the stack. The dashes in the middle of the stack effect description are just a visual aid to separate the state of the stack before and after the word executes. The parentheses are used as comment characters in Forth so the stack diagram is useful as documentation within the source code. Figure 5-3 shows the complete operation of the SWAP word in the form of a stack diagram.

> **NOTE** *Forth uses a table called a glossary to summarize new words. In Forth, everything is described in terms of common words—the power of analogy as a learning aid was not lost on the inventor of Forth.*

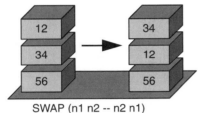

SWAP (n1 n2 -- n2 n1)

Figure 5-3. Using SWAP

Comments in Forth

Because pbForth is interactive, we've got to have some way of describing what you type at the terminal and what pbForth sends back. As a traditional courtesy, pbForth spits out an ok at the end of every line:

```
This is text you type
This is text from pbForth ok
```

> **NOTE** *Underlines within code listings indicate text printed by the computer (as opposed to input typed by the user).*

Every word in Forth is separated by at least one whitespace character, such as a space, a tab, or a new line. Avoid using tabs in your source code because this makes it hard to exchange the code with others. Comments are the text enclosed between parentheses, but they do not span new lines. Everything past a forward slash is a comment to the end of a line.

```
This is code ( this is a comment ) this is more code
This is code ( this is a comment to the end of the line
This is code / this is also a comment to the end of the line
```

> **NOTE** *You can test whether everything works by hitting the Return or Enter key a few times. The console should respond with an* ok *for every carriage return. Be aware of the fact that to conserve batteries, the IR tower shuts itself down about two seconds after the last character has been sent. When you first start typing, the tower may spit out some garbage that is then echoed to the console screen. This is perfectly alright. You might want to get into the habit of hitting Return a few times before typing any text to the console.*

Adding Definitions to the Dictionary

The pbForth interpreter is *case-sensitive*. This means that HELLO, Hello, and hello are all different words. Words that are part of a public interface are generally written in all uppercase letters, while private words are in mixed or lowercase letters.

Earlier in this chapter, under "The Forth Dictionary," I mentioned that the Forth dictionary stores words in the order they are defined. This may cause some confusion when you fix a definition and then try to run words that invoke the old definition. To illustrate this, create a word that prints out a simple greeting, the canonical "Hello world," and another word that calls it as follows:

```
: HELLO ." Hello World" ;
HELLO
Hello World ok
: SAY-HI HELLO ;
SAY-HI
Hello World ok
```

Now, if you redefine HELLO and call SAY-HI again, you get the *old* version of HELLO, because SAY-HI is still compiled in its definition.

```
: HELLO ." Greetings, earthling" ;
redefine HELLO ok
HELLO
Greetings, earthling ok
SAY-HI
Hello World ok
```

Remember to reload any definitions that are affected by the new word.

RCX Basics and Generating Output

After you have downloaded pbForth to the RCX, it is ready to accept input. Hit the return key a few times, and pbForth should respond with:

```
ok
ok
```

Now type in a few numbers and some random text and see what happens:

```
123 45 6
ok
78 fibblesnork
fibblesnork ? undefined word
```

The interpreter had no entry for `fibblesnork` and echoed it back with a question mark at the end.

The RCX has a rich set of functions built into the system firmware. They are based on documentation from Kekoa Proudfoot's definitive disassembly of the RCX ROM at `http://graphics.stanford.edu/~kekoa/rcx`. I extracted what I thought were the key routines from the ROM and created new Forth words to access them. As much as possible, I wanted the calling conventions for the new words to match those of the routines in the ROM. Using the working code in the ROM of the RCX meant that I did not need to develop these routines independently.

Back in the early days of hacking on VIC-20 and IBM-PC computers, programmers in BASIC used PEEK and POKE statements to get right at the hardware. The Forth equivalents are `@` (fetch) and `!` (store). The basic unit stored on the pbForth stack is a *cell*, which is 16 bits wide. A *cell address* on the RCX is a number that refers to a specific location in the memory. The `@` word takes a cell address and puts the memory contents at that specific address on the stack. On the other hand, the `!` word takes a stack item and stores it at the specified cell address. These words can be used to access RCX resources at a very low level and should be used with appropriate care.

Now we need some way of printing the results to the RCX's IR port and LCD. The pbForth firmware provides a simple set of operators to send output to the IR port, but because the IR tower tends to fall asleep, it's not much use for sending streams of data.

Our first glossary contains `@` and `!` as well as the standard output words in Forth.

`@`	`( a-addr -- x )`	`"fetch"`

Retrieves the cell value that is stored at a-addr and puts it on the stack as x.

`!`	`( x a-addr -- )`	`"store"`

Stores the value x into the cell at address a-addr.

`.`	`(n1 -- )`	`"dot"`

Prints the top of the stack as a signed number.

`U.`	`(u1 -- )`	`"u-dot"`

Prints the top of the stack as an unsigned number.

`."`	`( -- )`	`"dot-quote"`

Prints the string up to but not including the next double quote.

`EMIT`	`(n1 -- )`	`"emit"`

Prints the ASCII equivalent of n1.

`CR`	`( -- )`	`"c-r"`

Sends a carriage return to the output device.

So, if you wanted to print a result from a calculation, you could enter something like:

```
78 .
78 ok
```

If you need to send out a single ASCII character, then EMIT is what you need, like this:

```
HEX 41 EMIT
Aok
7 EMIT
(beep)ok
```

Your terminal won't actually show (beep), but the bell should ring because 7 is the ASCII character that rings the bell.

We'll discuss some of the other words in later chapters. Aside from the words that write output to the IR port, we also have the option of writing to the LCD or to the buzzer in the RCX to let us know how our software is performing. The material we cover in the next few pages is fundamental to understanding how to work with the RCX, so read it carefully.

The RCX is a high-performance embedded system, and like a high-performance airplane, you need to go through some basic preflight steps before you can take off. The words you need to know in order to get going on the RCX are described in the following glossary. They are organized according to the order in which they're likely to be added to the reader's vocabulary. The parameters for many of these words are discussed in Chapter 2.

RCX_INIT　　　　　　　　　　　(--)　　　　　　　　　　　"r-c-x-init"

Starts the low-level interrupt handlers and sets up the ROM routine data structures. Always use this word at the beginning of a session.

RCX_SOUND　　　　　　　　　　(-- addr)　　　　　　　　　"r-c-x-sound"

Returns the address of a variable which is can be used to store sound system query results.

SOUND_PLAY　　　　　　　　　　(s c --)　　　　　　　　　"sound-play"

Plays one of the seven pre-defined system sounds.

The legal hex values for code are

```
0x4003 Sound is queued
0x4004 Sound is unqueued
```

The legal values for sound are
```
0x0000 Blip
0x0001 Beep Beep
0x0002 Downward Tones
0x0003 Upward Tones
0x0004 Low Buzz
0x0005 Fast Upward Tones
0x0006 Low Buzz
```

SOUND_GET　　　　　　　　　　(addr --)　　　　　　　　　"sound-get"

Grabs the current state of the sound system and places the result in the buffer pointed to by a-addr. The result is zero if the system is idle (no sound is playing), or a non-zero value if it is busy.

LCD_NUMBER   (comma value format --)   "l-c-d-number"

The routine used to format values in the LCD.
The hex valued comma parameter has the following possibilities:

```
0x0000 Single digit to right of display, use with format = 0x3017
0x3002 No decimal point
0x3003 10th's decimal point
0x3004 100th's decimal point
0x3005 1000th's decimal point
```

The hex valued format parameter is used to determine where and how the value parameter is displayed:

```
0x3017 Single digit on right of display, use with comma = 0x0000
0x3001 Signed with no leading zeros
0x301F Unsigned with leading zeros
```

LCD_SHOW   (n --)   "l-c-d-show"

Turns on the LCD segment indicated by n.
The following hex values for n affect the corresponding display segments:

```
0x3006 standing figure
0x3007 walking figure
0x3008 sensor 0 view selected
0x3009 sensor 0 active
0x300a sensor 1 view selected
0x300b sensor 1 active
0x300c sensor 2 view selected
0x300d sensor 2 active
0x300e motor 0 view selected
0x300f motor 0 backward arrow
0x3010 motor 0 forward arrow
0x3011 motor 1 view selected
0x3012 motor 1 backward arrow
0x3013 motor 1 forward arrow
0x3014 motor 2 view selected
0x3015 motor 2 backward arrow
0x3016 motor 2 forward arrow
0x3018 datalog indicator
0x3019 progress indicator A
0x301a progress indicator B
0x301b battery low indicator
0x301c IR activity A
0x301d IR activity B
```

LCD_HIDE	(n --)	"l-c-d-hide"

Turns off the LCD segment indicated by n.

LCD_CLEAR	(--)	"l-c-d-clear"

Turns off all of the LCD segments.

LCD_4TH	(--)	"l-c-d-forth"

Turns the number portion of the LCD into a stylized logo. You must use your imagination to get 4th.

LCD_REFRESH	(--)	"l-c-d-refresh"

Sends the results of any LCD changing routines to the display. None of the LCD words will have any effect until LCD-REFRESH is called.

RCX_BUTTON	(-- addr)	"r-c-x-button"

Returns the address of a variable that can be used to store button query results.

BUTTON_GET	(addr --)	"button-get"

Puts the state of the buttons on the front panel of the RCX in the variable at addr.

Many of the parameters of the RCX routines are given in hexadecimal notation. If you are not familiar with hex notation, there is more information about this in "Signed versus Unsigned Numbers," later in this chapter. For now, type in the numbers as shown. Computer programmers use hex math frequently because it is an efficient notation for groups of 4 bits. After a while, you'll use hex as naturally as you use decimal notation.

The RCX Display System

The LCD has many segments, as shown in Figure 5-4. Each segment has its own code for use in the LCD_SHOW and LCD_HIDE routines described in the previous glossary. You can change only one segment at a time using these routines and then use LCD_REFRESH to make your changes apparent.

The LCD_NUMBER routine is a flexible way to send numbers to the RCX display. Depending on the decimal and number code you specify, you can format a number as signed or unsigned, with leading zeros or without, or set the single digit at the far right of the display. You can even tell the RCX where to put the decimal point. You must remember to use LCD_REFRESH to actually see your changes. The following

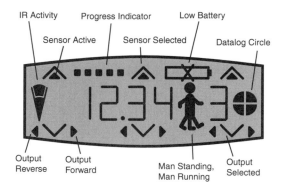

Figure 5-4. The LCD

example shows the effect of different "comma" codes on the number being displayed in the LCD:

```
RCX_INIT
HEX          \ Use hex for number display and entry
LCD_CLEAR
3007 LCD_SHOW LCD_REFRESH
3001 1234 301F LCD_NUMBER LCD_REFRESH
3002 1234 301F LCD_NUMBER LCD_REFRESH
3003 1234 301F LCD_NUMBER LCD_REFRESH
3004 1234 301F LCD_NUMBER LCD_REFRESH
```

The RCX display shows 4660 because it only displays decimal numbers, but we've entered 1234 as a hex number. The decimal equivalent of 1234 hex is 4660.

The RCX Sound System

The sound system in the RCX is capable of playing tones of arbitrary frequency and length, but this is not currently implemented in pbForth. Seven different systems sounds are available:

```
0x0000 Blip
0x0001 Beep Beep
0x0002 Downward Tones
0x0003 Upward Tones
0x0004 Low Buzz
0x0005 Fast Upward Tones
0x0006 Low Buzz
```

You can use them to let your robot tell you what it is up to. Using sound is a very effective method of debugging embedded systems—many desktop computers emit a series of beeps that can help a technician figure out what is going on.

When you type `RCX_INIT`, you should hear a little click from the RCX. Try the following lines to listen to the tones your RCX can emit:

```
RCX_INIT
HEX          \ Use hex for number display and entry
0 4003 SOUND_PLAY
1 4003 SOUND_PLAY
```

Numbers and Expressions

Forth uses *postfix* notation for its expressions, which users of Hewlett-Packard calculators are familiar with. Although you probably don't know it, you are likely more familiar with *infix* notation, where the operator is between the operands. When you write 4 + 3 you are using infix notation. In postfix notation, the operator comes *after* the operands.

This may seem like yet another weird aspect of Forth, but the main reason for using postfix is to omit the need for parentheses. If you want to solve a reasonably complex expression using infix notation, you have to work from the innermost parenthesis outwards, like this:

$$((4+3)\times 5 -\left(\frac{6}{3}\right) = 33$$

First you calculate 4 + 3, then multiply by 5 and subtract 6 / 3. This seems very simple, but your eyes and brain combine to make a powerful expression parser that must be somehow duplicated in software. By using postfix notation, you can get eliminate the parenthesis. Here is the same expression written for Forth:

```
 4 3 + 5 * 6 3 / -
```

Admittedly, it's harder for your eyes and brain to parse this, but it's much easier for the RCX! The stack is used to hold the intermediate result of 35 while we calculate 6 / 3 before subtracting it. This also provides some insight into why Forth programmers traditionally make little use of variables. In conventional languages, many variables are placeholders used to hold intermediate results during a calculation. Forth lets you have direct access to the data stack to store these transient values. Figure 5-5 clearly shows what is happening as we perform calculations on the stack. Numbers are *pushed* on to the stack, and operators *pop* them off.

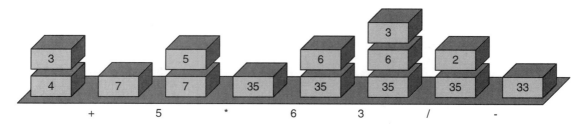

Figure 5-5. Using the stack for calculations

These are the basic math expressions you will use with pbForth:

`+`   `(n1 n2 -- n1+n2)`   `"plus"`

Adds the top two elements on the stack.

`-`   `(n1 n2 -- n1-n2)`   `"minus"`

Subtracts the top element from the second element.

`*`   `(n1 n2 -- n1*n2)`   `"star"`

Multiplies the top two elements on the stack.

`/`   `(n1 n2 -- quo)`   `"slash"`

Divides n1 by n2 leaving the quotient on the stack.

`/MOD`   `(n1 n2 -- rem quo)`   `"slash-mod"`

Divides n1 by n2 leaving a quotient and remainder on the stack.

`*/`   `(n1 n2 n3 -- quo)`   `"star-slash"`

Multiplies n1 by n2 to a 32-bit intermediate value, then divides by n3 and returns
the quotient.

`*/MOD`   `(n1 n2 n3 -- rem quo)`   `"star-slash-mod"`

Multiplies n1 by n2 to a 32-bit intermediate value, then divides by n3 leaving a
quotient and remainder on the stack.

In most cases, you'll use the four basic operators (addition, subtraction, multiplication, and division). The others, `/MOD`, `*/`, and `*/MOD`, are useful once you run
out of room in the range of numbers, which brings up another point about Forth—

it uses integer math. For those of you with ready access to high speed computers and calculators, floating point numbers seem like the only way to get the answer to a question. Most microcontrollers have no built-in floating point processor, so if you want to use this notation, extra software is required to implement it. With the extra software comes slower execution.

Forth programmers tend to think in terms of minimizing the hardware requirements for their application, so using faster integer math is a natural choice. The results of integer math do not have the same dynamic range as floating point, but they are usually good enough for typical RCX applications. A 16-bit integer can represent a range of 65,536 points. If you figure that knowing where your robot is to within 1 mm (about .040 in) is good enough, this represents about 65 m (about 200 ft). In reality, your resolution will be much worse than 1 mm, so 16-bit results are very good indeed.

Signed vs. Unsigned Numbers

The pbForth math system actually uses 16-bit signed integer math as the default. This means that the numbers range from –32,768 to 32,767. The addition and subtraction operators work on signed and unsigned numbers equally well, but multiplication and division only work on signed numbers.

A quick diversion for those of you interested in number systems will take the mystery out of these terms, as well as introduce binary and hexadecimal notation. If you understand number systems, you can skip this section. If you have a scientific calculator that does number conversions you can use it to work through the examples.

Everybody has heard that computers only think in terms of ones and zeros, but not many people know exactly what this means. In a nutshell, any single bit in a register or memory cell can hold either a one or a zero. This seems like a big restriction, so we end up grouping the bits to give us more combinations, and therefore bigger numbers. It's exactly the same as grouping the digits 0–9 in powers of 10 to make bigger numbers. Table 5-1 shows how each digit position in a numerical base corresponds to its weight in a number. The least significant or rightmost digit is in the 0th position.

Table 5-1. Bit Position Values

POSITION	BINARY	DECIMAL	HEXADECIMAL
0	1	1	1
1	2	10	16
2	4	100	256
3	8	1,000	4,096

Interpreting decimal numbers is so simple that we do it without even really thinking about it. If we want to interpret the decimal number 4,832, we say there are 2 ones plus 3 tens plus 8 hundreds plus 4 thousands. Binary and hexadecimal numbers are no different. The following diagram shows how to interpret a binary number.

1	0	1	1			Decimal
				2^0	1	1
				2^1	2	2
				2^2	4	0
				1^3	8	8
						11

Hexadecimal numbers are pretty much the same.

3	6	A	F			Decimal
				16^0	1	15
				16^1	16	160
				16^2	256	1536
				16^3	4096	12288
						13999

Note that this gives us only positive numbers. To make a number negative, the convention is to use the leftmost bit as a sign indicator. Zero is positive and 1 is negative. Signed integer math is also called 2's complement math. Let's use a simple example of all the combinations of 4 bits. The three number circles in Figure 5-6 illustrate how to convert positive and negative binary numbers to decimal. The leftmost circle shows the unsigned decimal numbers as they correspond to the binary bits on the center circle while the rightmost circle shows the signed decimal equivalents. To invert the sign of a binary number, simply invert all of the bits and add one.

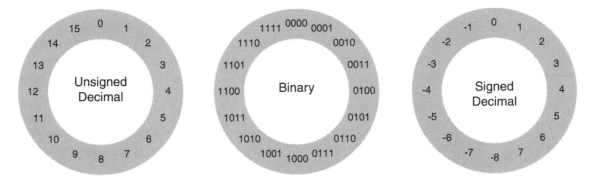

Figure 5-6. Signed and unsigned numbers

Numeric Base Conversion in Forth

You can use pbForth on the RCX to do the number conversions for you if you don't have a hex calculator handy. There is a system variable called BASE used to format output in whatever number system you like. The words HEX and DECIMAL set the conversion base. Here are a few conversion examples:

```
DECIMAL 43 U.
43ok
DECIMAL 43 HEX U.
2Bok
HEX 30 DECIMAL U.
48ok
DECIMAL -1 HEX U.
FFFFok
DECIMAL -1 HEX .
-1ok
```

Note that we had to use U. to get all of the digits of a signed number to print out. There is no binary conversion built in, but you can easily make your own like this:

```
DECIMAL
: BINARY 2 BASE ! ;
HEX 34 BINARY U.
110100ok
```

     If you accept the range of signed 16-bit integers, you will find that most equations can be scaled to give useful results in that range. Let's take the case of the RCX battery voltage. "Defining New Words for pbForth," later in this chapter shows how to retrieve the raw battery value, however, the formula to convert it to battery voltage is:

     Vbat = Vraw * 21,994 / 780

     The RCX uses this formula internally because it's essentially the same as using 28.1974 as the factor instead of 21,994 / 780. It's faster too. Let's assume a typical raw value of 286 and see what happens when we blindly type the following to Forth:

```
DECIMAL
286 21994 * 7780 / .
19
```

     This answer is obviously wrong, and the reason being that the first multiplication results in a *range overflow*, which means that the signed 16-bit range of results was exceeded. Once again, the creators of Forth anticipated this issue and created the */ operator. It multiplies two values and computes a 32-bit intermediate result, then divides this result by the third value to return a 16-bit quotient. In Forth, scaling is often done to provide accurate answers in fixed point math. As you develop more complex applications, this habit will become second nature. Let's see what we get when we use the */ operator:

```
DECIMAL
286 21994 780 */ .
8064
```

     This is correct: it is the battery voltage in millivolts.

     While we are on the topic of scaling numbers, it is interesting to see how microcontroller programmers handle transcendental numbers like pi, e, or the square root of two. It is a little known fact that almost any number can be approximated as a quotient of two numbers less than 32,768. In fact, the error is almost always less than 10E-6, which is far better than any measurements we can make with the RCX and its sensors. Table 5-2 shows the rational approximations for some common values, approximations for other common constants can be found in many good numerical methods texts.

Table 5-2. Rational Approximations for Common Values

NAME	VALUE	APPROXIMATION	ERROR
$\sqrt{2}$	1.4142...	19,601/13,860	1.8E-9
$\sqrt{3}$	1.7321...	18,817/10,864	2.4E-9
π (pi)	3.1416...	355/113	2.6E-7
e	2.7183...	28,667/10,546	1.5E-8

The process of finding a good approximation to a number is beyond the scope of this book, however, you should be able to accomplish it with trial-and-error and a bit of patience.

Defining New Words for pbForth

Most procedural languages let you define subroutines that you can call at any time. Subroutines let you package commonly used pieces of code to be easily used and maintained. The Forth language is no different—it lets you define new *words* for its dictionary. Here's a simple example that lets you format words for the display:

```
HEX
: SHOW_NUMBER ( n -- )
    3002 SWAP 301F LCD_NUMBER LCD_REFRESH ;
```

The HEX is simply there to let the RCX know that the numbers in the following input are in hex notation—it does not mean that the output is displayed in hex. You start a new word definition with the ":" (colon) and then follow it immediately with the name of your new word. Remember to leave at least one whitespace character between words in a definition. It is customary to put a short stack effect comment right after the name of the word. In this case, the diagram tells us that SHOW_NUMBER consumes exactly one value from the stack. The rest of the body just adds some parameters for the call to LCD_NUMBER. The end of the definition is indicated by the ";" (semicolon) and tells the compiler that the definition is complete.

Let's test out our new word with some values. From now on, we'll leave out the ok from pbForth for clarity.

```
DECIMAL
1 SHOW_NUMBER
10 SHOW_NUMBER
100 SHOW_NUMBER
1000 SHOW_NUMBER
```

```
10000 SHOW_NUMBER
```

Of course, because there are only four digits on the RCX display, numbers that are out of range display as 9999. That really is all there is to it! In the next section, we'll show you how to make your words perform repetitive or conditional operations, but for the time being, let's see what else we can do with some of the basic words we know so far.

The RCX_POWER and POWER_GET words are part of the power management system of the RCX that is explained in the next chapter. For now, we'll just use them without worrying about the details.

```
DECIMAL
: CALC_BATTERY ( raw -- mv )
  21994 780 */ ;

HEX
: SHOW_BATTERY ( -- )
  RCX_POWER DUP 4001 POWER_GET @
  CALC_BATTERY
  SHOW_NUMBER ;
```

This is a simple pair of definitions that tell us the battery voltage of our RCX every time we type SHOW_BATTERY.

The following glossary shows some of the basic stack manipulation words you will need to make more complex definitions:

DUP   (n1 -- n1 n1)   "dupe"

Makes a duplicate of the top element of the stack.

SWAP   (n1 n2 -- n2 n1)   "swap"

Exchanges the top two elements on the stack.

DROP   (n1 --)   "drop"

Deletes the top element of the stack.

OVER   (n1 n2 -- n1 n2 n1)   "over"

Puts a duplicate of the second stack element at the top of the stack.

ROT   (n1 n2 n3 -- n2 n3 n1)   "rote"

Rotates the top three elements on the stack so that the third element is brought to the top.

2DUP   (n1 n2 -- n1 n2 n1 n2)   "two-dupe"

Makes duplicates of the top two elements on the stack.

2DROP   (n1 n2 --)   "two-drop"

Deletes the top two elements of the stack.

You will use these stack manipulation words all the time. The list tells you everything you really need to know about these words; look for them in the examples in the following sections. Figure 5-7a and 5-7b shows some of the key stack manipulations in a graphical form. Eventually, you will be able to visualize the stack in your head as you write code.

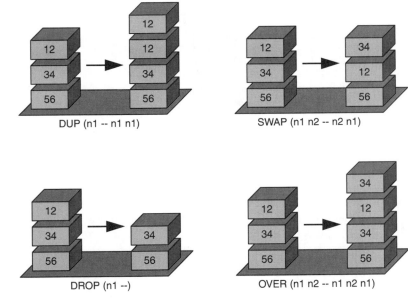

Figure 5-7a. Stack manipulations

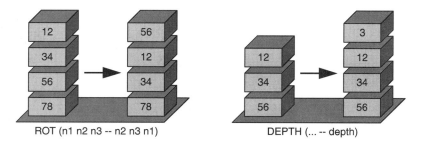

ROT (n1 n2 n3 -- n2 n3 n1)   DEPTH (... -- depth)

Figure 5-7b. Stack manipulations

Conditionals and Bitwise Operators in pbForth

With the material in the previous sections under your belt, you're ready for conditionals and looping. These operators are used to create programs that make decisions, rather than simply calculating the battery voltage or displaying a number.

Forth has a number of conditionals you can use in expressions. As we develop some of the concepts for conditional expressions, we'll also introduce some words for getting input from the RCX sensors.

Here's a quick example you can type in.

```
DECIMAL
0 1 > U.
0 ok
1 0 > U.
65535 ok
1 1 = U.
65535 ok
1 0 = U.
0 ok
```

You have probably figured out that when a condition is false the result is 0, and when it is true the result is 1. Actually, the Forth standard says that any non-zero value is true. Now we can introduce the IF statement and use it to make printing the output of a conditional more readable. The IF statement is compiler-only, which means it must be used inside a definition. You can't type it as input. It can be used as "IF do-this THEN" or "IF do-this ELSE do-that THEN". The IF portion evaluates a condition result on the stack. If it is non-zero, the code after the IF is executed. If an ELSE clause is present, it is executed if the condition result is 0. To make things clear, let's write a new word called SHOW_CONDITION to print either TRUE or FALSE depending on the condition on the stack, and then try it out on a few examples.

```
: SHOW_CONDITION ( n1 -- )
  IF ." TRUE" ELSE ." FALSE" THEN ;
0 1 > SHOW_CONDITION
FALSEok
1 0 > SHOW_CONDITION
TRUEok
1 1 = SHOW_CONDITION
TRUEok
1 0 = SHOW_CONDITION
FALSEok
```

Conditionals in Forth are of two basic types. They either compare the top two items on the stack against each other, or they compare the top item against 0. Besides the conditional operators, there are also the bitwise operators you would expect from any programming language. If you are used to programming in C (or C++), the bitwise operators might give you some grief. C distinguishes between bitwise and logical operations for AND and OR. If you write the logical AND expression (x && y) in C, and x and y are both non-zero, the result will be true. On the other hand, the bitwise AND expression (x & y) in C will give a non-zero result only if the corresponding bits in x and y are non-zero.

The AND and OR words in Forth are bitwise operators, so you need to be careful before using them in conditional looping. In particular, you may need to convert the bitwise number to a logical result before the conditional expression can be evaluated. A good example is in bit processing. Let's assume we have the results of two switches on the stack and we want to indicate whether both are pressed. The following sample code illustrates the problem with blindly using AND.

```
HEX
RCX_INIT

1 CONSTANT RUN_BUTTON
4 CONSTANT PRGM_BUTTON

: CHECK_BUTTONS ( button1 button2 -- )
  AND
  IF ." Both pressed"
  ELSE ." Both not pressed"
  THEN ;

RUN_BUTTON PRGM_BUTTON CHECK_BUTTONS
Both not pressed
```

The unhappy result is that even though we have numbers indicating true for both switches on the stack, the result of the bitwise AND is false. The correct way to process the values here is to convert the button presses to logical values, using `0=` to logically invert the numbers, and DeMorgan's Law to turn the AND into an OR, as shown here:

X and Y = NOT((NOT X) or (NOT Y))

The script is modified as follows to make it work properly:

```
: CHECK_BUTTONS ( button1 button2 -- )
  0= SWAP 0= OR 0=
  IF ." Both pressed"
  ELSE ." Both not pressed"
  THEN ;


RUN_BUTTON PRGM_BUTTON CHECK_BUTTONS
Both pressed
```

Now the RCX will print "`Both pressed`" as expected. Embedded systems programming is full of little pitfalls like this. Only experience and careful attention to detail will help you to avoid them.

The conditional and logical operators are described in more detail in the following glossary. Note that all comparisons (except `U<`) are based on signed arithmetic and only numbers in the range of -32,768 to 32,767 are valid. For the words that may take different kinds of numbers, "n" indicates a signed number, while "u" indicates an unsigned number.

`=`	`(n1 n2 -- f)`	`"equal"`

Sets f true if n1 and n2 are equal, and false otherwise.

`U<`	`(u1 n2 -- f)`	`"u-less-than"`

Sets f true if u1 is less than u2, and false otherwise.

`<`	`(n1 n2 -- f)`	`"less-than"`

Sets f true if n1 is less than n2, and false otherwise.

`>`	`(n1 n2 -- f)`	`"greater-than"`

Sets f true if n1 is greater than n2, and false otherwise.

`0=`	`(n1 -- f)`	`"zero equal"`

Sets f true if n1 equal to 0, and false otherwise.

0<   (n1 -- f)   "zero-less-than"

Sets f true if n1 is less than 0, and false otherwise.

AND   (n1 n2 -- n3)   "and"

Sets n3 to the bitwise AND of n1 and n2.

OR   (n1 n2 -- n3)   "or"

Sets n3 to the bitwise OR of n1 and n2.

XOR   (n1 n2 -- n3)   "x-or"

Sets n3 to the bitwise XOR of n1 and n2.

INVERT   (n1 -- n2)   "invert"

Sets n2 to the bitwise inverse of n1.

Basic RCX Sensors and Motors

Now we have almost enough material to do something interesting with a touch sensor and a motor. This chapter is only an introduction, so we don't go into much detail describing the words to control the RCX and its systems. The next chapter describes the words in more detail because we go through the exercise of designing the Seeker robot there. To do that, we need to know a lot more about how things work inside the RCX. Here is a glossary of the RCX words we use in the script.

MOTOR_SET   (power mode idx --)   "motor-set"

Sets the motor specified by an index of 0-2 to a power between 0-7. The allowed modes are:

1 forward
2 backward
3 stop
4 float

SENSOR_INIT   (--)   "sensor-init"

Initializes the sensor subsystem.

SENSOR_PASSIVE   (idx --)   "sensor-passive"

Sets the specified sensor to be a passive type. The touch and temperature sensors are passive.

SENSOR_TYPE   (type idx --)   "sensor-type"

Sets the sensor type to one of the following:

```
0 Raw sensor (useful for custom devices)
1 Touch sensor
2 Temperature sensor
3 Light sensor
4 Rotation sensor
```

SENSOR_MODE   (mode idx --)   "sensor-mode"

Sets the specified sensor to one of the following modes. Use common sense when combining different modes and types according to the following list:

```
0x0000 Raw mode
0x0020 Boolean mode
0x0040 Edge detection - every transition counts
0x0060 Pulse detection - only negative transitions count
0x0080 Percent of scale
0x00A0 Degrees Celsius
0x00C0 Degrees Fahrenheit
0x00E0 Angle detection
```

SENSOR_READ   (idx -- code)   "sensor-read"

Reads the specified sensor and returns a flag indicating success (0) or busy (other values).

SENSOR_BOOL   (idx -- bool)   "sensor-bool"

Retrieves the sensors current boolean data field. Note that this item will not change unless you actually call SENSOR_READ on the sensor first.

Now we'll use these words in the simple little script shown in Listing 5-1, which changes the motor's direction based on which buttons are pressed. It assumes we have a touch sensor on Port 1 (which we index as 0) that controls whether the motor is on or off. The other touch sensor is on Port 2 (which we index as 1) and it determines whether the motor turns forwards or backwards. The motor is on port A.

Listing 5-1. MOTORDIR.TXT–Controlling a motor with a touch sensor

```
\ MOTORDIR.TXT
HEX

: HANDLE_SENSORS_INIT
  RCX_INIT
  SENSOR_INIT
     0 SENSOR_PASSIVE
   1 0 SENSOR_TYPE
  20 0 SENSOR_MODE
     1 SENSOR_PASSIVE
   1 1 SENSOR_TYPE
  20 1 SENSOR_MODE ;

: HANDLE_SENSORS
  7 ( default power level )
  0 DUP SENSOR_READ DROP SENSOR_BOOL ( on or off? )
  IF   1 DUP SENSOR_READ DROP SENSOR_BOOL ( fwd or rev? )
       IF 1 ELSE 2 THEN
  ELSE 3 THEN    ( brake the motor )
  0 MOTOR_SET ;

HANDLE_SENSORS_INIT
HANDLE_SENSORS
```

This is a good example of how Forth encourages use of the stack for parameter passing instead of storing transient values in variables. The MOTOR_SET word requires the power level, mode, and motor index on the stack. The HANDLE_SENSORS word computes the parameters in that order. The state of the sensor at index 0 determines whether the motor is on or off (mode 3). If it is on, the state of sensor 1 determines whether the motor should turn forwards (1) or reverse (2). Finally, we can just put the motor index of 0 on the stack before calling MOTOR_SET. To test the word, type HANDLE_SENSORS while leaving the touch sensors in their proper state. This is a bit awkward, so type the word, then press the touch sensors with the fingers of one hand and hit the return key on the computer with the other.

Looping in pbForth

The example in the previous section forced us to type the word before it would read the buttons and change the state of the motor accordingly. Of course, this is not how we would do things in a real application. We need a way to execute a word over and over again in a loop without having to type it. It would also be nice if we could access the buttons on the RCX keypad itself to exit from the loop. The button words were defined earlier along with the LCD words. Here's a new word you can enter called RUN_BUTTON? that tells you the state of the **Run** button:

```
RCX_INIT
: RUN_BUTTON?
  RCX_BUTTON DUP BUTTON_GET @ 1 AND ;
```

Unfortunately, this simple word is actually *too* simple. It works fine when we test it at the terminal but will generally not work as expected in an actual application. This flaw will be revealed at the end of this chapter.

The looping words in Forth are of two basic types. There are *determinate* loops that execute a certain number of times, and *indeterminate* loops that execute as long as a condition is in a certain state. As with the IF-THEN-ELSE construct, the looping words must be used inside a definition, not at the command line. One application for a determinate loop is to display the contents of the stack without actually changing the stack. The ?DUP word will only copy the top stack item if it is non-zero. We only want to execute the DO loop if the depth of the stack is greater than 0. The following word .STACK will do a non-destructive stack print in a format similar to a stack effect diagram:

```
: .STACK ( -- )
  DEPTH ?DUP
  IF   0 DO DEPTH 1 - I - PICK U. LOOP
  THEN ." --" ;
```

An indeterminate loop can be used to run the HANDLE_SENSORS word until the **Run** button is pressed:

```
: HANDLE_SENSORS_TEST ( n -- )
  HANDLE_SENSORS_INIT
  BEGIN
    HANDLE_SENSORS
    RCX_BUTTON DUP BUTTON_GET @ 1 AND
  UNTIL ;

HANDLE_SENSORS_TEST
```

Now when you type `HANDLE_SENSORS_TEST`, the motor state is updated continuously depending on which of the touch sensors is pressed. The button fetching bug I mentioned is still lurking in this code, but it is not obvious. The following list summarizes the control-flow words in the Forth language:

`IF true_code THEN`   `( f -- )`   `"if-then"`

Executes true_code if the flag f is non-zero, otherwise does nothing

`IF true_code ELSE false_code THEN( f -- )`   `"if-else-then"`

Executes true_code if the flag f is non-zero, otherwise executes the false_code

`DO loop_code LOOP`   `( end start -- )`   `"do-loop"`

The DO word sets the loop index to start and executes loop_code at least once. When LOOP is encountered, the loop index is incremented by one, and if it is greater than or equal to end, the loop stops.

`DO loop_code n +LOOP`   `( end start -- )`   `"do-plus-loop"`

The DO word sets the loop index to start and executes loop_code at least once. When LOOP is encountered, the loop index is incremented by n, and if it is greater than or equal to end, the loop stops.

`BEGIN loop_code f UNTIL`   `( -- )`   `"begin-until"`

The loop-code is always executed at least once. If the value of the flag f is TRUE, the loop stops.

Using the Pushbuttons

The RCX has four pushbuttons on the front panel:

- Run

- View

- Prgm

- On–Off

Run, **View**, and **Prgm** are accessible to the BUTTON_GET word. The **On–Off** button is part of the power subsystem and is dealt with separately. In many cases, it would be nice to control your robot's actions to some extent using the pushbuttons on the front panel. The standard RCX firmware lets you cycle through the built-in programs using the **Prgm** button; it lets you look at sensor values using **View**; and **Run** starts or stops the currently running program.

We can do all of these things and more with a little clever Forth programming. The RCX word that deals with the RCX pushbuttons only returns the current state of the buttons. We might want to have some more advanced functions that debounce the switch state, as well as save switch press events when they happen.

> **NOTE** *The standard RCX firmware from LEGO is implemented using a round-robin scheduler. In simple terms, each of the tasks that the RCX needs to control are executed in turn until a cycle starts over again. Examples of tasks include updating motor states, checking sensor values, running RCX instructions, updating the LCD, and scanning pushbuttons. With the increased control that pbForth gives, you are also asked to take responsibility for some of the mundane house-keeping tasks.*

To process the pushbuttons effectively, we'll need to read them periodically and then save the events for later processing. It may not be possible to process the buttons when they are actually pressed, so we should save state changes as events in a buffer when they are detected. They can later be processed in the order that they occurred. Simply reading the switch state alone is bound to cause trouble. See if you can spot the error in Listing 5-2:

Listing 5-2. BUTTON1.TXT–Incorrect button processing

```
\ Button processing problem

: BUTTON_RUN? ( -- f )
  RCX_BUTTON DUP BUTTON_GET @ 1 AND ;

: TEST
  \ Wait for RUN button press to start
  BEGIN
    BUTTON_RUN?
  UNTIL
```

```
\ Wait for RUN button press to stop
BEGIN
  \ Add code to execute here...
  BUTTON_RUN?
UNTIL ;
```

If you can't figure out what's wrong here, don't feel bad. It took me the better part of an hour to spot the problem myself. The symptom was that the code in the second loop did not appear to run. Closer inspection showed that it actually did run, but only once. That was the critical piece of information. I forgot that the RCX processor was *much* faster at reading the pushbutton state than I was at letting go of the button. After the button was pressed and the first wait loop ended, the code in the second loop would run and detect that the switch was still pressed! It was almost impossible to release the switch in time, so the program would exit the second loop and return back to the interpreter.

Obviously, we need a way to read the buttons as well as handle and save state transitions. The other possibility would be to wait for the button to be released, but this would be awkward and would hold up the program from doing useful work. A better approach is to provide an Application Program Interface (API), which allows us to query the switch states and, at the same time, indicate whether a state change has actually occurred.

There is a straightforward algorithm for tracking changes in switch state with a single debounce. We need these four pieces of information to complete this task:

- CHG: True if a switch has changed state, false if not.

- CUR: The current switch sample value.

- PREV: The previous switch sample value.

- OLD: The oldest switch sample value.

The boolean formula for tracking the changed switch state is as follows:

CHG = ((OLD xor PREV)) and (not CUR xor PREV)

This is almost impossible to interpret without a chart. Table 5-3 shows a spurious switch press followed by a real switch press. Table 5-4 shows a spurious switch release followed by an actual release.

Table 5-3. Spurious Press Followed by a Real Press

OLD	PREV	CUR	OLD XOR PREV	NOT CUR XOR PREV	CHG
0	0	0	0	1	0
0	0	1	0	0	0
0	1	0	1	0	0
1	0	1	1	0	0
0	1	1	1	1	1

Table 5-4. Spurious Release Followed by a Real Release

OLD	PREV	CUR	OLD XOR PREV	NOT CUR XOR PREV	CHG
1	1	1	0	1	0
1	1	0	0	0	0
1	0	1	1	0	0
0	1	0	1	0	0
1	0	0	1	1	1

It is worth noting that the CHG state only indicates that a change has occurred. We still need to provide a way to read the current switch state for processing. We'll use the CREATE, CONSTANT, and VALUE mechanisms (described in the next chapter) to make a data structure to hold the button info, and add a simple API that reads and checks for switch events. In accordance with Forth conventions, the private structures and functions that are not typically used by the application are defined in lower case. We'll also make a ring buffer of switch events that is saved in the order in which they occurred. If the buffer fills up, newer switch presses are ignored. Listing 5-3 shows a complete button processing API, which correctly handles switches that are pressed for a long time.

Listing 5-3. BUTTONAPI.TXT–A complete button-processing API

```
\ BUTTONAPI.TXT - Improved button processing API

HEX

\ Typical ring buffer implementation. If empty, head
\ is equal to tail. If full, head is one less than
\ tail. Modulo araithmetic is used.

8 CONSTANT b_size \ Size of buffer in cells
0 VALUE    b_head \ Next index to store to
0 VALUE    b_tail \ Next index to read from

\ The switch buffer holds both the switch state and which
\ switches actually changed in the event.

CREATE b_buf
  b_size CELLS 2* ALLOT

\ RCX_BUTTON holds the current switch sample

0 VALUE b_prev    \ Holds the previous switch sample
0 VALUE b_old     \ Holds the oldest stable switch state

: b_put ( state chg -- )
  b_head DUP 1+ 8 MOD DUP
  b_tail =                        \ Check if full...
  IF   2DROP 2DROP                \ If yes, ignore the event
  ELSE TO b_head CELLS 2* b_buf + \ If not, store it
       SWAP OVER ! 1 CELLS + !
  THEN ;

: BUTTON_SCAN ( -- )
  b_prev DUP RCX_BUTTON
  DUP BUTTON_GET @
  DUP TO b_prev            \ Save the newest sample
  INVERT XOR 7 AND 7 =     \ Check if all buttons are stable
  IF   DUP b_old XOR ?DUP  \ Check if any buttons changed
       IF   OVER TO b_old  \ Save the stable changed state
            b_put          \ And save the event too
       ELSE DROP
       THEN
  ELSE DROP
  THEN ;
```

```
: BUTTON_EVENT? ( -- state chg )
  b_tail DUP b_head =              \ Check if empty
  IF   DROP 0 0                    \ If yes, return 0
  ELSE DUP 1+ 8 MOD TO b_tail      \ Else return event
       CELLS 2* b_buf + DUP
       1 CELLS + @ SWAP @
  THEN ;

\ Improved button processing program

: BUTTON_RUN? ( -- f )
  BUTTON_EVENT? AND 1 AND ;

: BUTTON_VIEW? ( -- f )
  BUTTON_EVENT? AND 2 AND ;

: BUTTON_PRGM? ( -- f )
  BUTTON_EVENT? AND 4 AND ;
```

You can now use the BUTTON_SCAN word periodically in your application to scan the button states, and then use the BUTTON_EVENT? word in your switch processing code to handle the button presses. As an example, let's use Listing 5-4 to redo the sample code in Listing 5-3 to make it only handle press events.

Listing 5-4. BUTTONTEST.TXT–Using the button API in an application

```
\ BUTTONTEST.TXT - Improved button processing problem

HEX

: TEST_BUTTON
  RCX_INIT
  1 4003 SOUND_PLAY   \ Beep-beep

\ Wait for RUN button press to start
  BEGIN
    BUTTON_SCAN BUTTON_RUN?
  UNTIL
  3 4003 SOUND_PLAY    \ Upward tones

  \ Wait for RUN button press to stop
```

```
BEGIN
  \ Code inside loop goes here
  BUTTON_SCAN BUTTON_RUN?
UNTIL
2 4003 SOUND_PLAY ;  \ Downward tones
```

After you enter TEST_BUTTON at the console, the RCX emits two beep tones. It then waits for you to press the **Run** button, after which it will sound a series of rising tones. Pressing the **Run** button a second time will cause the downward tones to sound and the word is then finished executing. Note that even if you keep the button pressed, the scanning algorithm requires you to release the button before the next press is detected.

Another thing you might have noticed is that after entering TEST_BUTTON, the RCX does not respond to text from the console. This is because the TEST_BUTTON word takes complete control of the RCX. The interpreter is not scanning the IR port for new characters.

Summary

In this introductory chapter, we have discussed some of the history of Forth, and why it is ideally suited for interactive development on a microcontroller with limited resources. The basic syntax of Forth was introduced, along with key features that differentiate Forth from other languages. These include the dictionary, the stack, and the ability to interact with the interpreter and the compiler.

From there, we expanded the discussion to include the basic features of the RCX and how to access them using pbForth. The LCD, the buzzer, and the motor control words were introduced with example scripts. We also took a side road into hexadecimal notation and signed/unsigned numbers. Finally, we gave an example of a common embedded systems problem with processing pushbuttons.

The next chapter will guide you through the design process of a real application—a simple robot that scans for bright lights and seeks them out. We'll improve on basic ideas as we go along, emphasizing the interactive nature of robot development. The main thing to remember as you learn pbForth is to bite off small pieces. Once you have mastered a particular idea or programming construct, play around with it to see how it works and what the limits are. And above all, have fun.

Programming Seeker in pbForth

SEEKER IS THE STANDARD ROBOT PLATFORM used throughout this book. In this chapter, we'll go through the steps required to get basic functionality out of the chassis. We'll emphasize the interactive and incremental nature of designing software to go with your robot.

When designing a robot system, the mechanical, electronic, and software elements must be integrated. On real-world assignments, such as industrial assembly robots, the design teams for each part of the robot will brainstorm ideas in the early stages of the project. The project manager will coordinate and monitor the progress of the design to ensure that the work of the mechanical team does conflict with that of the electrical or software teams.

When you design an RCX robot, think of yourself as the project manager. You are responsible for making sure the sensors give the software enough information to control the motors properly. You control the basic form of your chassis, what sensors you need, and how the software will eventually drive the motors. The RCX system makes some of the mechanical ideas easier to implement, but reading the Construction chapter in *Dave Baum's Definitive Guide to LEGO MINDSTORMS* (Apress, 2000) will help if you are inexperienced in the ways of the LEGO brick. After you have built a few robots with the parts in the RCX kit, you might have more ideas to try out. Chapter 2 provides great background information on how the input systems for your RCX work. Chapters 9 and 10 deal with the basic electronics concepts involved in designing specialized sensors. You will be able to use pbForth to take advantage of the standard and custom sensors. This chapter is really a design case study, and if you follow along with your model of Seeker you will get a feel for how the process works. Afterwards, you will have enough skills to use pbForth to interface to just about any robot design you can implement with the RCX. In the next section, "Making Seeker Move," I'll present the process of how to build up a vocabulary of motor control words in some detail. The sequence of trying out a concept, building a simple script, and then testing and optimizing it will become second nature to you. The goal of any programming session should be to come away with a few words that both meet the needs of the application and might also serve as the framework of a future project.

We are assuming that you've read over the introductory material on pbForth in the previous chapter, as well as Chapter 2. If anything in the sample code is unclear, please go back to those chapters for more information. If you have not already done so, building Seeker now (see Chapter 3) would be a good idea. The next section goes through all of the steps required to get Seeker running, and it's a lot easier to figure out what is going on if you have a real robot to work with.

Making Seeker Move

The easiest part of this project is getting the robot to move. When a tracked vehicle runs both tracks in the same direction it travels in a straight line. When they run in opposite directions, the robot will spin in place. In practice, the left and right drive motors will spin at slightly different speeds, so the robot will tend to veer off to one side. There are ways around this problem using advanced drive techniques, but we won't implement them here. Besides, this is an example of a real-world problem that a designer must take into account.

> **NOTE** *To make things easy to test without having to worry about losing the RCX off the edge of your desk, just place it upon a couple of LEGO bricks.*

To be mobile, the robot must do five things:

- Go forward

- Go backward

- Spin left

- Spin right

- Stop

Listing 6-1 shows a simple way you might write these five control words in pbForth. We're assuming that the drive motors are connected to ports A and C, as in the earlier Seeker instructions. Remember, if your robot does not move as expected, you can reverse a motor by turning the connector 180 degrees or by changing the motor direction code as depicted in the scripts that follow. Also, recall from the previous chapter that RCX_INIT is required to get the RCX internal drivers running for features such as motor control.

Listing 6-1. DIFFMOTOR1.TXT–First attempt at differential drive control words

```
\ DIFFMOTOR1.TXT - DIFFERENTIAL DRIVE CONTROL WORDS

RCX_INIT

: BOT_FORWARD ( -- )
  7 1 0 MOTOR_SET
  7 1 2 MOTOR_SET ;

: BOT_REVERSE ( -- )
  7 2 0 MOTOR_SET
  7 2 2 MOTOR_SET ;

: BOT_LEFT    ( -- )
  7 2 0 MOTOR_SET
  7 1 2 MOTOR_SET ;

: BOT_RIGHT   ( -- )
  7 1 0 MOTOR_SET
  7 2 2 MOTOR_SET ;

: BOT_STOP    ( -- )
  7 3 0 MOTOR_SET
  7 3 2 MOTOR_SET ;
```

The more economical programmers among you will immediately notice that there is a lot of similarity in each of these words. It must be possible to take advantage of this to make things a bit cleaner and more elegant. In Forth, pulling common code out of multiple words is called *factoring*, which is the same thing we do when pulling common factors out of an algebraic expression. The same code in factored form is shown in Listing 6-2.

Listing 6-2. DIFFMOTOR2.TXT–Factored differential drive control words

```
\ DIFFMOTOR2.TXT - FACTORED DIFFERENTIAL DRIVE CONTROL WORDS

RCX_INIT

: BOT_MOTOR_SET ( left right -- )
  7 SWAP 0 MOTOR_SET
  7 SWAP 2 MOTOR_SET ;
```

```
: BOT_FORWARD ( -- )
  1 1 BOT_MOTOR_SET ;

: BOT_REVERSE ( -- )
  2 2 BOT_MOTOR_SET ;

: BOT_LEFT    ( -- )
  1 2 BOT_MOTOR_SET ;

: BOT_RIGHT   ( -- )
  2 1 BOT_MOTOR_SET ;

: BOT_STOP    ( -- )
  3 3 BOT_MOTOR_SET ;
```

Note that the BOT_xyz words have not changed their stack effects, only the implementation inside the words has changed. By pulling all of the common code into a new word called BOT_MOTOR_SET, we just need to pass the left and right direction settings and BOT_MOTOR_SET does the rest of the work for us. The result being some code savings and a slight speed penalty, but the real benefit is that we can easily change the motion control words to accommodate changes in the connections. For example, if we decide to use motor port B instead of C for the right-side track, we make the following change. Remember to reload the rest of the bot control words to ensure that the definitions are updated.

```
: BOT_MOTOR_SET ( left right -- )
  7 SWAP 0 MOTOR_SET
  7 SWAP 1 MOTOR_SET ;
```

We can now easily test the operation of Seeker by typing at the console BOT_LEFT, BOT_RIGHT, and so on. When I tested the code the first time, I found that forward and reverse were exchanged, but that left and right were OK. I just changed the definitions of BOT_FORWARD and BOT_REVERSE and reloaded the script. Once I was convinced the motor control words were correct, I saved the script for use later.

Displaying Motor States

Now that we have the motors doing what we want, we might try to update the display to indicate how things are going. NQC and RCX Code automatically update the display indicators for you, while pbForth forces you to do it yourself. While it's a bit tedious, it also gives you good control over exactly what is displayed.

> **NOTE** *It's good programming practice to write down your ideas and any system information you can think of before you start coding. Understanding the problem completely will often make the solution obvious.*

Instead of doing it the hard way first, we'll design the motor display words using a factored approach right from the beginning. We'll probably want to pass the motor index and a direction parameter to this word, and it would be smart if it accepted parameters in the same order as MOTOR_SET, for reasons that will soon become clear.

Referring back to the previous chapter, the display codes for the motor indicators are shown in the following Table 6-1.

Table 6-1. Motor Indicator Display Codes

MOTOR	ACTIVE	FORWARD	REVERSE
0	0x300E	0x3010	0x300F
1	0x3011	0x3013	0x3012
2	0x3014	0x3016	0x3015

It looks like there is a very simple arithmetic rule we can take advantage of here; namely, for any display indicator, we just multiply the motor index by three and add the base value. We also want to establish some rules for displaying the four motor states because this will help us to write the definition of our new word.

- For the FLOAT state, turn off all the indicators.

- For the FORWARD state, turn on the active and forward indicators.

- For the REVERSE state, turn on the active and reverse indicators.

- For the BRAKE state, turn on the active, reverse, and forward indicators.

To see if we're on the right track with this, let's try a few things on the interactive console. The ok from the RCX has been removed for clarity.

```
HEX
300E LCD_SHOW LCD_REFRESH
3010 LCD_SHOW
300F LCD_SHOW LCD_REFRESH
300E LCD_HIDE LCD_REFRESH
```

Note that the display does not change unless you use the LCD_REFRESH word. To help with readability, we need to define some constants for the motor directions we will allow. Don't worry about the length of the names and the memory space in the RCX. The long name only takes up space where it is defined using the CONSTANT word. When you use the new word later, the Forth compiler in the RCX translates it into an efficient bytecode for you. You don't need to define constants for everything, just the words you will frequently use. The motor directions will be used all over the place, so we should use a constant. The LCD segment names are buried in the new word we're writing, and the idea is that we won't need to see the details, so we don't really need a constant for them. If you're using the TclTk GUI that comes with pbForth, it will strip extra comments and whitespace from the program as you upload it, so don't be afraid to use them. Listing 6-3 contains the new words required to update the motor display indicators.

Listing 6-3. SHOWMOTOR1.TXT–Updating the motor indicators on the LCD

```
\ SHOWMOTOR1.TXT - MOTOR INDICATOR MANIPULATION

HEX
RCX_INIT

\ Define the motor direction constants

1 CONSTANT MOTOR_FORWARD
2 CONSTANT MOTOR_REVERSE
3 CONSTANT MOTOR_BRAKE
4 CONSTANT MOTOR_FLOAT

\ MOTOR_SHOW_xyz sets the LCD segments for a specific
\ direction and motor

: MOTOR_SHOW_FORWARD ( idx*3 -- )
    DUP 300E + LCD_SHOW
    DUP 3010 + LCD_SHOW
        300F + LCD_HIDE ;

: MOTOR_SHOW_REVERSE ( idx*3 -- )
    DUP 300E + LCD_SHOW
    DUP 3010 + LCD_HIDE
        300F + LCD_SHOW ;

: MOTOR_SHOW_BRAKE ( idx*3 -- )
    DUP 300E + LCD_SHOW
    DUP 3010 + LCD_SHOW
        300F + LCD_SHOW ;
```

```
: MOTOR_SHOW_FLOAT ( idx*3 -- )
    DUP 300E + LCD_HIDE
    DUP 3010 + LCD_HIDE
        300F + LCD_HIDE ;


: MOTOR_SHOW ( dir idx --   )
  3 *        ( dir idx*3 -- )
      OVER MOTOR_FORWARD = IF MOTOR_SHOW_FORWARD
  ELSE OVER MOTOR_REVERSE = IF MOTOR_SHOW_REVERSE
  ELSE OVER MOTOR_BRAKE   = IF MOTOR_SHOW_BRAKE
  ELSE SWAP MOTOR_FLOAT   = IF MOTOR_SHOW_FLOAT
  ELSE DROP
  THEN THEN THEN THEN ;
```

The MOTOR_SHOW word is an example of a nested IF structure. It's intimidating to look at, but if you use them sparingly and are careful to format them for readability, nested IF statements can be very powerful. Another option is to use table lookup or vectored execution to select the word to execute, which is described in the following sidebar. You might also wonder why we did not put LCD_REFRESH inside the MOTOR_SHOW word. The reason is that it is likely that other motor and sensor indicators need updating, and it's best to refresh the LCD all at once to save time.

Vectored Execution of Forth Words

The use of a table of function pointers is an alternative to nested IF structures in many programming languages. Forth is no exception. The use of a table lookup to select the word is slightly more complicated and makes you do some work up front, but it's generally faster than a nested IF structure. The idea is to make a table of the execution points of the MOTOR_SHOW_xyz words and then use the direction index to pick the right one.

When you type a word like RCX_INIT or LCD_REFRESH the interpreter looks up the word, determines its address, and executes it. You can do the same thing.

```
HEX
3004 1 SOUND_PLAY
3004 1 ' SOUND_PLAY EXECUTE
```

The ' (tick) word will try to find the SOUND_PLAY word in the dictionary. If found, the execution address is left on the stack, where EXECUTE will use it to run the word. So it's clear we can set up a table with the execution addresses, but how will we store them?

We can make a new word that returns the address of the first empty memory cell after the definition using the CREATE word. The entries are compiled and added to the table using the "," (comma) word.

Each execution address uses up one cell of memory, or 16 bits. The memory in the RCX is byte addressed, so we'll need to convert the index to the cell offset. Finally, tables or arrays in computer land always start with element zero, but our direction indexes start at 1. We can either put in a dummy cell or subtract one from the index to make everything work. I usually put in a dummy cell if it makes the code easier to understand. Here is the new MOTOR_SHOW word.

```
\ Improved MOTOR_SHOW

CREATE MOTOR_SHOW_VECTOR
' MOTOR_SHOW_FLOAT    ,  \ Dummy entry for dir=0
' MOTOR_SHOW_FORWARD ,
' MOTOR_SHOW_REVERSE ,
' MOTOR_SHOW_BRAKE    ,
' MOTOR_SHOW_FLOAT    ,

\ NOTE if dir is ANYTHING other than 0,1,2,3,4 this
\       routine will crash the RCX

: MOTOR_SHOW ( dir idx --   )
  3 *        ( dir idx*3 -- )
  SWAP CELLS              \ Calculate the correct entry
  MOTOR_SHOW_VECTOR +     \ Point at the entry in the table
  @ EXECUTE ;             \ Fetch it, then execute it
```

The process of creating the table is done at compile-time. The MOTOR_SHOW word is now shorter and takes up less memory as a result. It is also faster because it does not have to evaluate all the conditionals.

At this point, the reason for keeping the parameter list the same as the MOTOR_SET word may be obvious: we can fix BOT_MOTOR_SET to automatically update the display when the motor state changes. The new word is shown in the following example:

```
: BOT_MOTOR_SET ( left right -- )
  7 SWAP 0 2DUP MOTOR_SHOW MOTOR_SET
  7 SWAP 2 2DUP MOTOR_SHOW MOTOR_SET ;
```

The MOTOR_SET word wants (power dir idx --) on the stack, and MOTOR_SHOW just needs the (dir idx --), so a simple 2DUP is enough to copy the top two elements without affecting the requirements for MOTOR_SET. More importantly, we do not need to save the parameters in variables, they are copied directly onto the stack as needed.

The final script that puts it all together is shown in Listing 6-4. Note that because we use vectored execution, we don't need to use the motor constants anymore. In fact, we have defined an API, which lets us control Seeker and its motor displays using a collection of abstracted words that tell us exactly what the robot is doing. It would be a stretch to think that BOT_LEFT did anything *other* than turn the robot to the left!

Listing 6-4. DIFFMOTOR3.TXT–Motor control and display words using vectored execution

```
\ DIFFMOTOR3.TXT - words to manipulate the motors and indicators

DIFFMOTOR
MARKER DIFFMOTOR

HEX
RCX_INIT

\ MOTOR_SHOW_xyz sets the LCD segments for a specific
\ direction and motor

: MOTOR_SHOW_FORWARD ( idx*3 -- )
    DUP 300E + LCD_SHOW
    DUP 3010 + LCD_SHOW
        300F + LCD_HIDE ;

: MOTOR_SHOW_REVERSE ( idx*3 -- )
    DUP 300E + LCD_SHOW
    DUP 3010 + LCD_HIDE
        300F + LCD_SHOW ;

: MOTOR_SHOW_BRAKE ( idx*3 -- )
    DUP 300E + LCD_SHOW
    DUP 3010 + LCD_SHOW
        300F + LCD_SHOW ;

: MOTOR_SHOW_FLOAT ( idx*3 -- )
    DUP 300E + LCD_HIDE
    DUP 3010 + LCD_HIDE
        300F + LCD_HIDE ;

\ Improved MOTOR_SHOW
```

```
CREATE MOTOR_SHOW_VECTOR
' MOTOR_SHOW_FLOAT    ,  \ Dummy entry for dir=0
' MOTOR_SHOW_FORWARD ,
' MOTOR_SHOW_REVERSE ,
' MOTOR_SHOW_BRAKE    ,
' MOTOR_SHOW_FLOAT    ,

\ NOTE if dir is ANYTHING other than 0,1,2,3,4 this
\       routine will crash the RCX

: MOTOR_SHOW ( dir idx --   )
  3 *        ( dir idx*3 -- )
  SWAP CELLS            \ Calculate the correct entry
  MOTOR_SHOW_VECTOR +   \ Point at the entry in the table
  @ EXECUTE ;           \ Fetch it, then execute it

\ FACTORED DIFFERENTIAL DRIVE CONTROL WORDS

: BOT_MOTOR_SET ( left right -- )
  7 SWAP 0 2DUP MOTOR_SHOW MOTOR_SET
  7 SWAP 2 2DUP MOTOR_SHOW MOTOR_SET ;

: BOT_FORWARD ( -- )
  1 1 BOT_MOTOR_SET ;

: BOT_REVERSE ( -- )
  2 2 BOT_MOTOR_SET ;

: BOT_LEFT    ( -- )
  1 2 BOT_MOTOR_SET ;

: BOT_RIGHT   ( -- )
  2 1 BOT_MOTOR_SET ;

: BOT_STOP    ( -- )
  3 3 BOT_MOTOR_SET ;
```

Leaving Markers in the Dictionary

When you load this script for the first time, you may get a

```
DIFFMOTOR ? undefined word
```

response from pbForth when it's interpreting the DIFFMOTOR string. To make memory management easier internally, pbForth puts all of its definitions into a linked list structure. The bytecodes that the Forth machine interprets are actually the addresses of the words in the linked list. Removing an entry and shifting all the addresses would be a nightmare, so it's not done. It is much easier to simply clear the wordlist from a known point to the end of the dictionary.

Think of the dictionary as a loose-leaf binder. Initially, the binder contains definitions for Forth's built-in words, like HEX, SWAP, etc. Each page also has a number, which corresponds to the bytecode for the word on the page. As you add definitions, you add pages to the end of the binder. The compiler checks the dictionary from back to front for words you use in your definition, and notes the page number of the first matching word it finds. Obviously, as you add more definitions to the dictionary, it will get full. What we need is a way to set a bookmark in the dictionary so we can discard all of the definitions past the mark.

The solution is the MARKER word, which takes a string as input, in this case DIFFMOTOR. The next time you type DIFFMOTOR, the RCX will delete all the words from the most recent definition back to just before the use of MARKER. It's as if you had ripped out all of the pages up to and including the marker from your binder. It will essentially forget all of the words you defined after (and including) the marker. (As an interesting historical aside, some of the original Forth implementations had a word called FORGET.)

Note that only the pbmax.srec image has MARKER defined. This is an optional word that is not included in the minimal pbForth firmware image.

In case you are wondering how much space this script (or any other) takes up in the RCX, you can use the word HERE to get the current location of the dictionary pointer before the script is loaded. You can use it again to get the location after loading the script. Here's a typical result:

```
DECIMAL
HERE DUP U.
46456 ok
( Load the script )
HERE DUP U.
46964 ok
SWAP - U.
508 ok
```

The U. word is used here because we want the address to be printed as an unsigned number. This seems to be a pretty big number for such a small amount of code, but if you count all of the letters in the definitions, you'll see that we end up using about 130 bytes for the names alone. Because the only names we will ever use in other definitions are the robot motion control words, all of the others can be shortened. For now, we'll leave them alone so that we can understand the code better.

Making Seeker See and Feel

Now that we can make Seeker move at will, we're ready to make it see and feel its environment. This section requires some understanding of the material in Chapter 2 to make use of the sensor mode and type information. We'll work out a few words for setting up sensor inputs under pbForth, and then we'll add words to read and display the results.

The Touch Sensor as Detector

The simplest sensor type is the touch sensor. It is a passive sensor that has two states from a user's point of view—open and closed. The use of the sensor in an application is determined by the mode of operation, such as raw, boolean, edge-count, pulse-count and so on. Your robot can tell if it has hit something, or count the number of times it has hit something depending on the mode. In most cases, however, you want the default operation for the sensor, so we'll engage in some interactive testing with the touch sensor to help us figure out the form our new words should take. Before starting on this, let's put a touch sensor on Port 1—remember that this is index 0 for pbForth. If you have already built Seeker (and hopefully, you have by now), the touch sensor is already on Port 1. Listing 6-5 is an interactive session with the RCX, which tries to clarify how the touch sensor works in boolean mode. Note that you can always get the raw sensor value using SENSOR_RAW.

Listing 6-5. Interactive demonstration of touch sensor operation

```
HEX
RCX_INIT
SENSOR_INIT

0 SENSOR_PASSIVE
1 0 SENSOR_TYPE
20 0 SENSOR_MODE

\ Read the sensor in the "open" mode
0 SENSOR_READ DROP 0 SENSOR_BOOL U. 0 SENSOR_RAW U.
0 3F8 ok
```

```
\ Press the sensor and read it in the "closed" mode
0 SENSOR_READ DROP 0 SENSOR_BOOL U. 0 SENSOR_RAW U.
1 2C ok
```

On Seeker, the front bumper works "backwards" because it is normally closed. When Seeker hits an obstacle, the bumper moves in and the touch sensor opens up. We'll show you how to turn this around later in this section.

The index 0 certainly shows up a lot, and it's pretty clear that most of the business of configuring and reading a sensor is pure repetition. Also, you can use the SENSOR_BOOL, SENSOR_RAW, and SENSOR_VALUE words as many times as you like after SENSOR_READ. This is because they only retrieve the values that are calculated after SENSOR_READ, which does the work of converting the raw reading into useful values. With this in mind, it's fairly easy to design a few words that make setting up and using a touch sensor easier. Listing 6-6 shows how to simplify the process of creating and using a touch sensor in boolean mode.

Listing 6-6. TOUCH.TXT–Touch sensor creation and manipulation words

```
\ TOUCH.TXT - TOUCH SENSOR CREATION AND MANIPULATION

HEX
RCX_INIT
SENSOR_INIT

: SENSOR_BOOL_MAKE ( idx -- )
  DUP SENSOR_PASSIVE
  1  OVER SENSOR_TYPE
  20 SWAP SENSOR_MODE ;

: SENSOR_BOOL? ( idx -- f )
  DUP SENSOR_READ DROP SENSOR_BOOL ;

: SENSOR_BOOL_SHOW ( state idx -- )
  2* 3009 + SWAP
  IF   LCD_SHOW
  ELSE LCD_HIDE
  THEN ;
```

It is a common convention in Forth that words that end in a "?" return a TRUE/FALSE indication of their meaning. In this case, we return a TRUE (non-zero) value if the touch sensor is pressed in, and FALSE (zero) otherwise. If your touch sensing mechanism works "backwards," it's easy to add a 0= to invert the meaning of SENSOR_BOOL?. In fact, this is what we'll need to do to get Seeker's touch sensor to work properly.

It is also a common convention that words follow a noun/verb format. In other words, we indicate the thing the word operates on, and then what it does.

Finally, it is good practice to add RCX_INIT and SENSOR_INIT to scripts that need them. It's probably not necessary to put them into every script, but it makes for less typing when you're testing.

By now, you'll recognize what SENSOR_BOOL_SHOW does, it just sets or clears the active indicator for the specified sensor index. Remember to use LCD_REFRESH to actually change what the LCD shows.

The Touch Sensor as Counter

We can explore some other ways of using the touch sensor with scripts that display the number of pulses or edge transitions a sensor makes. Fortunately, the RCX firmware has built-in routines that debounce the input signal and take care of the counting for us. Chapter 2 has detailed information on how to set the slope parameter for a sensor to customize its operation. This is more important when you start building and using your own custom sensors. Listing 6-7 is a script that sets up a sensor in counting mode.

Listing 6-7. TOUCHCOUNT.TXT – Setting up a sensor in counting mode

```
\ TOUCHCOUNT.TXT - set up a counting touch sensor

HEX
RCX_INIT
SENSOR_INIT

: SENSOR_COUNT_MAKE ( idx -- )
  DUP SENSOR_PASSIVE
  1  OVER SENSOR_TYPE
  60 SWAP SENSOR_MODE ;

: SENSOR_COUNT_GET ( idx -- n f )
  DUP SENSOR_READ DROP DUP SENSOR_VALUE SWAP SENSOR_BOOL ;

: SENSOR_COUNT_SHOW ( n state idx -- )
  SENSOR_BOOL_SHOW
  3002 SWAP 301F LCD_NUMBER ;

: SENSOR_COUNT_TEST
  RCX_INIT
  SENSOR_INIT
  0 SENSOR_COUNT_MAKE
```

```
BEGIN
  0 SENSOR_COUNT_GET
  0 SENSOR_COUNT_SHOW
  LCD_REFRESH
  EKEY?
UNTIL ;
```

Load this script and run SENSOR_COUNT_TEST from the console. The program expects a touch sensor on port 1. If you're using the Seeker bumper to test this with, every time you press and release the bumper you'll see the little black triangle near the sensor connector turn on and the count in the display will increase by one. If you press any key on the console, the test script stops and the familiar ok prompt will come back after you hit return a few times. Notice that the test word is simply built up out of words we defined and tested interactively.

The Raw Light Sensor

Now we'll get the light sensor going. Once we have that, we can start putting the words we have defined into use in controlling our robot. The light sensor is described in detail in Chapter 2, so here we'll just discuss the software aspects. We can easily make up a similar script to test the light sensor—in fact, it's so easy that we'll simply copy the touch sensor script and change certain names and constants. The script in Listing 6-8 assumes the light sensor is hooked up to Input 2.

Listing 6-8. LIGHT.TXT – Light sensor creation and manipulation words

```
\ LIGHT.TXT - LIGHT SENSOR CREATION AND TESTING

HEX
RCX_INIT
SENSOR_INIT

: SENSOR_LIGHT_MAKE ( idx -- )
  DUP SENSOR_ACTIVE
  3  OVER SENSOR_TYPE
  80 SWAP SENSOR_MODE ;

: SENSOR_LIGHT_GET ( idx -- n )
  DUP SENSOR_READ DROP SENSOR_VALUE ;

: SENSOR_LIGHT_SHOW ( n idx -- )
  2* 3008 + LCD_SHOW
  3002 SWAP 301F LCD_NUMBER ;
```

```
: SENSOR_LIGHT_TEST
  RCX_INIT
  SENSOR_INIT
  1 SENSOR_LIGHT_MAKE
  BEGIN
    1 SENSOR_LIGHT_GET
    1 SENSOR_LIGHT_SHOW
    LCD_REFRESH
    EKEY?
  UNTIL ;
```

This script works pretty much like SENSOR_COUNT_GET. It just updates the display with the current value of the light sensor. The display updates so fast that you probably only see a blur of digits unless the sensor is pointing at a fairly steady light source. We can fix this in one of two ways. The first is a timer that increases the interval between readings, and the second is to average more readings and increase the interval between updates. The advantage of the second method is that we are more immune to transient light spikes that might throw off the light-seeking algorithms. The next section explores how to use the values returned by the sensor to make control decisions in our robot.

Averaging the Light Sensor

One of the techniques used to smooth out noise in sensor readings is averaging. An inexperienced programmer might make a large array of values, fill it with data, and continuously average it using a sliding window through the data points. One way to reduce the amount of calculation is to initialize the buffer sum once, then add a new reading to the total and subtract the value it is replacing. This is better, but still wastes a lot of memory. The idea of a *weighted average* can be used to reduce both memory and arithmetic requirements for smoothing data.

If we know something about the sampling rate and the amount of noise to expect from the sensor, we can do simple arithmetic to calculate how to weight our samples. But first we'll need to do some experiments with the light sensor.

We can use the RCX timers and a counter to get an idea of the sampling rate. Recall from Chapter 2 that the RCX gets a reading from a new channel every 3 ms, so there is no point in sampling faster than about 333 times a second. In the section titled "Low-Resolution Timers" you'll see that a tight loop in pbForth is much faster than this.

The idea behind a weighted average is to give more importance to the average of previous readings than to the current reading. Think of this in terms of a bucket, a cup, and a supply of water that may vary in temperature from cold to hot. We may want to control the water temperature coming from the tap but ignore any brief fluctuations. Let's assume that the water has been cold up until now and we fill up the bucket from the tap. This corresponds to initializing our filter. It's important to initialize a filter with a reasonable value, otherwise the response of the system might be unpredictable. The bucket represents the current average water temperature. One cup represents the current water temperature sample, which has been changed to hot. The second cup is used to transfer water as follows:

1. Fill the cup with water from the bucket and dump it out.

2. Fill the cup with water from the tap, dump it into the bucket and stir.

Depending upon the difference in size between the sample cups and the bucket, the temperature in the averaging bucket will rise slowly or quickly. It also makes a difference how often you transfer samples to the averaging bucket. Many small samples will have the same result as a few large samples. Unfortunately, large samples of water temperature will make the average change quickly, while small samples tend to make the average change very slowly. This is one of the classic tradeoffs in engineering, where changing one variable has a direct effect on another. The trick is finding the ideal balance between the two that makes your design work properly.

The equation that represents this averaging technique is

$$NewAvg = \frac{((OldAvg \times (Weight - 1)) + Value)}{Weight}$$

Listing 6-9 demonstrates the use of weighted averages. It has a new construct, called a VALUE, which behaves like a CONSTANT at run-time, but can be changed like a VARIABLE. We'll also see how to implement a simple data structure in Forth that can take data items and encapsulate them, insulating the application from the implementation of the structure. Finally, we'll introduce the idea of a *defining word*, which lets you extend the compiler to allow it to create new words.

Listing 6-9. FILTER1.TXT – Filter creation and manipulation words

```
\ FILTER1.TXT - FILTER CREATION AND MANIPULATION

: FILTER_CREATE ( "name" )
  CREATE
  0 ,    \ Initial average
  1 , ;  \ Initial weight
```

```
: FILTER_INIT ( weight avg a-addr -- )
  SWAP 2 PICK * OVER !
  CELL+ ! ;

: FILTER_GET ( a-addr -- avg )
  DUP @ SWAP CELL+ @ / ;

: FILTER_PUT ( value a-addr -- )
  SWAP OVER FILTER_GET -
  OVER @ + SWAP ! ;

\ Now we can test the filter - but we need the light
\ sensor words in LIGHT.TXT loaded first!

HEX
RCX_INIT
SENSOR_INIT
1 SENSOR_LIGHT_MAKE

FILTER_CREATE LIGHT_FILTER

8 1 SENSOR_LIGHT_GET LIGHT_FILTER FILTER_INIT

: TEST_FILTER
  BEGIN
    1 SENSOR_LIGHT_GET LIGHT_FILTER FILTER_PUT
    LIGHT_FILTER FILTER_GET
    3002 SWAP 301F LCD_NUMBER
    LCD_REFRESH
    EKEY?
  UNTIL ;
```

Our bucket/cup analogy gives us the two elements we need to implement a filter in software. The bucket is the average, and the ratio between the size of the bucket and cup is the weighting factor, or weight for short. The basic data structure for our filter needs only two elements, a current average, and the weight you want to apply to a new value. We'll hide the exact implementation of the underlying structure by providing the *interface words* listed in the following glossary to communicate with the filter. The idea here is that we'll want to make our words general, so they can be used over again. There isn't much point in making a specialized word for a weighted average filter, especially because it can be useful in many robotics applications.

FILTER_CREATE   (name)   "filter-create"

Allocates space for a new filter structure. The name of the filter is read from the input stream. When the name is invoked later, it will return the address of the filter structure for the interface words.

FILTER_INIT   (weight average addr --)   "filter-init"

Sets up the initial values the filter will use. Rather than use separate words for setting the initial average and the weight factor, this word does both.

FILTER_GET   (addr -- average)   "filter-get"

Retrieves the average value of the current filter.

FILTER_PUT   (value addr --)   "filter-set"

Puts a new sample into the filter for processing.

The code for filter words and an example of their use is shown in Listing 6-9. There is one very important point worth mentioning here: because Forth uses fixed-point math, the average cannot respond to small changes due to truncation errors. As an example, let the old average be 46, the weight is 8, and the new value is 49. Plugging the values into the averaging formula, we get

$$NewAvg = \frac{(46 \times (8-1)) + 49))}{8}$$

$$NewAvg = 46.375$$

Because Forth uses fixed-point math, the result is truncated to 46. It will take a new value of 54 before the new average goes up at all. To get around this problem, we prescale the average up by the weight and rearrange the formula as follows:

$$NewAvg \approx \frac{((OldAvg \times Weight) - OldAvg + Value)}{Weight}$$

> **NOTE** *This is one of the neat little numerical tricks in embedded systems design. To avoid division and multiplication every time we need to add a new value to the average, we keep OldAvg*Weight in the filter. Hiding the implementation behind the API makes for good programming because we can easily change things as needed without breaking existing routines.*

To "slow down" the response of the filter, increase the weight factor. I'll leave it as an experiment for you to change the weight and then observe the different response on the LCD to `TEST_FILTER`.

Using the Timers

Timers are useful in many different aspects of robotics. We can use them to wait for specific time intervals, or to calculate how long something takes. This section contains a gentle introduction to timers and how they might be used. In one case, we'll use them to turn on a motor for a specific time period. In another, we'll use timers to measure how long it takes to run a pbForth word.

High-Resolution Timers

Let's do some interactive experiments with the timers to see if we can get a handle on how to design the words we need to test the run-time of a Forth word. Once again, in Forth it's easy to try new ideas to get a proof of principle before spending hours designing and coding a system. As usual, the RCX responses are underlined. Because we are working with timers, the exact values returned depend upon the time elapsed since the `timer_SET` command, thus don't be surprised if you see different numbers from the RCX.

```
RCX_INIT
ok
HEX
ok
400 0 timer_SET
ok
0 timer_GET U.
24B ok
0 timer_GET U.
D7 ok
0 timer_GET U.
0 ok
```

In the next example we're figuring out how the high-resolution timers work. The RCX System Software implements ten high-resolution countdown timers. They count at 100 ticks per second and stop when they hit zero. You set them to the value of the interval you want to time, and then test them periodically to see when they have expired. The `TEST_timer` word updates the LCD with the current value of the timer. The `DELAY` word sits in a tight loop for the specified number of 0.01-second ticks until it's done. Listing 6-10 shows how to use the high-resolution timers to wait for a specific time.

Listing 6-10. TIMER1.TXT – Using high-resolution timers for a timed delay

```
\ TIMER1.TXT - TESTING THE HI_RES TIMERS

RCX_INIT
HEX

: TEST_timer ( n idx -- )
  SWAP OVER timer_SET    ( idx -- )
  BEGIN
    DUP timer_GET          ( idx n1 -- )
    3002 OVER 301F LCD_NUMBER LCD_REFRESH
    0=                     ( idx n1 -- )
  UNTIL DROP ;           ( -- )

: DELAY ( ticks )
  0 timer_SET
  BEGIN 0 timer_GET 0= UNTIL ;

: TEST_DELAY ( ticks )
  7 1 0 MOTOR_SET
  DELAY
  7 3 0 MOTOR_SET ;

DECIMAL
1000 0 TEST_timer
```

After you type the last line (or upload it from a script) you should see the number display on the RCX count down from 1,000 to 0 and stop. Because the high-resolution timers tick 100 times a second, the countdown should last very close to 10 seconds. Unfortunately the numbers go by so quickly you won't be able to see them very clearly.

Try different tick values for TEST_DELAY and see how Seeker's left track turns on for the exact time. By using very small values, we can "jog" Seeker in a tight circle, which we'll need as we look around for our light source, as in "The Light Sensor and Thresholds," later in this chapter.

Low-Resolution Timers

Next, we'll try the lower-resolution timers. They tick 10 times a second, but that's plenty of resolution for what we need to do here. We need to remember that these low- resolution timers count up and return to 0 at 32,767. To avoid having to check for rollover of arbitrary timer settings, we can set the timer to 0 at the start of an interval and only check if we're past the desired interval. These timers are better suited, however, to elapsed time measurements.

The following script includes an example of how to use low-resolution timers to test the run-time of words. All you do is get the execution address of the word to test and save it. Then run WORD_TIME with the number of times to run the word. The result is displayed on the LCD. Just remember to start testing with a small number of iterations and then work up to bigger values to get a more precise estimate of run-time.

The timing tester in Listing 6-11 uses *vectored execution,* which was discussed in the sidebar, "Vectored Execution of Forth Words," earlier in this chapter. This means that we can store the address of any word in a variable or value and execute it later. Besides being useful in this particular application, vectored execution is useful for choosing one word to execute from many others.

Listing 6-11. TIMER2.TXT – Using low-resolution timers to check execution time

```
\ TIMER2.TXT - WORD RUN_TIME TESTER

0 VALUE WORD_UNDER_TEST

\ REMEMBER - THE WORD YOU ARE TESTING MUST BE STACK NEUTRAL
\            IT CANNOT LEAVE ANYTHING ON THE STACK OR
\            CONSUME ANYTHING

'' LCD_REFRESH TO WORD_UNDER_TEST

RCX_INIT
HEX

: WORD_TIME ( n -- )
  0 0 TIMER_SET
  0 DO WORD_UNDER_TEST EXECUTE LOOP
  0 TIMER_GET

  3002 SWAP 301F LCD_NUMBER LCD_REFRESH ;

DECIMAL
1000 WORD_TIME
```

After you load this script, the LCD should show 0016, which indicates that 1,000 iterations of LCD_REFRESH took about 16 ticks of the low-resolution timer, or about 1.6 seconds. This means that 1 iteration of LCD_REFRESH will take about .0016 seconds.

One very important thing to remember about words that you test is that they must be *stack neutral* because they are executing inside a loop. In other words, they cannot leave anything on the stack because it would quickly overflow; they cannot consume anything from the stack, because they would deplete the stack. You can get around this by enclosing your word within another word that sets up or cleans up the stack after it runs.

Here's another sample of word run-time testing:

```
DECIMAL
: TEST_PLUS
  1 2 + DROP ;

' TEST_PLUS TO WORD_UNDER_TEST
10000 WORD_TIME
```

Running this script we see that it only takes about 5 ticks. Put another way, we can get about 20,000 additions plus the stack setup done in one second—that's *fast*. Similarly, we can run about 25,000 motor set words in one second:

```
DECIMAL
: TEST_MOTOR_SET
  1 7 4 MOTOR_SET ;

' TEST_MOTOR_SET TO WORD_UNDER_TEST
25000 WORD_TIME
```

As you can see, pbForth gives you the ability to run your code very quickly.

The Light Sensor and Thresholds

Now that we have the basic building blocks for using the light sensor and the timers, we can assemble them into a useful robot. The operation of Seeker will be as follows:

1. Spin slowly and determine the average light level while still keeping track of the brightest light.

2. Find the bright light again and point toward it.

3. Move towards the bright light. If the light disappears, try to find it by swinging slightly left and then right.

4. If Seeker bumps into an obstacle, back up, and return to Step 1.

5. If Seeker can't find the original bright light, return to Step 1.

Let's assemble the parts now and test the robot behavior as we go along. The process we're going through here is exactly the one I used when designing this application for the book. Incremental changes were made, tested, and then added to the master script that controlled the robot. It's important to remember that you will be uploading scripts to the RCX all the time, so making sure that the IR port is visible can be a bit of a challenge.

We have little control of Seeker's actual heading, or even how long it will take to spin around. We'll make two values we can adjust to the most important environmental condition—the type of floor covering. The robot will find it harder to turn on a carpeted surface, while a very slick surface will cause slippage. One of the two values will control the number of steps that the robot uses to turn in a full circle, and the other controls the size of each step. Forth has traditionally utilized CONSTANTs and VARIABLEs to store items we don't want to juggle around on the stack. A constant puts a number on the stack when it is executed, but the value cannot be changed. A variable puts the address of its contents on the stack, which must then be fetched from that address. It is, of course, possible to change a variable's value, but the requirement to fetch the number every time leads to messy source code. ANSI Forth introduced a third storage type, which is a VALUE. This new data type behaves like a constant, but you can change its contents using the TO word. We'll see VALUE in use in the script shown in Listing 6-12.

Listing 6-12. SCAN1.TXT – Scanning for the peak light reading

```
\ SCAN1.TXT - PEAK SCANNER FOR THE SEEKER
\
\ REQUIRES: DIFFMOTOR3.TXT LIGHT.TXT FILTER1.TXT

    0 VALUE SCAN_CURRENT_PEAK
32767 VALUE SCAN_CURRENT_MIN
    8  VALUE SCAN_TURN_DELAY
   30 VALUE SCAN_STEPS


\ The SCAN_FOR_PEAK word will put the highest value
\ it finds in its scan into SCAN_CURRENT_PEAK

RCX_INIT
SENSOR_INIT
1 SENSOR_LIGHT_MAKE

\ And make a filter for the light sensor average too

FILTER_CREATE SCAN_AVERAGE
16 1 SENSOR_LIGHT_GET SCAN_AVERAGE FILTER_INIT
```

```
: SCAN_FOR_PEAK
  \ Initialize the peak detector
  0     TO SCAN_CURRENT_PEAK
  32767 TO SCAN_CURRENT_MIN

  SCAN_STEPS 0 DO
    \ Now figure out if we need to store the new peak
    \ or minimum values

    1 SENSOR_LIGHT_GET

    DUP SCAN_AVERAGE FILTER_PUT

    DUP SCAN_CURRENT_PEAK >
    IF  DUP TO SCAN_CURRENT_PEAK
    THEN

    DUP SCAN_CURRENT_MIN <
    IF  DUP TO SCAN_CURRENT_MIN
    THEN

    DROP

    \ Now spin the robot to the left for some time
    BOT_LEFT
    SCAN_TURN_DELAY 0 timer_SET
    BEGIN
      0 timer_GET 0=
    UNTIL
    BOT_STOP
  LOOP ;
```

This word will execute to completion if you type SCAN_FOR_PEAK–that's because the pbForth interpreter does not regain control until the end of this word. You'll probably find that the robot does not make exactly one full turn. You now can exercise your power as project manager and tune the SCAN_TURN_DELAY and SCAN_STEPS values to get the performance you are looking for. The current setup will give us 20 steps of 100 ms each, which ends up at around 2 seconds total. You might expect the bot to stop between samples, but the other code around the delay loop takes so little time that the robot appears to move continuously.

You can grab the peak value that the RCX collected in its scan by typing "SCAN_CURRENT_PEAK ." or grab the minimum value by typing "SCAN_CURRENT_MIN ." at the console. The next thing to do is find the peak value again. We'll make the word return a true/false flag so we can determine if the peak was found. It would be a good idea to add some tolerance around the peak value so we can take into account variable brightness as we wander around.

> **NOTE**   *You might notice that the language I'm using implies that we are the robot! This is another important trick in getting your creations to work. Playing computer is a method used by every professional programmer—it helps them to fully understand the code and what it is doing. Often, simply showing code that does not work to another programmer and walking them through it makes the problem obvious.*

The word we need can scan to the left or to the right, looking for a brightness value that is within some threshold of the peak. We'll need to add the threshold as a new value to the system. The scan direction and number of steps should be parameters to the word. Finally, the word should return true or false depending on whether or not the bright light was found. Listing 6-13 combines all of these ideas into a single word that we can use to make Seeker find the peak light value.

Listing 6-13. SCAN2.TXT – Finding the specified peak light reading

```
\ SCAN2.TXT - PEAK FINDER FOR THE SEEKER
\
\
\ REQUIRES: DIFFMOTOR3.TXT LIGHT.TXT FILTER1.TXT SCAN1.TXT

 3 VALUE SCAN_PEAK_THRESH

: FIND_PEAK ( dir steps -- f )

  \ Now set the threshold as the difference between the
  \ average and the peak

  SCAN_CURRENT_PEAK SCAN_AVERAGE FILTER_GET
  - 2 / 1 + 4 MIN TO SCAN_PEAK_THRESH

  0 ROT ROT ( 0 dir steps --)    \ Set up failure

  0 DO
    \ Now figure out if we have found the peak or
    \ a brighter light

    1 SENSOR_LIGHT_GET
```

```
SCAN_CURRENT_PEAK SCAN_PEAK_THRESH - >

\ If the current reading is bigger than the peak
\ minus the thresh, we have a new light to follow.

IF   SWAP 1+ SWAP LEAVE
THEN

\ We have not found it yet, stop and spin the bot...

DUP IF BOT_RIGHT ELSE BOT_LEFT THEN

SCAN_TURN_DELAY 0 timer_SET

BEGIN
  0 timer_GET 0=
UNTIL
BOT_STOP

LOOP

DROP ;
```

Let's test the code so far. If you tested SCAN_FOR_PEAK previously, the peak value we're looking for should now be stored. Now type "0 10 FIND_PEAK" and the robot should spin to the left for up to ten scans and stop if it points toward a light source within the threshold of the peak. You can type "." to see if your robot actually found the light.

You can tune the algorithm to your particular conditions by changing the VALUEs we created earlier. We have set it up so that the threshold is set to half the difference between the peak and the average, or 4, whichever is smaller.

At this point, we have the ability to scan around for a new peak, as well as scan until we find a light that is within some tolerance of the peak. We have tested the words interactively and tuned our constants to the site conditions. Now we can design an algorithm that will make the robot run autonomously. We should, however, put the touch sensors to some use. The idea being that when the robot hits an obstacle, it should back up and make another scan for a bright object. This is easy to do by checking to see if we've hit an obstacle after moving the bot forward for a bit. If we have hit something, we'll just back up and rescan for the peak. The script in Listing 6-14 checks to see if we've hit something.

Listing 6-14. BUMPER.TXT – Finding and avoiding obstacles

```
\ BUMPER.TXT - THE SEEKER'S OBSTACLE AVOIDANCE
\
\ REQUIRES: DIFFMOTOR3.TXT TOUCH.TXT

DECIMAL

0 SENSOR_BOOL_MAKE

\ The SEEKER_AVOID just backs the bot up for 1 second

: SEEKER_AVOID ( -- )
  BOT_REVERSE
  100 0 timer_SET
  BEGIN 0 timer_GET 0= UNTIL
  BOT_STOP ;

\ The CHECK_BUMPER word reverses the sense of the touch
\ sensor before deciding to back up. Returns TRUE if
\ we've hit an obstacle.

: CHECK_BUMPER ( -- f )
  0 SENSOR_BOOL? 0= DUP
  IF SEEKER_AVOID
  THEN ;
```

There is nothing terribly difficult about this, except for the fact that Seeker's bumper works backwards to a normal touch sensor, which means it is active when the sensor reads open. In this case, the 0= construct is enough to turn the logical value of the switch around.

Finally, Listing 6-15 presents the entire Seeker script that will turn our little creature into an autonomous robot.

Listing 6-15. The finished seeker application

```
\ SEEKER.TXT - THE SEEKER APPLICATION
\
\ REQUIRES: SCAN1.TXT SCAN2.TXT BUMPER.TXT BUTTONAPI.TXT

: SEEKER

  RCX_INIT
  SENSOR_INIT
```

```
0 SENSOR_BOOL_MAKE
1 SENSOR_LIGHT_MAKE

BEGIN
  BUTTON_SCAN BUTTON_RUN?
UNTIL

SCAN_FOR_PEAK

BEGIN
  0     \ Assume we can't find the peak
        \ Scan back and forth to look for the peak

  6 1 DO
    I 1 AND I 6 * FIND_PEAK
    IF DROP 1 LEAVE
    THEN
  LOOP

  \ Now check the bumper, if we've hit something or
  \ we can't find the peak, indicate false

  CHECK_BUMPER
  IF   DROP 0
  THEN

  \ If we find the peak move forward, otherwise scan
  \ around and look for a new peak

  IF   BOT_FORWARD
       12 0 timer_SET
       BEGIN
         BUTTON_SCAN
         0 timer_GET 0=
       UNTIL
       BOT_STOP
  ELSE SCAN_FOR_PEAK
  THEN

  \ Keep doing this until the RUN button is pressed

  BUTTON_RUN?
UNTIL ;
```

You will need to type SEEKER at the console every time you want to start the robot, then press **Run** to start the big scanning loop. When you want Seeker to stop, just press **Run** again. You may need to hold the **Run** switch for a while because Seeker might be busy trying to find the peak and it doesn't check for the **Run** switch until it finishes the current find sequence.

Summary

We have developed a non-trivial application in pbForth for making the Seeker robot perform a simple task. You might expand on the code by inverting its behavior to look for dark spots. You can also add sounds to help you get more information back as to what Seeker is doing.

We have only scratched the surface of what pbForth can do. If you choose to explore Forth in more detail, you will find that you can easily create large arrays for data logging or mapping, use cooperative multi-tasking, and even do complex signal processing. But for most applications, the basics we have learned here are sufficient.

Have fun exploring the world of robotics, try all of the languages, and learn as much as you can about the RCX internals. One of the great things about the RCX is that you can comprehend the entire device. The more you know about it, the more control you have over it.

LegOS

Luis Villa

Part Three

Introduction to LegOS

LEGOS, LIKE NQC AND PBFORTH, is an alternative programming environment for the RCX. Unlike the other environments, legOS is designed around the standard and popular C language, which has been used and refined for nearly thirty years. Markus L. Noga created legOS; and although there have been a number of other contributors, Markus wrote most of the code. Markus maintains the original legOS Web site at `http://noga.de/legOS`. However, legOS development has migrated to SourceForge (`http://legOS.sourceforge.net/`) in order to support a larger community of developers. The SourceForge site is the central collection point for all of the newest legOS files, documents, and development work.

So Why LegOS?

Programming in C on the RCX has its tradeoffs. On the one hand, if you already know C, the combination of C and legOS offers you a great deal of flexibility, power, and efficiency that can't be matched by the other MINDSTORMS languages. For example, unlike the limited number of variables offered by the standard firmware, C provides an essentially unlimited number of variables. The programmer also has access to useful data types like matrices and arrays, along with the ability to reuse code that was originally written for other platforms.

In addition to these features of the C language, legOS supports your code by providing a number of library functions that allow direct access to the hardware, which gives the programmer a level of control that can't be matched by any of the other environments. When you aren't accessing the hardware directly, legOS provides many traditional operating system features, like preemptive multi-tasking and a networking layer. You can even generate random numbers so that your robot can be truly unpredictable. With the power provided by legOS, and the flexibility offered by C, you can develop virtually anything you dream of writing on a computer.

> **NOTE** *The current version of legOS (as of the date of publication) is 0.2.4. However, legOS is constantly being modified, so you should check the Web site at* `http://legOS.sourceforge.net` *for the most up to date version of legOS, as well as the newest information and documentation. Furthermore, legOS is Free Software. Because it is licensed under the Mozilla Public License, anyone who wants to (including you) can modify or add to it. SourceForge is the place to go if you want to contribute to this effort.*

So What's the Catch?

There are a few catches to using legOS. First and foremost, you need to know or learn C. While the basics of the language are pretty straightforward, it can be difficult to take full advantage of because it is a complex and sophisticated language with many intricacies. If you don't know C, there are a couple of things you can try to help you learn it. Many programmers find that the best way to learn a language is to study code that someone else has written. Hopefully, the example code in this book is simple and clear enough to at least help serve that purpose. There are also a great deal of C tutorials online. I strongly suggest going to the Google directory listing at `http://directory.google.com/Top/Computers/Programming/Languages/C/Tutorials` and trying the newest links there.

If you prefer the more thorough treatment that a book can provide, *Practical C Programming,* by Steve Qualline, has been a favorite of mine. *Programming C: A Modern Approach,* by K.N. King, is also highly recommended by a variety of sources on the Web. Of course, once you've started, nothing beats writing lots of code and seeing what works.

Secondly, even if you know C, you'll still have to install and configure the tools necessary to compile and download your programs. This is getting easier (particularly on the Windows platform) but isn't seamless yet.

Unfortunately, if you aren't on Windows or Linux, it is not currently possible to run legOS at all. MacOS does not have the necessary command line environment, and complications with I/0 have made it difficult to port the download tools to other Unix platforms like Solaris. On the bright side, legOS is known to work on non-Intel versions of Linux (as a result of the standardized IO.)

So, How Does it Work?

Unfortunately, with power comes complexity. As a result, legOS is a system of many parts. It can be boiled down to three main pieces:

- OS

- Compiler

- Program loader

LegOS itself is basically a set of libraries that is compiled using gcc and downloaded to the robot with firmdl before you download your own programs. The compiler is a recompiled version of the GNU C Compiler (gcc.) This is used to compile the legOS and your programs into H8 assembly that the RCX can execute. Finally, there are the firmdl3 and dll programs. Once you have used the compiler to create an executable out of your code, these two programs download legOS and your executable (respectively) from your computer to the robot.

Let's explore the interplay of these four tools (gcc, firmdl3, dll, and legOS) in more detail, by getting the robot ready to run with a sample program. This section assumes that you've already installed the necessary tools correctly and built the kernel, as described in Appendix E.

The first step is to use firmdl3 to download the kernel to the RCX. You can do that by executing the following command in your legOS home directory:

```
util/firmdl3 boot/legOS.srec
```

This should install the legOS kernel in your RCX. When it's done, you'll see the LCD man, and a dash (–) in the rightmost spot on the LCD. To make sure the kernel has been loaded correctly by the RCX, press the **Prgm** button. You should see "NONE" in the LCD. If not, it's possible that the download failed. If that is the case, try it again while adding –s after the firmdl3 command. This will be slower, but more reliable.

You can also use the following options with firmdl3 to change its behavior:

`--tty=TTY`: Set TTY to the correct port if you connect the tower to a different port than the default. The default is `/dev/ttyS0` under Linux and `COM1` under Windows.

`--fast`: Download quickly. This is the default.

`--slow`: Download slowly. If you Sare having problems with downloading, you may want to try this, as it is more reliable under a wider range of lighting conditions.

Table 7-1 specifies some of the most common error messages that firmdl3 will return in case of failure. Note that a few of these start with `/dev/ttyS0`. On your system, this will show whatever port firmdl3 was actually trying to contact: by default on Linux, this is `/dev/ttyS0`, but on Windows systems it will usually be `COM1`. Of course, if you use –tty to specify a different port, the error message will reflect this.

Table 7-1. Common Error Messages for firmdl3

ERROR	DIAGNOSIS
`/dev/ttyS0: Permission denied`	You do not have sufficient permission to write to the port. This may be the default under many Linux distributions. You will have to become root, and either use firmdl3 as root or execute the following command: "chmod +222 /dev/ttyS0".

Table 7-1. Common Error Messages for firmdl3 (Continued)

ERROR	DIAGNOSIS
`/dev/ttyS0: Input/output error`	Most likely, the tower is not plugged into the specified port. May also indicate that the tower is low on batteries. To fix, either plug it into the specified port or use –tty=TTY to change the specified port (as mentioned earlier in this section).
`no response from RCX`	Either the RCX is still turned off, or possibly the tower battery level is low.
`unlock firmware failed`	Indicates slight corruption in the download. Use firmdl3 to download the firmware again.
`delete firmware failed`	Indicates that legOS is still present on the RCX. To remove it so that the download can succeed, either take out the batteries (in case of a hard freeze) or press the **Prgm** button while holding down the **On-Off** button.

Now that you have a kernel in the robot, let's test it by compiling a simple demonstration program:

1. Create a directory (I'll call it ch7) within your legOS directory.

2. Copy the Makefile from legOS/demo/ to your new legOS/ch7 directory.

3. Type the following listing into a file named simple.c within the legOS/ch7 directory:

```
/* simple.c */

int main(int argc, char *argv[])
{
  return 0;
}
```

4. Enter the ch7 directory, and type "`make simple.lx`". By default, this will look for the simple.c file and compile it into legOS's binary format. Once it is done, your ch7 directory should contain simple.o and simple.lx.

The .o file isn't particularly useful most of the time, but the .lx file is legOS's binary format—the file that actually gets downloaded to the RCX. When you are compiling your own programs, all you need to do is create the program yourfilename.c, copy the Makefile into your directory, and the command "`make yourfilename.lx`" will compile it. It is important to note that this directory must be a subdirectory of legOS/. Otherwise, your compile will fail because of Makefile problems.

> **NOTE** *All of the sample programs in this book may be downloaded from the book's Web site at* `http://www.apress.com/.`

If you are running Linux, you may want to put symbolic links to dll and firmdl3 in more convenient places than util/ . I find it useful to put a link to dll in the directory in which I write and compile my programs (ch7/ in this case) and a link to firmdl3 into my legOS/ directory to make it quicker to download a new kernel when I need one. If you have followed the build instructions for Windows, these should already be in your path.

Now that we've compiled a .lx file, it's reasonably straightforward to get the code into the robot. First, turn on the RCX and go to your legOS directory and type

```
util/dll ch7/simple.lx
```

This will load simple.lx into the first program slot. LegOS has eight program slots, and by adding –pX after dll, you can download your program into the desired slot. Once you've downloaded the program, hit the **Prgm** button until the digit on the right hand side of the LCD shows the number of the slot that you've downloaded the program into. (By default, this is slot zero.) Once you've selected it, hit the **Run** button, and the program will execute.

> **NOTE** *There is only one significant .dll error:* `error-deleting program.` *This is, unfortunately, a catch-all error, meaning that when you get it, it could be any of a large number of problems. The most important things to check are that your IR tower is correctly connected, the RCX is actually on (don't laugh— I've done it several times), and no program is currently running on the RCX.*

Now that we've compiled a sample program and downloaded it to the robot, let's look at the structure of the program itself.

This snippet is the simplest possible legOS code that will compile. As you can see, there isn't much to it. Like most C programs on a Unix system, every legOS program must start with a `main()` function that takes two arguments and returns an integer. Because the programs are called from within legOS (instead of the command line), the two arguments to main are actually never used. However, they are still required, for internal compatibility purposes. Beyond this `main()` function, no other code is actually required in a legOS program. Nevertheless, you'll probably want to add a little bit more, so that the program will actually do something. The rest of this chapter will take a look at the various operating system functions you can use within your programs.

Basic LegOS Functions

The core of legOS is, of course, the library of functions that provide access to the various features of the RCX and the OS. For convenience, I'll divide these functions into three main categories:

- Output functions

- Input functions

- Program control

Outputs

Let's start by looking at code that will allow us to interact with the outside world. These are primarily the motors and the LCD. While the motors are probably essential to just about every robot you'll build with the RCX, it is also extremely important to learn how to use the LCD. It is basically your only tool for debugging legOS programs. As a result, if you want to write sophisticated programs, you'll have to understand the LCD and use it well.

Motors

Motor control is straightforward. There are two sets of functions: one set that controls the direction of the motors and another set that controls their speed. The direction functions are of the form `motor_x_dir(MotorDirection dir)`, where x is the letter of the motor (a, b, or c) and "dir" is one of four strings: off, fwd, rev, and brake. This is slightly different than what you may be used to, because legOS collapses *direction* and *mode* (in the language of Chapter 2) into the single concept of direction. In this notation, brake is the same as what Chapter 2 refers to as "off," while off is what that same section refers to as "floating." This mixing also means that, unlike the normal firmware, when a motor is switched to a different mode, the motor will forget its previous direction.

The speed functions are similar. They look like `motor_x_speed(speed)`, where x is again either a, b, or c, and the speed is a number between 0 and the constant `MAX_SPEED`. `MAX_SPEED` is 255 by default. So, unlike the standard firmware's 8 power levels, legOS has access to 255 (a speed of 0 leaves the motor turned off). Generally speaking, this is overkill—on most surfaces, the 1/8 power increments that the normal software uses are completely sufficient and provide as much control as is necessary. However, this level of detailed control can be very useful as it allows you to linearly scale your power output to smoothly link math to outputs.

Let's look at a simple piece of example code in Listing 7-1.

Listing 7-1. motors.c

```
/* motors.c */
#include <unistd.h>
#include <dmotor.h>

int main(int argc, char **argv)
{

  int k;

  /*start the motor*/
  motor_a_dir(fwd);
  motor_a_speed(MAX_SPEED);

  /*slow down the motor gradually*/
  for(k=MAX_SPEED;k>=0;k--)
    {
      /*slow the motor down a notch*/
      motor_a_speed(k);
      /*this function makes the robot wait for 20 milliseconds.*/
      /*more details on it later*/
      msleep(20);
    }

  motor_a_dir(off);
  return 0;
}
```

You'll note that this code steps the motor speed down in very small increments, which can't be done in the standard RCX environment. It also turns off the motor at the end of the program. This is unnecessary in this case, because the OS will shut off the motors after the OS retakes control of the robot. However, it is a good habit to get into, because it is the end of the program (and not the function!) that turns off the motors. If you don't pay attention to this detail, your motors are likely to run until your robot goes into a wall.

> **NOTE** *Many legOS functions are made available to your program through various header (aka .h) files. In order to use the functions, you'll have to* #include *the correct files. Each section will have a note like this one near the top, noting which file you should include to get that functionality. To access the motors, for example, you should* #include <dmotor.h>.

The LCD

Unlike the standard firmware, legOS allows direct control of the LCD. Every individual segment down to the arms of the running man can be turned on and off individually. In most cases, this level of control is unnecessary and higher level functions can be called from your program to take care of the details. However, the flexibility is there if you ever need it. The most important LCD functions are listed next, with the most frequently used functions first.

- cputs(char *string) is perhaps the most commonly used LCD function. Send it a string (no more than five letters, of course) and it will push the characters to the LCD. This is left justified—a single character printed with cputs will appear on the left side of the LCD.

- lcd_int(int x) pushes the int x to the screen. This can be very useful for debugging your code—for example, printing out the values of sensors. This is right justified. Note that this takes an int—if you pass it an unsigned int that is larger than the range of an int, you'll get strange behaviors.

- lcd_clear()Clears the LCD. While not always necessary, it can be a good idea to call this function before attempting to write something to the screen, since it doesn't necessarily overwrite the characters that were previously on the screen.

- cls() is similar to lcd_clear(), but clears only the LCD letters and not the walking man and other symbols.

- cputw(unsigned int x) outputs a value in hexadecimal notation. If you are comfortable with hex, then this can be useful, since it can represent values between 0 and 65,535. Whereas lcd_int() is effectively limited to four digits (-9,999 to 9,999) by the size of the LCD, and limited by the size of an int to roughly ±32KB. (More on this in the Advanced legOS chapter.)

- `dlcd_show(segment)` and `dlcd_hide(segment)` are very low-level functions that take as arguments the names of specific pieces of the screen, like LCD_ARMS, and turn those locations on and off. Each of the previous calls (like `lcd_int()` and `cputs()`) are actually just functions that call variants of these two functions, which turn a large number of specific segments on and off for you. The complete list of LCD segment names is in the dlcd.h include file.

- `lcd_refresh()` is an older function that is still useful under certain circumstances. Technically speaking, the functions I've already described do not actually write to the LCD, but rather to a buffer in memory. In its default configuration, legOS automatically flushes this buffer to the LCD, but if you want more control, you can turn this feature off and control the flushing of the buffer to the screen yourself with `lcd_refresh()`. For more on how to configure the OS in this way, check out the advanced legOS chapter of this book.

NOTE   *To access the higher level LCD functions, you should* #include *<conio.h>. If you want to explore more on your own, or use only the lower level LCD functions, you should take a look at* dlcd.h. *This is included within* conio.h, *so there is no need to* #include *both files.*

The sample program lcd.c shown in Listing 7-2 contains examples of a couple of these features. First, we access a specific segment of the LCD—in this case, the arms of the walking man. Then we clear the screen and use a higher level call (cputs) to put two similar (but not quite the same) messages on the screen. Keep a close eye on the second two messages: you'll notice that H and O are the only letters in this group that actually change from lower to upper case. This isn't a bug, it's just a limitation of using text in a small LCD screen. Keep this limitation in mind if you have problems decoding the LCD later.

Listing 7-2. lcd.c

```
/* lcd.c */
#include <unistd.h>
#include <conio.h>

int main(int argc, char **argv)
{
  int k;
  /*make our man wave hello*/
  for(k=0;k<=5;k++)
```

```
  {
    cls();
    dlcd_show(LCD_ARMS);
    msleep(200);
    dlcd_hide(LCD_ARMS);
    msleep(200);
  }

/*now he says hello*/
cputs("hello");
msleep(1000);

/*now he says it differently*/
/*notice: not too differently*/
cputs("HELLO");
msleep(1000);
cls();

return 0;

}
```

One thing to keep in mind as you write code is that in certain applications, if you aren't careful, successive calls to the LCD will quickly overwrite each other making it impossible to read any of them. For example, in a for loop, if you expect useable data to be outputted, it is probably insufficient to call "cputs" repeatedly. The RCX is fast enough that each loop will finish quicker than you can read the output of the previous loop. In fact, if you write and erase something fast enough (less than 10 ms) the item may never make it to the screen at all. To get around this, just use the msleep() call that I used in the motor example. As you'll see in slightly more detail later, that call puts your function to "sleep" for the specified number milliseconds. I find that it takes about 200 ms for a person to read a two-digit integer, but your experiences may vary.

> **NOTE**   *As you'll see later in this chapter under "Program Control,"* msleep() *is found in* unistd.h, *which is why* unistd.h *is included in* lcd.c.

One other important thing to remember is that under certain circumstances the OS will take over the LCD and print out its own messages. For example, the OS generally keeps the LCD stick figure walking in order to indicate OS activity. In addition, if you interrupt the program with the **Run** button, the OS will clear the screen. However, at other times when you might expect the OS to clear the screen (like when the program exits!) it won't. That's why I use the `cls()` function at the end of this program to remove the "HELLO" from the screen and make it more obvious that control has moved to the OS.

Inputs

Now that we can interact with the outside world using the motors and gain insight into our robot with the LCD, we can also take a look at the input functions that allow a program to get data and extract meaning from the outside world and from the user. These functions control both the sensors that other programs have been using to get information and the buttons on the front of the RCX, which are customizable under legOS.

> **NOTE** *To access the sensors, you should* `#include <dsensor.h>`.

Raw Sensors

Recall that each sensor returns a raw value that is then interpreted into something "meaningful." In legOS, the raw values are accessed directly by way of three constants: `SENSOR_1`, `SENSOR _ 2`, and `SENSOR_3`. The legOS kernel updates all three of these virtually continuously. This is different from the normal firmware, which samples the sensors at a fixed rate and can therefore miss changes that occur more quickly than the sampling interval. This allows programs that use legOS to respond more quickly to small changes in the environment. For example, legOS can read rotation sensors with reasonable accuracy at nearly 5000 revolutions per minute (rpm). The standard firmware can only do 1250 rpm, because it samples less frequently. Similarly, legOS users have found that they can build extremely fast line-following robots, because they can read and adjust to inputs at speeds at which an RCX Code-controlled robot would run off the line.

> **NOTE** *When you use* `SENSOR_X`, *the value returned is a hexadecimal word that may have a value from 0-0xffff. (0xffff is hexadecimal notation for the decimal value 65,535.) Because 0xffff is very large, if you want to output the raw value of a sensor to the screen, use* `cputw()` *instead of* `lcd_int()`.

Touch Sensors

The constants TOUCH_1, TOUCH_2, and TOUCH_3 each read 1 if the sensor is pressed and 0 if it is not pressed. These are just simple macros that act on the raw sensor values. Like the three raw sensor constants, these constants are continuously and automatically updated. It is important to remember that these variables are handled differently from touch sensors in the standard firmware. First, the OS doesn't need to be "informed" what type of sensor is attached to the sensor port. The touch sensor variables will return a simple boolean value (1 or 0, for true and false, respectively), no matter what is attached to the port—touch sensor, light sensor, or regular plastic brick. The second thing to remember is that unlike the complex sampling done by the standard firmware, legOS simply decides whether or not the raw value is above a certain threshold, and then reports that as the answer. In my experience, this works fine, because in most applications the touch sensor gets firmly depressed—when your robot runs into a wall, for example. However, should you wish to have finer control, you may want to use the raw values directly.

Using TOUCH_1 in code is pretty straightforward. The touch.c program shown in Listing 7-3 uses it in a simple if statement. If the sensor is pressed, the value of TOUCH_1 is 1, thus the if statement makes the man wave. Otherwise, his arms are hidden.

Listing 7-3. touch.c

```
/*touch.c*/
#include <unistd.h>
#include <conio.h>
#include <dsensor.h>

/*make our man wave hello*/

int main(int argc, char **argv)
{
  while(1)
    {
      /*when we are touching the button, wave*/
      if(TOUCH_1)

        {
          dlcd_show(LCD_ARMS);
        }
```

```
      /*if we aren't, don't*/
      else
        {
          dlcd_hide(LCD_ARMS);
        }
    }
  return 0;
}
```

Light Sensors

The light sensor constants are (unsurprisingly) LIGHT_1, LIGHT_2, and LIGHT_3. Like the raw and touch sensor values, these are constantly updated values. They are scaled so that you'll get small integer values roughly between 50 (for dark) and 300 (for light).

Aside from the values of the lights, it is important to mention the functions that switch the light sensor between active and passive modes. To set the mode, use the functions ds_active(&SENSOR_X) and ds_passive(&SENSOR_X), where X is the number of the light sensor. Make sure to use the &–if you don't, no error message will be generated and you'll wonder why your light is still on or off.

Listing 7-4 is a simple program that uses these functions to do a simple test on the brightness of the light source it points towards. If the light falls below the prescribed level, the program will output "dark," if it is brighter, it will show the actual light reading.

Listing 7-4. light.c

```
/*light.c*/
#include <unistd.h>
#include <conio.h>
#include <dsensor.h>

int main(int argc, char **argv)
{
  /*Turn on the sensor*/
  ds_active(&SENSOR_2);

  while(1)
    {
      /*test to see if it is dark out*/
      if(LIGHT_2<150)
```

```
      {
        cputs("dark");
        msleep(10);
      }
    /*if not, say exactly how bright it is*/
    else
      {
        lcd_int(LIGHT_2);
        msleep(10);
      }
  }


  /*go back to the OS*/
  cls();
  return 0;
}
```

As you can see, using the values is straightforward. Just treat the LIGHT_2 value as you would any other variable and use the equal (=), less than (<), and greater than (>) operators to compare it to other values. The only difference from a normal variable, of course, is that instead of setting the value yourself, the OS sets it.

You'll note that the function ds_passive() is not used at the end of the program. LegOS takes care of this bookkeeping detail and does similar work for motors.

Buttons

Unlike the standard firmware, under legOS you can check the status of certain buttons on your RCX and use them for whatever purposes you'd like.

BUTTON NAME	LEGOS NAME
View	BUTTON_VIEW
Prgm	BUTTON_PROGRAM

With these two names (BUTTON_VIEW and BUTTON_PROGRAM), use RELEASED(dbutton(), variable) and PRESSED(dbutton(), variable) as functions. They'll return 1 if they are in the correct state (PRESSED or RELEASED) and 0 if they are not. Because PRESSED is the same as "not RELEASED" only one of these functions is necessary, but they are both included to allow you to ensure the clarity of your code.

It is important to remember that legOS does not debounce buttons when they are accessed in this way. You'll have to make your program wait for the bounce on its own. Alternately, if you don't want raw access to the buttons, there is a getchar() function in the dkey.h file. This function will wait until a single button has been pressed and return an integer that represents the button that was pressed. The relevant values are:

BUTTON NAME	GETCHAR() VALUE
View	4
Prgm	8

The getchar() function can't handle multiple button presses at once, so if you want to be able to use key combinations, you'll have to handle those with the raw button information.

> **NOTE** *Under older versions of legOS, all four buttons on the front of the RCX could be accessed in the same way as **View** and **Prgm**. In fact, if you look through the legOS source code, you'll note that the **On-Off** and **Run** buttons still have values associated with* PRESSED(), RELEASED(), *and* getchar(). *However, because the OS uses these keys, they are no longer available directly to the programmer in the same manner.*

Listing 7-5 shows how you might use these functions in a program.

Listing 7-5. button.c

```
/*button.c*/

#include <unistd.h>
#include <conio.h>
#include <dlcd.h>
#include <dsensor.h>
#include <dbutton.h>
#include <dkey.h>

int main(int argc, char **argv)
{
  int temp;
```

```
    /*wait until program is pressed*/
    while(RELEASED(dbutton(),BUTTON_PROGRAM))
      {
        cputs("prog");
      }
    cls();
    sleep(1);

    /*now wait until view is pressed*/
    while(RELEASED(dbutton(),BUTTON_VIEW))
      {
        cputs("view");
      }
    cls();
    sleep(1);

    /*wait until any button is pressed*/
    temp = getchar();

    /*show us which one got pressed*/
    if(8==temp)
      {
        cputs("prog");
      }
    else
      {
        cputs("view");
      }
    sleep(1);
    cls();

    return 0;
}
```

Quite simply, the program prompts the user to press a specific button. RELEASED() is then used to tell whether or not a specific button has been pressed. While those two loops are ongoing, pressing the other button will have no result because RELEASED() and PRESSED() are tied to the specified buttons. Once that is done, the program uses getchar(). At that point, either button can be pressed and the results returned.

NOTE *To access the button-related functions, you should* #include <dbutton.h> *and* #include <dkey.h>.

Program Control

If you've read through the various demo programs for input and output, by now you've seen a few examples of functions, such as `msleep()`, which are used for program control in legOS. We'll explain them here and discuss certain other functions.

> **NOTE** *To access the legOS control functions, you should* `#include <unistd.h>`. *This is true for all the various control functions listed next, unless specifically noted.*

The sleep Functions

As you saw in the LCD example, a common and useful pair of functions is the set of time functions, `sleep()` and `msleep()`. These functions each take an integer, and when called, put the program to sleep for the specified number of seconds or milliseconds. In a multi-threaded program, only the thread calling the function will be put to sleep. Otherwise, the whole program will wait until the allotted time has passed. You saw this behavior, for example, in light.c (Listing 7-4), where a small `msleep(10)` was used to prevent the LCD from flickering during extremely fast rewrites, even though the robot wasn't doing anything else during those "sleeping" periods.

It is important to note that `msleep()` shouldn't be used as a timer if exact time is important, because the OS waits the specified number of seconds and then executes the next line of code only after the current task is finished. For example, if you ran a bumper thread and a light-sensing thread at the same time (as we will do in the seeker.c program later in this chapter), an `msleep(50)` in the bumper thread would sleep for 50 ms and then wait until the light-sensing thread finished its task. In most cases, such a delay should be negligible, but under certain circumstances it might be important. As a result, it is safe to use these functions liberally throughout your code, but you will need to examine them more closely if you experience strange timing problems with threaded programs.

The wait_event() Function

The second important time management function to consider is the `wait_event()` function. This function is used to make a program wait until a particular event has occurred. For example, in the light seeker that we'll see at the end of this chapter, the robot has to wait until the bumper is touched. A `wait_event()` call is used for this, much like the `until()` function in NQC.

The function takes two arguments. The first is the location of a function (of type `wakeup_t`), which returns true or false. And the second argument is a string that can be passed to that function. Calling wait_event(my_function, data) will call wakeup_t my_function(data) repeatedly, until wakeup_t my_function(data) returns a "true" (non-zero) value. Until the function returns true, the thread won't do anything except the wait_event(). Once a true value is returned, the thread can continue on its merry way.

As an example, let's look at Listing 7-6. This program waits until the touch sensor has been touched, then takes control of the robot.

Listing 7-6. wait.c

```c
/*wait.c*/
#include <conio.h>
#include <unistd.h>
#include <dsensor.h>
#include <dlcd.h>

/*
 * we must take the argument,
 * but we don't have to use it
 */

wakeup_t touch_wakeup(wakeup_t ignore)
{
  return(TOUCH_1);
}

int main(int argc, char *argv[])
{
  /*a message from the robot*/
  cputs("touch");
  msleep(500);
  cputs("me");

  /*the event itself*/
  wait_event(touch_wakeup, 0);

  /*we are done*/
  cputs("yay");
  sleep(1);
  /*return to the OS*/
  cls();
  return 0;
}
```

As you can see, the wait_event call in this code calls a simple function that merely returns the value of the touch sensor. Once the button has been pressed, the program will stop waiting and "yay" will appear on the screen. While this example is a simple function (with an obvious use), wait_event() calls can have many other uses. For example, with the rotation sensors, you can wait until your robot has traveled a certain distance. Or, if you wanted to expand on the seeker.c program at the end of this chapter, you could wait until the light sensor passed a certain threshold and have the robot do a small victory dance. It is important to remember that you can pass values to a wait event: for example, you can pass a threshold value to a light-sensing wait_event, or pass a specific count to a rotation-sensing wait_event.

Threading with execi() and Friends

Finally, let's cover threading. As you've already noticed in the NQC portion of Chapters 3 and 4, it is difficult to write an interesting program on the robot if your programs can't figuratively walk and chew gum at the same time. LegOS programs accomplish this by using threads. A *thread* is basically a separate function or set of functions, which run side by side with other threads. Under legOS, threads are created by using the execi() function call. For example, the Seeker program used later creates one of its threads as follows:

```
driving_thread = execi(&basic_driver,0,0,PRIO_NORMAL,
                        DEFAULT_STACK_SIZE);
```

As you might tell from the example code, execi() takes five parameters. In most cases, only the first is important. This first parameter is the location of the function that you'd like to use as the separate thread. In the example, this is &basic_driver. Generally speaking, this is an ampersand (&) and the name of the thread function. Like main(), any function that is used as a separate thread must take two arguments—int argc and char *argv[]. You can use these parameters to pass information to a new thread, or you can ignore them, but either way they must be included in the declaration of the function. One other important note: the functions that you start the thread with (basic_driver() in this example) must be of return type int. Otherwise you'll get compiler errors.

The second and third arguments are the values to be passed to the new thread. In this case, I had no information to pass to basic_driver(), so the second and third arguments were both zero. If you do need to pass information to your new threads, the information you pass as the second and third arguments of execi() will be in argc and argv when the new function is called.

The fourth argument to execi() is the priority of the task. There are three things to keep in mind when assigning this number. First, the OS is not as efficient when multiple threads have the same priority. So, keep these unique—only one thread should have priority one, only one thread should have priority two, and so on. Second, threads with a lower priority will get executed after threads with a higher priority. Because (generally) all threads always get executed, this isn't terribly important. The third point is the default set of priorities: PRIO_LOWEST, PRIO_NORMAL, and PRIO_HIGHEST. These are defined to be 1, 10, and 20, respectively. I have used PRIO_NORMAL here, but as long as you use positive numbers less than 20, you should be fine. This last note is important, since priorities equal to or greater than PRIO_HIGHEST may not be properly killed by the OS.

The fifth and final argument is the stack size in bytes. Under most conditions, it is best to use DEFAULT_STACK_SIZE for this, unless you have a very good idea of how much stack the thread is going to use and are in extreme need of a few extra bytes. If you don't know what stack is, don't worry about it—DEFAULT_STACK_SIZE (which is 512) is fine for all but the most memory-starved threads.

Once you've used execi() to create a new thread, there are a couple of things to keep in mind. First, execi() will return a process ID number in the form of an argument of type pid_t, which you should save to a global variable (for example, a variable declared outside of a function so that it is accessible to every function.) When the time comes to end that thread (say, as the result of a button press or light sensor activation), use the kill(pid_t threadid) function to kill the thread, passing it the process ID that you got from execi(). For example, the bumper thread uses kill(driving_thread) to end the light-seeking behavior after the bumper has been hit.

As of legOS 0.2.x, the kernel is preemptive in its multi-tasking. This means that the scheduler should automatically and regularly switch back and forth between the threads you have created in this fashion. If you want more precise control of your threads by explicitly giving control back to the kernel: yield(), sleep(), and msleep() explicitly return program control to the scheduler so that it can wake up the next thread. However, using these commands for this purpose should be unnecessary.

> **NOTE** *LegOS also has support for semaphores, which allow communication between threads. If you are experienced with them, take a look through* legOS/ include/semaphore.h *to see the interface that legOS uses for semaphores. It should be quite familiar to most experienced Unix programmers.*

The LegOS Seeker

Now that we've seen the basic building blocks of a legOS program, it's time to combine them into a complete program for the Seeker robot presented in Chapter 3. This robot won't be exactly the same as that Seeker bot, because it will use a couple of legOS's features so to make it more interesting and capable. LegOS's superior memory handling will give our robot a sense of history, and the random() function will make it slightly less predictable. However, integrating these things will make the robot behave slightly differently (particularly when it first starts), so don't be surprised if it doesn't work exactly like the NQC version does.

When you look at seeker.c (shown as Listing 7-7) one of the first things you may notice is the use of random() in the bumper code. The two calls to random() are used to generate random numbers, which allows a legOS-powered robot to actually surprise you. In this case, when the robot bumps into a wall, it "guesses" the better way to back up. Though it's not really that important in this application, for other uses, like genetic algorithms, random numbers are absolutely necessary. Used wisely, the element of unpredictability can make any robot more interesting.

Listing 7-7. seeker.c

```
/* seeker.c*/

#include <conio.h>
#include <stdlib.h>
#include <unistd.h>
#include <dsensor.h>
#include <dmotor.h>
#include <dlcd.h>
#include <time.h>

#define BUMPER !TOUCH_1
#define EYE LIGHT_2
#define HISTORY_SIZE 100
#define MAX_COMMAND 2
#define LOCATE_COMMAND 1

/*global process IDs*/
pid_t driving_thread;
pid_t bumper_thread;
pid_t light_thread;

/*A small array to record history*/
int local_history[10];

/*big history*/
int room_history[HISTORY_SIZE];
```

```
/*other useful universal variables*/
/*this is poor form but more reliable*/
long int threshhold = 0;
long int local_average = 0;

/*next turn direction*/
char next_direction;

/*dummy variable*/
wakeup_t dummy = 0;

/*
 *   bumper press functions
 */

wakeup_t bumper_hit_wakeup(wakeup_t data)
{
  return BUMPER;
}

wakeup_t bumper_release_wakeup(wakeup_t data)
{
  return BUMPER;
}

wakeup_t threshhold_wakeup(wakeup_t data)
{
  return(EYE>threshhold);
}

/*
 * Big block of motor commands
 * provides simple functions to cleanup later code.
 */

void run_motors()
{
  motor_a_speed(MAX_SPEED);
  motor_c_speed(MAX_SPEED);
}
```

```
void go_forward()
{
  motor_a_dir(fwd);
  motor_c_dir(fwd);
  run_motors();
}

void go_back()
{
  motor_a_dir(rev);
  motor_c_dir(rev);
  run_motors();
}

void spin_left()
{
  next_direction = 'r';
  motor_a_dir(fwd);
  motor_c_dir(rev);
  run_motors();
}

void spin_right()
{
  next_direction = 'l';
  motor_a_dir(rev);
  motor_c_dir(fwd);
  run_motors();
}

void stop_motors()
{
  motor_a_speed(0);
  motor_c_speed(0);
  motor_a_dir(brake);
  motor_c_dir(brake);
}

void change_direction()
{
  /*judging from next direction, turn*/
  if('l'==next_direction)
    {
      spin_left();
    }
```

```
        else
          {
            spin_right();
          }
      }


  /*this finds the index of the largest integer in the array*/
  int query_array(int an_array[], int query_type)
  {
    int k = 0;
    int max_value = 0;
    int max_index = 0;
    for(k=0;k<HISTORY_SIZE;k++)
      {
        if(an_array[k]>max_value)
          {
            max_value = an_array[k];
            max_index = k;
          }
      }


    /*if we want to get the location of the max*/
    if(LOCATE_COMMAND==query_type)
      {
        return max_index;
      }


    /*if we want to get the value of the max*/
    else
      {
        return max_value;
      }
  }


  /*move old values down, insert old value at 0*/
  void local_history_update(int new_entry)
  {
    int k = 0;
    for(k=9;k>0;k--)
      {
        local_history[k]=local_history[k-1];
      }
    local_history[0]=new_entry;
    return;
  }
```

```
/*get the average of the array*/
int local_history_average()
{
  int total = 0;
  int k = 0;
  for(k=0;k<10;k++)
    {
      total+=local_history[k];
    }
  return (total/10);
}

/*
 * Here we record history and find the brightest spot.
 * Once found, we try to return to it..
 */

void history_calibration()
{
  int initial_max = 0;
  int k = 0;

  /*status report*/
  cputs("calib");
  msleep(100);

  /*here we spin for 3 seconds, taking light readings.*/
  spin_left();
  for(k=0;k<HISTORY_SIZE;k++)
    {
      room_history[k] = EYE;
      msleep(30);
    }
  stop_motors();

  /*find roughly where we found the brightest spot*/

  initial_max = query_array(room_history, MAX_COMMAND);

  lcd_int(initial_max);
  msleep(100);
```

```
/*set the threshhold to a reasonable fraction of the max value*/
threshhold = (initial_max*85)/100;

spin_right();

/*test to see if the local values are ~= max value*/

wait_event(&threshhold_wakeup, dummy);

/*We've found it, so let's announce that.*/
stop_motors();
cputs("found");
sleep(1);

/*what exactly did we find, anyway?*/
lcd_int(threshhold);
sleep(1);

  return;
}


/*
 * This function drives the motor by default.
 * Should be killed when another thread wants to take control.
 * Simple strategy:
 * If we are getting brighter or staying the same, we are OK.
 * Otherwise, we should sweep back and forth until we find a bright
 * spot again.
 */

int basic_driver(int argc, char *argv[])
{
  time_t sweep_start_time, current_sweep_length;
  int bright_spot_not_found;

  go_forward();

  while(1)
    {
      /*check the rolling average of readings*/
      local_average = local_history_average();

      /*are we getting brighter?*/
      if(EYE>=local_average)
```

```
    {
      lcd_int(local_average);
      local_history_update(EYE);
    }

/*uh-oh, we just got darker*/
/*lets sweep back and forth*/
else
  {
      stop_motors();

      /*get a new threshhold*/
      threshhold = local_average;

      /*we haven't found anything yet*/
      bright_spot_not_found = 1;

      /*initialize the length of the sweep to 1/10 second*/
      /*remember, it doubles each time, so it grows quickly*/
      current_sweep_length = 100;

      while(bright_spot_not_found)
        {
          /*prepare to do a scan*/
          cputs("scan");

          /*what time did we start at?*/
          sweep_start_time = sys_time;

          /*that last try didn't work, let's sweep the other way*/
          change_direction();

          /*sweep left or right for current_sweep_length ms*/
          while(sys_time < (sweep_start_time + current_sweep_length))
            {
              /*test to see if we are bright enough*/
              if(threshhold_wakeup(dummy))
                {
                  /*we found it!*/
                  cputs("found");
                  bright_spot_not_found = 0;
                  break;
                }
            }
```

```
                /*haven't found it, double the length of time we go back*/
                current_sweep_length *= 2;
                /*also, we'll reduce the threshhold by 10%*/
                threshhold *= 90;
                threshhold /= 100;
              }
            /*ok, so we've found the spot. Let's go.*/
            go_forward();
          }
        /*wait some time before sampling again*/
        msleep(100);
      }

    /*so the compiler doesn't complain*/
    return 0;
}


/*
 * This thread tests for the bumper and
 * takes control of the robot when that occurs.
 */

int bumper_driver(int argc, char *argv[])
{
  while(1)
    {
      wait_event(&bumper_hit_wakeup, dummy);

      /*we've hit something. Better stop moving.*/
      kill(driving_thread);
      stop_motors();

      lcd_clear();
      cputs("BUMP");

      /*let's back up a little bit*/
      go_back();
      msleep(500);

      /*pick a direction*/
      if(random()&(0x1))
        {
          spin_left();
        }
```

```
      else
        {
          spin_right();
        }
      /*wait to spin a reasonable distance*/
      msleep(250);

      /*now lets press forward again*/
      go_forward();
      msleep(250);
      stop_motors();

      /*restart the light seeking.*/
      driving_thread = execi(&basic_driver,0,0,PRIO_NORMAL,
                             DEFAULT_STACK_SIZE);
    }

  /*so the compiler doesn't complain*/
  return 0;
}

int main(int argc, char *argv[])
{
  /*initialize the light sensor*/
  ds_active(&SENSOR_2);

  /*initialize the random number generator*/
  srandom(LIGHT_2);

  /*initialize history and try to orient ourselves*/
  history_calibration();

  /*start the control threads*/

  driving_thread = execi(&basic_driver,0,0,PRIO_NORMAL,
                         DEFAULT_STACK_SIZE);
  bumper_thread = execi(&bumper_driver,0,0,PRIO_NORMAL+1,
                         DEFAULT_STACK_SIZE);

  return 0;
}
```

The difference between the behavior of this program and the behavior of the NQC-based Seeker at the beginning of the program can be attributed to legOS's superior handling of variables. Because we can store and access a lot of data instead of making the user calibrate the robot at the beginning, the program causes the robot to circle for roughly three seconds and stores one hundred light readings into an array. It then backs up to find the location of the brightest spot it encountered. While not perfect, this gives the legOS robot a much better start than the pseudo-random walk of the NQC robot. Once it gets going, the robot keeps track of its last ten light readings. If the current reading dips below the average, the robot knows it is going into a darker spot and attempts to change direction by sweeping back and forth. Each time, it will look twice as far, doubling back upon itself to prevent turning all the way to one side or the other. These "doubling backs" (and in fact, all movement in the program) were calibrated on carpet, so if your robot moves too fast, simply find the `run_motors()` function and adjust the speed.

The two "history" arrays demonstrate two key powers of legOS: the use of multiple variables and flexible data structures. All robots need a sense of "history" if they want to move around well, and it is difficult to establish that without the data structures to organize information. This flexibility will become even more important as you add more sensors to your robot, and is very helpful for applications that need to do complex math, such as neural networks.

Conclusion

Hopefully, this chapter has served to show the basics of legOS. You should now be able to write solid legOS programs that use the basic functionality of the language. In the next chapter, we'll cover some advanced topics in legOS, such as using the rotation sensors and floating point math. Using the basics from this chapter plus the new ideas, we'll explore another interesting application for legOS—a learning robot.

Advanced LegOS

THE PREVIOUS CHAPTER COVERED the vast bulk of the functionality of legOS. If you've read it, you should be able to write some interesting legOS programs. However, there are still a few gaps in your legOS knowledge. In this chapter, we'll look at a more advanced application for legOS, and the legOS functionality needed to support it and other advanced legOS programs. Once you've completed this chapter, you will be ready to explore the full potential of legOS.

Rotation Sensors

Before delving deeper into the mysteries of legOS, we should tackle a more mundane topic—rotation sensors. Long the bane of legOS users, the rotation sensor code in legOS finally reached production quality with legOS 0.2.3. They are now quite reliable, and reasonably straightforward to use. They are also versatile and provide an easy way for robots to measure angles, rotations, distance, or speed. The sample program in Listing 8-1 is a simple one that counts the number of times the rotation sensor has been turned.

> **NOTE** *Like the sensors described in the previous chapter, using the rotation sensors requires the inclusion of* dsensor.h. *As usual, this can be done by inserting* #include <dsensor.h> *at the top of your code.*

Listing 8-1. rotation.c

```
/* rotation.c */

#include <conio.h>
#include <unistd.h>
#include <dsensor.h>
/*
 * main
 */
```

```
int main(int argc, char **argv)
{
  /* turn it on */
  ds_active(&SENSOR_2);
  ds_rotation_on(&SENSOR_2);

  /* calibrate it to 0 */
  ds_rotation_set(&SENSOR_2,0);
  msleep(100);

  while(1)
    {
      lcd_int(ROTATION_2);
      msleep(20);
    }
}
```

Remembering that the rotation sensor is an active sensor, the first thing this code (and any rotation sensor code) must do is turn on the sensor itself with ds_active(&SENSOR_X). Once that is done, ds_rotation_on(&SENSOR_X) initializes the rotation sensor. Both of these steps are required. After that, we can at any time calibrate the sensor to any starting point we want, by calling ds_rotation_set(&SENSOR_X, value). It is helpful to remember that while this value is usually 0 (because we typically only want to count rotations), it can be set to other values as well.

> **NOTE** *Because of the way that rotation state is tracked in the OS, after calling* ds_rotation_set, *it is important to call* msleep(100) *in order to ensure that the value that you use is actually exactly what the sensor gets set to. Otherwise, it may be off by one or two. If this is unimportant to you (for example, if you plan to count hundreds or thousands of rotations instead of 20, as we will when we discuss Trailerbot) then it is perfectly safe to skip the* msleep *call.*

Once the sensor has been set up with these three functions, we can use ROTATION_X just as we've used LIGHT_X and TOUCH_X previously. Rotation sensors have a resolution of 16 ticks per revolution, so two full rotations would be read as a value of 32. Generally speaking, rotation sensors are quite reliable. However, the rotation sensor will not always update correctly if control of the program stays with another thread for too long. This isn't usually a problem. Multi-tasking is much improved in legOS 0.2.x, and the processing of interrupts has also improved, so the kernel should count all rotation sensor changes with no problems. The second potential problem is that rotation sensors don't function well if the RCX batteries get too weak. If it looks like you're losing counts—in other words, if `ROTATION_X` doesn't appear to change when the rotation sensor moves, or doesn't change enough—try replacing the batteries and your results should markedly improve.

Sound

One of the more entertaining features of legOS is the sound driver, although it is not incredibly useful (especially when compared to the rotation sensor). The RCX speaker is the last piece of hardware that this chapter will cover. It's not your home stereo system, but it does have a surprising range of tones and can produce some recognizable music.

> **NOTE** *To access the speaker, you should use* `#include <dsound.h>`.

To play a sound or series of notes with legOS, you must first characterize the sound or notes as a series of `note_t` structures. Each `note_t` contains a pitch and a duration. Pitches are specified from a list of tones in the `dsound.h file`, each of which has the form `PITCH_XY`, where X is the note (A, C, D, etc.) and Y is the octave (1-8). Durations can be specified in two ways: either as multiples of sixteenth notes (for example, a half note would be given as 8) or, more conveniently, through the use of some `#defines`, which are defined as the multiples for common notes like `WHOLE`, `HALF`, `QUARTER`, and `EIGHTH` notes.

Once the notes have been defined, they need to be put into a vector of `note_ts`. That vector is then passed to the function `dsound_play()`, which plays the vector. A number of auxiliary functions are available and defined in `dsound.h`; for example, `dsound_set_duration()` sets the length of a sixteenth note in milliseconds, which allows you to control the pace of music played by the RCX. Another important function is `dsound_playing()`. It returns true if music is playing, and false otherwise. This is important because `dsound_play()` returns as soon as it is called, therefore multiple calls to `dsound_play()` might overlap each other if `dsound_playing()` is not used first as a test.

The example shown in Listing 8-2 uses a snippet from the Mitch Ryder song "Devil with a Blue Dress on" to demonstrate how all of these functions work.

Listing 8-2. sound.c

```c
/*sound.c*/

#include <dsound.h>

/*array of notes that make up the refrain*/
/*of Devil with a Blue Dress*/

static const note_t devil[] = {
  { PITCH_G4, QUARTER },
  { PITCH_G4, QUARTER },
  { PITCH_G4, QUARTER },
  { PITCH_G4, QUARTER },
  { PITCH_G4, HALF },
  { PITCH_G4, HALF },

  { PITCH_G4, HALF },
  { PITCH_G4, HALF },
  { PITCH_G4, HALF },
  { PITCH_G4, HALF },

  { PITCH_F4, QUARTER },
  { PITCH_F4, QUARTER },
  { PITCH_F4, QUARTER },
  { PITCH_F4, QUARTER },
  { PITCH_F4, HALF },
  { PITCH_F4, HALF },

  { PITCH_F4, HALF },
  { PITCH_PAUSE, HALF },
  { PITCH_PAUSE, HALF },
  { PITCH_PAUSE, HALF },

  { PITCH_E4, QUARTER },
  { PITCH_E4, QUARTER },
  { PITCH_E4, QUARTER },
  { PITCH_E4, QUARTER },
  { PITCH_F4, HALF },
  { PITCH_F4, HALF },

  { PITCH_E4, HALF },
  { PITCH_E4, HALF },
  { PITCH_F4, HALF },
  { PITCH_F4, HALF },
```

```
  { PITCH_E4, QUARTER },
  { PITCH_E4, QUARTER },
  { PITCH_E4, QUARTER },
  { PITCH_E4, QUARTER },
  { PITCH_F4, HALF },
  { PITCH_F4, HALF },

  { PITCH_E4, HALF },
  { PITCH_PAUSE, HALF },
  { PITCH_PAUSE, HALF },
  { PITCH_PAUSE, HALF },
  { PITCH_END, 0 }
};


int main(int argc,char *argv[]) {

  /*The default makes this a really, really slow song*/
  /*So, we speed it up a little bit.*/
  dsound_set_duration(40);

  /*now, we play it*/
  while(1) {
    dsound_play(devil);
    wait_event(dsound_finished,0);
    sleep(1);
  }

  return 0;
}
```

"Devil" is a very fast-paced song, so we have to use `dsound_set_duration()` to shorten the length of the notes. While 40 milliseconds (ms) doesn't sound long, remember that this is for a sixteenth note—the quarter notes in the tune are 160 ms and the half notes are 320 ms, which are considerably longer periods of time. The `dsound_finished()` function used in the call to `wait_event` is essentially a wrapper function (also found in `dsound.h`) around `dsound_playing()`. It ensures the previous sound snippet has finished before we start playing it again.

> **NOTE** *If you have the Ultimate Accessory Pack for MINDSTORMS, you have one other piece of hardware: the LEGO Remote Control. While the remote is not yet officially supported by legOS, at least a couple of people have reported success using it and it seems likely that it will be supported by the time this book reaches shelves. As always, check* http://legOS.sourceforge.net/ *for the latest news on this and other legOS updates.*

Math in LegOS

One of the big advantages of using legOS over the standard firmware is the ability to do a lot of math. The next two sections will explain two wrinkles that make math in legOS slightly more complex than just "x = y + z."

Floating Point

As you may have already noticed if you have tried to do math in NQC, the RCX is normally limited to integer math (for example, math without decimal points.) This is because the Hitachi chip the RCX is based on has no Floating Point Unit (FPU), the section of a processor dedicated to floating point math.

In most cases, there are simple workarounds for this problem. For example, in seeker.c (and in NQC programs), operations like multiplying by .85 (for the threshold calculation) are done first by multiplying by 85 and then dividing by 100. For most applications, this approach is sufficient. In fact, experienced embedded systems designers such as Ralph Hempel (author of the pbForth chapters in Part Two of this book), argue that most math, even in complicated programs, should be done without using floating point. However, for programmers used to the flexibility of a desktop, this approach may seem a little backward. Furthermore, it makes it easy to make mistakes (one early version of seeker.c multiplied by 10 and divided by eight in an attempt to get 80%).

Luckily, Kekoa Proudfoot has written a small floating point library that can be linked into legOS for those times when floating point math is either simpler or more necessary. In fact, as of the 0.2 series, legOS is set up to automatically include the library whenever you use a `double` or `float` in your code. Even though it is now automatic (and as a result, simple to use) there are still a few reasons to consider avoiding using these numeric types when you write large programs.

First, the entire library is linked to your .lx file, not the legOS kernel. While this makes the kernel more flexible, it means, for example, that a program which counts from 1 to 2^{16} using an `int` requires about 92 bytes of memory, while the same program using a `double` and doing no math except addition uses 980 bytes. As mentioned previously, this isn't usually a problem because the 32KB accessible by legOS is a surprisingly large amount. However, if you want to use legOS for something sophisticated, the linkage of the library into your .lx file is definitely something to keep in mind.

The other detriment to floating point math is the speed of the operation. While this difference isn't noticeable most of the time, in math intensive applications, floating point emulation will slow down your program. For example, calculating x*0.85 in floating point is roughly fifty percent slower than calculating (x*85)/100 in integer math. In most cases, this difference won't be noticeable, but in some uses it can be significant.

Type Sizes

Perhaps the most insidious bugs I've ever had to track in a legOS program stemmed from a simple source: misunderstanding the size of variable types when using gcc and legOS. For instance, the example in the preceding section (where int x is multiplied by 85) can easily cause an error if x is too large. Why? Well, because an int in legOS is only 16 bits, it has an upper bound of only about 32,000. If you try to fill an int with something larger than that (say, 85*400, or 0xffff in the case of sensor raw values), you'll get no error messages and many garbage numbers. The solution is, of course, very simple—just use a long int instead of an int. Despite the simple solution, this can be an irritating problem to debug, so make this trick one of the first things you try if numbers mysteriously change to values you don't expect.

Because the normal source for these values (limits.h, a compiler file) is incorrect in the cross-compiler source, I've included a table of type sizes.

TYPE	SIZE IN BYTES	UPPER BOUND	LOWER BOUND
int	2	32,767	-32,768
unsigned int	2	65,535	0
long int	4	2,147,483,647	-2,147,483,648
float	4	Depends on amount of accuracy necessary.	
double	4	Depends on amount of accuracy necessary.	

LegOS Network Protocol (LNP)

While legOS generally exceeds the standard firmware in flexibility and power , there has traditionally been one gaping hole—the ability to communicate back and forth with the PC. This period is coming to a close. LegOS has its own networking protocol: LegOS Network Protocol, or LNP. If you look closely at the source, you'll note that LNP is already used in firmdl3 and dll to make downloads faster and more reliable. More importantly, you can now access LNP-enabled RCXs from computers running Linux, thanks to the work of Martin Cornelius. He has written two pieces of code (LibLNP and the LNP Daemon, or LNPD), which allow programmers to write Linux programs that access the IR tower and the robots.

> **NOTE** *LibLNP and LNP Daemon are Linux-specific tools. However, shortly before this book went to print, Yannis Jeannotat released a similar set of tools for Windows, allowing LNP-enabled robots to be accessed from Visual C++, MS Java, and other Windows programming environments. You can find links to these new tools (called, appropriately enough, WinLNP) at* `http://legOS.sourceforge.net/files/windows/winLNP/`*.*

The model for these tools is reasonably straightforward. The LNP daemon is a continually running process that prevents the IR tower from shutting off and brokers requests between a program running on the PC and the program on the RCX. LibLNP is the set of interfaces that allow the Linux program to contact the daemon and send messages to the RCX. This is a very flexible model: any number of programs can access the daemon while running on the PC, and because every legOS kernel can have its own LNP address, you can communicate with up to eight different RCXs at once. For further details, download the package from `http://legOS.sourceforge.net/files/linux/LNPD/` and read the README and .h files.

LegOS Debugging

Unfortunately, debugging legOS programs is often the low point of the process of coding for legOS. This is usually the case for any serious programming exercise, of course, but you haven't really known pain until you've tried to debug a large program on a five character LCD screen using an OS that can be a bit unstable. With those problems in mind, here are a few things from my experience that may help with debugging:

- **Frequently output variables**. Because there are no formal debugging tools for legOS (such as gdb), there is no way to trace the values of variables except by dumping them to the screen as often as possible. By this I mean as often as every other line, even when the intervening lines are something simple like "x = y * z." Remember, even simple operations like this can bite when you're used to working with 32-bit integers that are suddenly 16 bit. Frequently dumping variables can help you figure out exactly which line of "perfect" code is actually the culprit.

- **Label variables as you dump them**. Integers flashing by on the screen are too easy to lose track of. To help, I often use a function that takes a label and a variable value as arguments, then outputs them to the screen with `msleep()` calls of appropriate length between them. A simple function like this can condense four lines of code (`cputs`, `sleep`, `lcd_int`, `msleep`) into one line, making your code more readable, while still getting all the necessary information onscreen .

- **Make variables global**. While generally considered bad programming form for larger programs, it can help keep things simple, which should be a primary goal when writing shorter programs (as most of your legOS programs will probably be.)

- **Download the kernel again**. It has been my experience that starting from scratch by using firmdl3 to download a new kernel is sometimes the answer to obscure or difficult problems. Why this is the case is not clear, but it is possible that certain kernel operations are not thread-safe and may cause data corruption within the kernel. Also, you can't mix and match kernels and .lx files: if you've compiled an executable against one kernel and then rebuilt the kernel, you may be able to download the program but it will probably die mysteriously.

- **When in doubt, post your code and your symptoms to** `lugnet.robotics.rcx.legos@lugnet.com`. This is the online gathering place for most of the legOS developers and serves as a good place to ask questions and get answers. There are some very knowledgeable folks there—they've helped me a ton.

Above all, don't give up. While trying to create a sophisticated program with legOS can be frustrating, the results can be very rewarding.

Trailerbot

As noted, the strengths of legOS lie in the ability to do math, store large numbers of variables, and use all the features of the C language. Trailerbot uses all of these features. As result, it not only pushes the limits of what the RCX is physically capable of, but it serves as a great demonstration of the kind of complex work that can be done with legOS, given time and skill.

Trailerbot is a variation on a class project from CPS 196, a legOS-based course taught at Duke University in the Fall of 1999 It was intended at that time to demonstrate a strategy in artificial intelligence (AI) called reinforcement learning. Despite its new home in the RCX, the Trailerbot is a variation of a traditional experiment in learning robots: the pole balancing robot or inverted pendulum problem. In traditional versions of the problem, a pole mounted on a robot must be kept balanced straight up in the air. Because the RCX really can't compute that quickly, we lay the pole on its side, and it becomes a trailer for the RCX to attempt to push in a straight line without jackknifing. What makes the task interesting is that instead of explicitly telling the robot what to do, it is programmed to learn on its own, beginning with a limited set of information about itself and the outside world.

Using the analogy of a trailer introduces some inevitable terminology problems. Normally, you pull a trailer instead of pushing it; you only push it when you go backwards. To clarify, when I say the robot or trailer is "going forward," I mean that the motors are pushing towards the trailer, and not pulling it, which is how trailers normally "go forward." The same "flipping" of terms applies to backing up—when I say backing up, I mean that the robot is moving away from the trailer. Also, because "forward" is toward the motor ports, the "right" side of the robot is the side with the **On-Off** and **View** buttons, and a right turn rotates the robot in that direction.

Building Trailerbot

Trailerbot uses a rotation sensor not included as part of RIS 1.0 (#9719) or RIS 1.5 (#9747). You may find a rotation sensor in the Ultimate Accessory Set (#3801) or you may purchase it individually from LEGO Shop-At-Home (1-800-453-4652). Aside from the rotation sensor, the rest of Trailerbot can be built with the parts contained in either RIS 1.0 or RIS 1.5.

Trailerbot consists of two parts: the main body and a trailer. Actually, the term "trailer" is a misnomer because the goal of Trailerbot is to push (rather than pull) its trailer, thus the trailer is in front of the main body. Two wheels at the front end power the main body and a skid supports the rear end.

First, construct the body's frame as shown in Figures 8-1 and 8-2.

Figure 8-1. Step 1

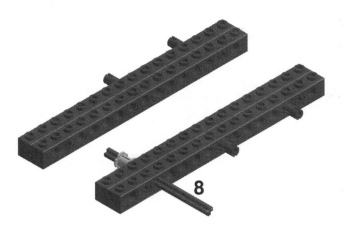

Figure 8-2. Step 2

Next, build the skid, shown in Figures 8-3 to 8-5, and the hitch, shown in Figure 8-6.

Figure 8-3. Step 3

Figure 8-4. Step 4

Figure 8-5. Step 5

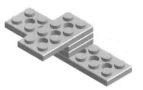

Figure 8-6. Step 6

Continue by adding the skid and hitch to the frame, along with the support for the motors as depicted in Figures 8-7 to 8-9.

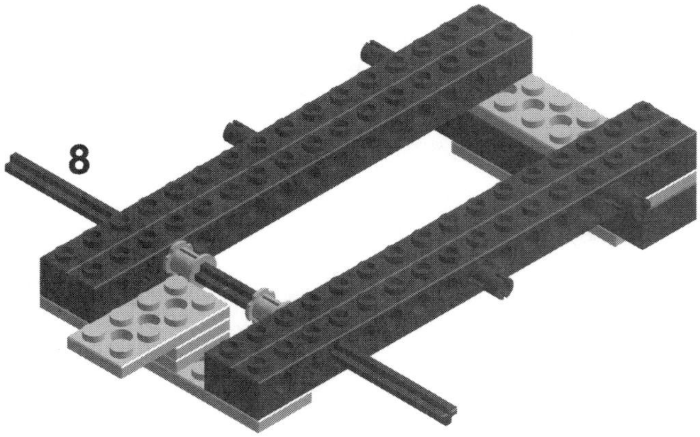

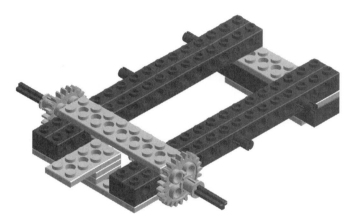

Figure 8-7. Step 7

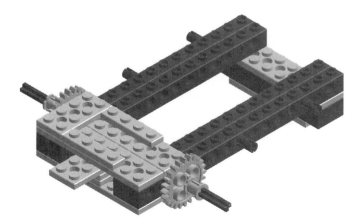

Figure 8-8. Step 8

Figure 8-9. Step 9

The motors, the RCX, and most of the wiring is added next, as shown in Figures 8-10 and 8-11. Be sure to use 24-tooth gears on the motors so they can mesh with the gears on the axles below. Pay careful attention to the orientation of the motor wires—if not placed properly, Trailerbot may not move forwards when the RCX turns on both motors in the forward direction. Although not critical to Trailerbot's operation, a light sensor is added so the random number generator can be seeded with an external value. The completed body is shown in Figure 8-12 with the addition of tires and several 1×6 beams to hold everything together.

Figure 8-10. Step 10

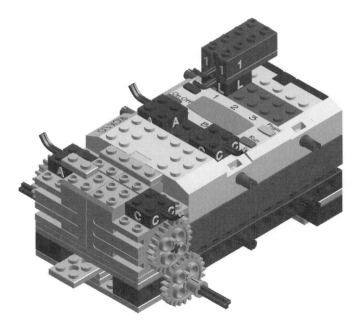

Figure 8-11. Step 11

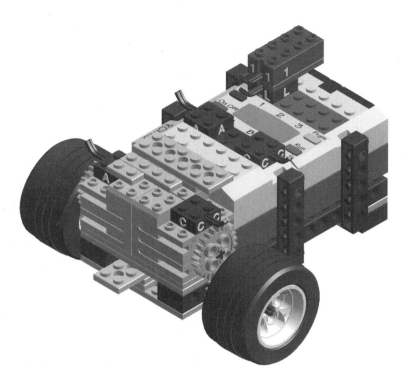

Figure 8-12. Step 12

Construction of the trailer begins is shown in Figure 8-13 with a #8 axle and a bushing. One end of the bushing is circular while the other end has a small notch in it. Most of the time it doesn't matter which way a bushing is put onto an axle, but in this particular case it is important that the notched side faces up. A few more pieces are added to the axle as shown in Figure 8-14. Don't worry about the spacing between pieces—they will be adjusted after the trailer is attached to the body.

Figure 8-13. Step 13   *Figure 8-14. Step 14.*

The trailer is completed in Figures 8-15 to 8-17. Be sure to use the smallest wheel—larger wheels won't be able to spin freely.

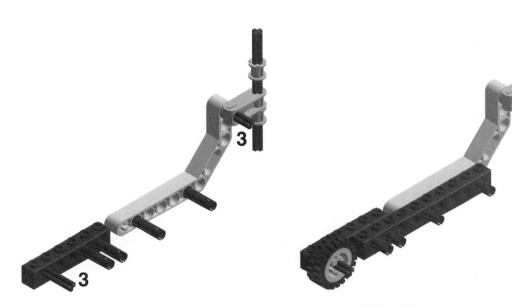

Figure 8-15. Step 15

Figure 8-16. Step 16

Figure 8-17. Step 17

The trailer is attached to the main body (as shown in Figure 8-18) by feeding the bottom of the trailer axle through the hole in the body's hitch. A 2×4 TECHNIC plate (a plate with holes in it) should be added to secure the top end of the axle to the body. This may require some minor adjustment to the bushings on the axle. Once completed, the bottom bushing should rest on the hitch, and the top bushing should be just below the newly added 2×4 TECHNIC plate. The trailer itself should be able to pivot easily left and right. If it does not, the top bushing is probably pressed too tightly against the top plate—slide it down a bit.

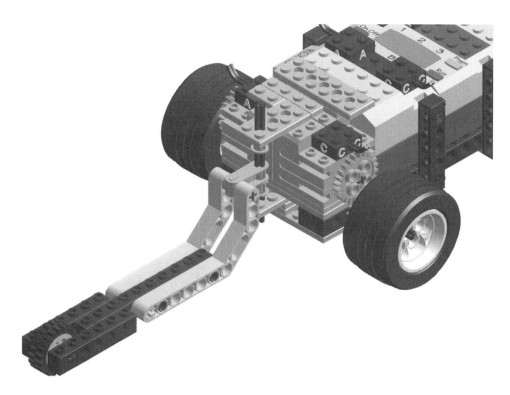

Figure 8-18. Step 18

Trailerbot uses a rotation sensor to determine the position of its trailer. This is done by attaching an 8-tooth gear to the rotation sensor, then meshing this gear with a 24-tooth crown gear placed at the top of the trailer axle. As the trailer swings left or right, the crown gear will turn, which will then spin the rotation sensor. The rotation sensor and crown gear are added in Figures 8-19 to 8-21. The crown gear might need slight adjustment to mesh smoothly with the rotation sensor's gear.

4

Figure 8-19. Step 19

Figure 8-20. Step 20

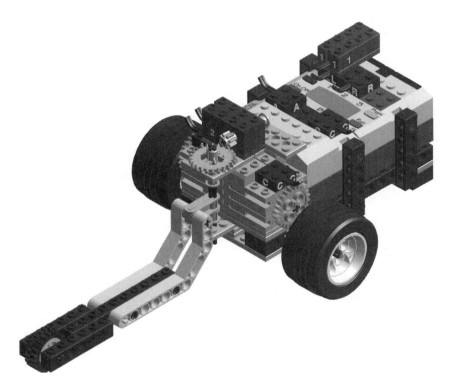

Figure 8-21. Step 21

The rotation sensor has a resolution of 16 steps per rotation, or 22.5 degrees per step. However, the meshing of the crown gear and 8-tooth gear provides a gear ratio of 3:1, thus the rotation sensor will measure the position of the trailer with a resolution of 7.5 degrees.

How Trailerbot Learns

Trailerbot uses a specific type of reinforcement learning algorithm, called Q learning, to understand how to push around the trailer. In a nutshell, this means that the code does two things. First, the robot uses trial and error to learn the probability that an action (such as turning or backing up) will lead to a specific state (for example, jackknifed or straight). Second, it tries to figure out which action will give it the greatest probability of staying straight. This is complicated, but it will become more clear as we step through the code.

> **NOTE** *Trailerbot's algorithm is not strictly Q learning, but it is pretty close to the "real thing." To get the lowdown on Q learning complete with lots of actual math, check out* http://www.cs.cmu.edu/afs/cs/project/jair/pub/volume4/ kaelbling96a-html/node25.html *or* http://envy.cs.umass.edu/~rich/book/6/ node6.html.

Q learning is a good choice for this application because it learns best when there aren't many options. In fact, as we'll see, the code takes special steps to refine and distill what the robot knows about the world.

Seeing the World

As you may have noticed from building the robot, it really doesn't have much information about what is going on around it, except for the lone rotation sensor. This sensor is geared up to give us about 20 "clicks" of resolution between the left jackknifed position and the right jackknife. We won't use all of this resolution because the robot would be overwhelmed. Instead, we'll use the function shown in Listing 8-3 to "water down" what the robot sees into information it can deal with more easily.

> **NOTE** *Because the actual code for Trailerbot is long (nearly 600 lines) I won't show it in its entirety in the text. Additionally, because the comments are long (frequently longer than the code itself) I've removed them in many cases in order to make the code presented here more readable. To run the program, download the sample programs from the book's page on the Apress Web site:* http:// www.apress.com. *The program for Trailerbot is called trailerbot.c.*

Listing 8-3. Creating manageable rotation.

```
/*
 * Function to convert rotation from 0-19
 * to a more manageable 0-4
 */
```

```
int norm_rotation(int real_value)
{
  switch(real_value)
    {
      /*right jackknife*/
    case -1:
    case 0:
    case 1:
    case 2:
      return 0;
      /*leaning toward the right*/
    case 3:
    case 4:
    case 5:
    case 6:
      return 1;
      /*centered!*/
    case 7:
    case 8:
    case 9:
    case 10:
    case 11:
    case 12:
      return 2;
      /*leaning towards the left*/
    case 13:
    case 14:
    case 15:
    case 16:
      return 3;        /*left jackknife*/
    case 17:
    case 18:
    case 19:
    case 20:
      return 4;
      /*if none of these, big error*/
    default:
      /*to be easily visible on LCD*/
      cputs("ERROR");
      sleep(1);
      return -1;
    }
  /*to get rid of compiler warning*/
  return 0;
}
```

The `switch` statement is a handy construct in C. In this case, it gets used to make a simple converter from what the rotation sensor "sees" to more meaningful information for the robot.

Controlling Actions

One of the strengths of being human is that we learn things from one situation and apply that learning to others. MINDSTORMS robots don't have that property (even with legOS, oddly enough). So, like the rotation sensor being filtered down to five inputs, we have to limit the robot to a choice of six outputs:

- Front/back

- Hard right/hard left

- Soft right/soft left

We control these movements with the block of motor control command code shown in Listing 8-4:

Listing 8-4. Controlling movements with motor control commands.

```
/*
 * Big block of motor commands
 * provides simple functions to cleanup later code.
 */

void run_motors()
{
  motor_a_speed(MAX_SPEED);
  motor_c_speed(MAX_SPEED);
}

void go_forward()
{
  motor_a_dir(fwd);
  motor_c_dir(fwd);
  run_motors();
  msleep(100*TURN_MULTIPLIER);
}
```

```
void go_back()
{
  motor_a_dir(rev);
  motor_c_dir(rev);
  run_motors();
  msleep(150*TURN_MULTIPLIER);
}

void soft_left()
{
  motor_a_dir(fwd);
  motor_c_dir(fwd);
  motor_a_speed(MAX_SPEED);
  motor_c_speed(MAX_SPEED/2);
  msleep(75*TURN_MULTIPLIER);
}

void soft_right()
{
  motor_a_dir(fwd);
  motor_c_dir(fwd);
  motor_a_speed(MAX_SPEED/2);
  motor_c_speed(MAX_SPEED);
  msleep(75*TURN_MULTIPLIER);
}

void hard_right()
{
  motor_a_dir(rev);
  motor_c_dir(fwd);
  motor_a_speed(MAX_SPEED);
  motor_c_speed(MAX_SPEED);
  msleep(100*TURN_MULTIPLIER);
}

void hard_left()
{
  motor_a_dir(fwd);
  motor_c_dir(rev);
  motor_a_speed(MAX_SPEED);
  motor_c_speed(MAX_SPEED);
  msleep(100*TURN_MULTIPLIER);
}
```

```
void stop_motors()
{
  motor_a_speed(0);
  motor_c_speed(0);
  motor_a_dir(brake);
  motor_c_dir(brake);

  /*to conserve batteries*/
  msleep(500);
  motor_a_dir(off);
  motor_c_dir(off);
}
```

Unfortunately, these commands don't cross over between floor surfaces very well. You may have to adjust them to be more appropriate functions for your floor. Luckily, adjusting them is pretty simple—find TURN_MULTIPLIER (defined near the top of the code) and fiddle with it. A value of seven works pretty well on my carpet, and I've used a four on my hardwood floors. Having said this, don't worry about adjusting them too much—one of the benefits of having your robot learn (instead of having you teach) is that if something doesn't work well, the robot will learn and stop doing it. So, if hard_right() turns your robot 180 degrees because your floor is smoother than carpet, the robot will learn that hard_right() always jackknifes and should stop avoid such a turn in the future.

Defining the World with Constants and Arrays

Now that we've figured out how the robot interacts with the world, we should try to understand how the robot keeps track of the world. Generally speaking, all the important information is stored in global arrays or #define statements at the beginning of the code, which appears in Listing 8-5 (without the comments).

Listing 8-5. Tracking the world in global arrays or #define statements.

```
#define ANGLES 6
#define MOVEMENTS 6

#define FAR_RIGHT 0
#define FAR_LEFT 4

#define TURN_MULTIPLIER 5
```

```
#define EPSILON_MAX .60
#define EPSILON_MIN .10
#define EPSILON_DECAY .02
double epsilon = EPSILON_MAX;

#define ALPHA .20
#define GAMMA .90
#define KAPPA 10

#define HEAVEN 5
#define HEAVEN_REWARD 20

enum movement
{
  HARD_LEFT, SOFT_LEFT, FORWARD, SOFT_RIGHT, HARD_RIGHT, REVERSE
};

double steering_results[ANGLES][MOVEMENTS][ANGLES];
double q_score[ANGLES][MOVEMENTS];
```

The first set of #defines and the last set of arrays are probably the most important information here. ANGLES is the number of values the robot can get from the rotation sensor. Remember, we're limiting the number to five (the range 0–4) with the norm_rotation() function. However, the code makes ANGLES equal to these five states plus one more. As you can see, the rotation sensor will never read 5, so the robot will never make it to this "extra" state. For now, all you need to know about this extra state is that it exists to trick the robot—by inserting it into ANGLES, we tell the robot that this state exists, and it never knows that it can't get there. The reason for this trickery will be explained later, in the Q Score section. The two special constants are also related to this state—HEAVEN indicates that the state is in the "fifth" rotation sensor state (that can't be reached) and HEAVEN_REWARD tells the robot that, should it ever get to HEAVEN, it will be well rewarded.

Similar to the mapping of trailer orientations to ANGLES, each of the six basic motions (such as hard_right) is mapped to MOVEMENTS. The two arrays, steering_results and q_score, are the "memory" of the algorithm. Think of steering_results as a table where the robot can look up its current angle (the first index), ask about a specific movement (the second index), and find out the probability that this movement will get it to other angles (the third index). Basically, this information is stored so that once the robot knows where it wants to go, it can figure out the best way to get there from where is currently located.

The q_score array is similar. In it, the robot will look up the angle it is currently in (the first index), ask about possible movements (the second index), and get back the Q score of each movement. Simply put, the higher the Q score, the more desirable the associated pairing of angle and movement is. The `q_score` array then stores the information about that desirability.

The three Greek letters (ALPHA, GAMMA, and KAPPA) and the epsilon definitions are parameters that control the learning process itself. We'll look at them in more detail once we plunge into the algorithm in the Q Score section.

Most of the other constants defined in this section of code are pretty straightforward. The movement `enum` and FAR_LEFT and FAR_RIGHT are ways to link the world to specific numeric values that can be used as indexes for the arrays we have already defined.

Moving Trailerbot

Once the robot has been set up and initialized, it must begin to explore the world and interpret what it learns. In Trailerbot, this occurs in the `move()` function. Every call of the `move()` function results in one movement and one update of `steering_results`, as shown in Listing 8-6.

Listing 8-6. Calling `move()` *functions and updating* `steering_results`.

```
void move()
{
  int i;

  /*variable to use in figuring out the "best" option*/
  int max_q_score = 0;
```

```
/*what do we do next? store it here*/
/*we init to -1 as an error*/
int next_movement = -1;

/*Where we started.*/
/*We don't use ROTATION_2 all the way through in case it changes.*/
int initial_angle = norm_rotation(ROTATION_2);

/*Where we ended up.*/
int new_angle;

/*Show the current angle*/
cputs("ANGLE");
msleep(200);
lcd_int(initial_angle);
msleep(500);

/*
 * Most of the time, we do the "correct" thing
 * by finding the best q_score of our possible options.
 * On the off chance that norm_random() is low (or EPSILON is high ;)
 * we then "explore" by choosing a random movement.
 */

if(norm_random() > epsilon)
  {
    /*We are doing what the table tells us to.*/
    cputs("real ");
    msleep(500);

    for(i=0; i<MOVEMENTS; i++)
      {
        if(q_score[initial_angle][i] > max_q_score)
          {
            max_q_score = q_score[initial_angle][i];
            next_movement = i;
          }
      }
  }
else
  {
    double temp;
    /*We are just picking something at random.*/
    cputs("rand ");
    msleep(500);
```

```
        /*pick one. Any one.*/

      temp = norm_random();
      next_movement = temp*MOVEMENTS;

      /*show what we do next*/
      lcd_int(next_movement);
      sleep(1);
   }


/*what happens if next_movement never gets changed?*/
/*we'd hate to do HARD_LEFT over and over again*/
/*so we choose randomly*/

if(-1==next_movement)
  {
    double temp;
    temp = norm_random();
    next_movement = temp*MOVEMENTS;
  }

/*having chosen a movement, lets do it*/
switch(next_movement)
  {
  case HARD_LEFT:
    cputs("HL   ");
    hard_left();
    break;
  case SOFT_LEFT:
    cputs("SL   ");
    soft_left();
    break;
  case FORWARD:
    cputs("FWD  ");
    go_forward();
    break;
  case SOFT_RIGHT:
    cputs("SR   ");
    soft_right();
    break;
  case HARD_RIGHT:
    cputs("HR   ");
    hard_right();
    break;
```

```
  case REVERSE:
    cputs("REV  ");
    go_back();
    break;
  default:
    /*this is an error and should never be reached*/
    cputs("ERROR");
    sleep(1);
    stop_motors();
    break;
  }

/*Once we've started, we'd better stop*/
stop_motors();

/*Allows us to read direction*/
msleep(500);

/*This is here just to make the next function cleaner*/
new_angle = norm_rotation(ROTATION_2);

/*Where are we now?*/
cputs("NEW  ");
msleep(200);
lcd_int(new_angle);
msleep(500);

/*
 * Since we know that "next_movement" took us from "initial_angle"
 * to new_angle (ROTATION_2), we store that increased probability.
 */

steering_results[initial_angle][next_movement][new_angle] += ALPHA;

/*here we re-norm so that the sum of the probabilities is still 1*/
for(i=0; i<ANGLES; i++)
  {
    steering_results[initial_angle][next_movement][i] /= (1+ALPHA);
  }
```

```
/*The last thing we do is reduce Epsilon*/
if(epsilon > EPSILON_MIN)
  {
    epsilon-=EPSILON_DECAY;
  }

}
```

For the robot, exploration is always a mix of doing what it thinks is "right" and (occasionally) trying something random to see what happens. As you can see in the section of code that uses epsilon, the percentage of time the robot chooses a random direction is set in epsilon. If the random number generated is more than epsilon, the robot chooses the "best" option by looking it up in the Q table. It determines this best movement by looking up where it is (initial_angle) in the q_score array and then going through the array until it finds the MOVEMENT with the highest Q value. This is, of course, not necessarily the best option; the first time around, all Q values are still zero, thus the robot defaults to a random choice.

If the random number generator picks a value less than or equal to epsilon, a random choice is made. Balancing the random and "learned" is difficult: if the robot is random too often, it will often make poor decisions even after it has learned what to do, but if it is not random enough, it will learn very slowly. In order to balance this, we use the values EPSILON_MAX, EPSILON_MIN, and EPSILON_DECAY. By setting EPSILON_MAX high, the robot starts randomly, learning as it goes. In code not shown here, the robot reduces epsilon by EPSILON_DECAY every time the code is called. In this way, the robot becomes less random as it learns more. With any luck, by the time epsilon equals EPSILON_MIN, the robot will have learned some reasonably intelligent behavior and won't have to make as many mistakes as it continues to learn.

After the movement has been chosen, the move() function continues by using a switch statement to issue the command to move. Once it has moved, the robot has to figure out where it went! That's not so tough (it simply calls ROTATION_2 again). However, the robot can't just throw away that information. It has to store it to better understand the results of its actions. It does this by adjusting the probabilities in steering_results to reflect the fact that it started in initial_angle, performed next_movement, and ended up in new_angle. The constant ALPHA controls the rate of this update: a higher alpha makes the table update faster, but it also means that one wacky result (say, a bump in the floor, or an angle directly on the boundary between two angle measurements) can have a disproportionate impact on Trailer-bot's learning.

As this cycle is repeated over and over again, the table will gradually grow to reflect reality more accurately. For example, the first time the robot is jackknifed and goes backward, it will begin to understand that "backing up when I am jackknifed leaves me straight again," and the more often that occurs, the more the interaction will be strengthened. Similarly, the robot should also learn that "going forward when I am pointed forward leaves me going forward." However, statements like these are only half the battle—the robot has to learn that it wants to go forward and avoid jack-knifing. This is where the Q scores come in.

Q scores

Technically speaking, Q scores are the "expected value" of an angle/movement pair. In other words, if the robot makes a movement from an angle, can it expect to be rewarded where it ends up? And what can it expect from the movement after that? This is a cool algorithm because it is farsighted: the robot looks not only at the immediate reward, but also attempts to understand what options it will have one movement into the future. Furthermore, because the algorithm is run over and over again, it is effectively recursive—it looks not only one turn into the future, but many turns. Maintaining the Q scores is the responsibility of q_score_update(), which is shown in Listing 8-7.

Listing 8-7. Maintaining Q Scores

```
void q_score_update()
{
  /*loop variables. Lots of them.*/
  int i, j, k, l;

  /*three variables for later*/
  float reward;
  float q_sum;
  float max_q_score;

  for(i=0; i<ANGLES; i++)
    {
      for(j=0; j<MOVEMENTS; j++)
        {
          /*are we doing a bad thing?*/
          if((i>=FAR_LEFT)||(i<=FAR_RIGHT)||(REVERSE==j))
            {
              reward = 0;
            }
          /*are we in "heaven?"*/
          else if(HEAVEN==i)
            {
              reward = HEAVEN_REWARD;
            }
```

```
                    /*if not, we get rewarded normally*/
                    else
                      {
                         reward = 1;
                      }

                    /*
                     * This code "looks ahead" to see two things:
                     * 1) What possibility do we have of getting to
                     *     all possible angles?
                     * 2) Once we get to those angles, what is the best
                     *     possible outcome?
                     * These two pieces of information are combined and
                     * stored in q_sum.
                     */

                    q_sum = 0;

                    for(k=0; k<ANGLES; k++)
                      {
                         max_q_score = 0;
                         for(l=0; l<MOVEMENTS; l++)
                           {
                             if(q_score[k][l] > max_q_score)
                               {
                                  max_q_score = q_score[k][l];
                               }
                           }
                         q_sum += (steering_results[i][j][k]*max_q_score);
                      }

                    /*store the new expected q_score*/
                    q_score[i][j] = reward+(GAMMA*q_sum);
                }
            }
        }
```

Basically, this code has two parts. Each of these parts is called for every member of the q_scores array. Each member of the array represents a potential future combination of angle and movement. It doesn't matter whether or not the robot has been in that combination, we have to study it in case the robot needs to know about it in the future. The first part is quite straightforward: if the robot were to find itself in this position, would it be jackknifed or backing up? If either one is true, it doesn't get rewarded. Now we check to see if this position is in "heaven."

If so, we reward it with a very high value. If it is neither jackknifed nor in Heaven, it would have to be going forward, so it would get a reward of one. Once this is done the real meat of the algorithm occurs.

The reasoning behind this second part is tricky but effective. In the outer loop, the algorithm looks at all possible outcomes (the five angles). The inner loop finds the best possible Q score that could occur from each of those angles. The best possible score is then multiplied by the probability that the robot would end up in that particular angle. This way, if an angle would be impossible to get to in one move (say, the probability of reaching the left side jackknife from the far right side) then the robot more or less ignores the `q_score` of that location. On the other hand, `q_scores` that are very likely to occur (no matter how poor the reward) get weighted more heavily.

The weighted scores are then added to the reward to create the new `q_score` for that particular angle/movement pair. This is moderated by GAMMA: if GAMMA is large, the future becomes more important. If the future is very important, then the robot can be tempted to do interesting things. For example, one robot I watched while testing this program decided to jackknife itself repeatedly because it learned that it could reliably get from jackknifed to almost jackknifed. Because the future was so important, the fact that it didn't get a reward when it was jackknifed was mitigated by the high probability that it could get rewarded at the next turn.

We use the concept of "heaven" here because initially when the probabilities of going to all locations are equal, the Q score of "heaven" will be high and the robot will try very hard to reach if. To do this, it will explore and try new things; in the process it will gain more information about its environment. As it continues to explore, not only will it benefit from the new information it stores, it will also slowly realize that it will never get to "heaven." As it learns this fact (in other words, as the probabilities for reaching heaven that are stored in `steering_results` drop to zero), the robot will stop randomly looking for heaven and focus on what it now knows are "correct" behaviors with a high probability of a good outcome.

The `q_score_update()` function needs to be called repeatedly because each time it is, the algorithm looks farther into the future. This results in a more accurate depiction of reality (at least, as far as can be said of a model like this). KAPPA controls how many times it is called after each move(). KAPPA should be set to at least 10; higher values will create better results, though the effects may not always be clearly visible.

Running Trailerbot

When Trailerbot first runs, it prompts the owner to help calibrate the rotation sensor. This is very important: if the sensor is miscalibrated, the rest of the program will get bad data and function poorly. Begin with the trailer jackknifed to the right by turning it clockwise until it contacts Trailerbot's body, then start the program. The message "start at right" should appear on the LCD. After a slight pause, the phrase "now center" will be displayed, at which point you should move the trailer to a centered position. After another brief pause the LCD will display what position it thinks the trailer is in. If the display shows the value "2" (the code for "centered") then calibration was successful, otherwise the program will have to be stopped and re-started.

Once that is done, the program does nothing other than call move() and q_score_update() repeatedly. At this point, the user really can't do much except sit back, watch, and perhaps occasionally move things out of the robot's way. This can be an exercise in patience: each set of calls to q_score_update() takes about ten seconds and learning usually isn't visible for a couple of minutes. Furthermore, this is not a completely reliable process. Because there is so much inherent randomness in the learning process, Trailerbot (and other robots that use reinforcement learning) often "learns" strange and interesting patterns. For example, sometimes Trailerbot will learn that traveling in a circle is a safe way to keep scoring points, especially if the mechanism and terrain make it difficult to travel in a straight line. Other times Trailerbot may get jammed in a jackknife for quite some time because it needs to randomly "guess" that backing up is good before it knows that it is a "good" thing in the long term. Because Trailerbot works by guessing randomly (at least initially), the robot may occasionally be unlucky and choose a series of movements that work poorly and don't allow it to learn. If this happens, the robot can look awfully silly.

Learning from Learning

Even the worst failures will often demonstrate some learning. Failures often repeat in the same patterns because they haven't yet stumbled into better opportunities. As you become more familiar with the algorithm, you'll spot these patterns more easily. For example, many times the Trailerbot will learn that going in a circle is a very stable way not to jackknife. Because it is rarely, if ever, punished when traveling in a circle, the circle gets strongly reinforced and Trailerbot never bothers to "discover" the joys of a straight line. Similarly, if TURN_MULTIPLIER is too low, or if the batteries are weak, soft turns may not move the robot at all. This may seem like a failure. However, to the robot this is a success: no movement means no jackknifing, thus the robot will probably quickly learn that anything other than a soft turn is a waste of time.

Furthermore, many of the robots will be "lucky" enough to learn the right patterns and learn how to correct themselves just as a real driver would. Watching these robots (particularly as they learn) is fascinating and will make your patience worthwhile. This is not a perfect program—there isn't a perfect AI anywhere yet, let alone on a system with only 32KB of RAM. Despite its imperfections, Trailerbot offers a glimpse into the possibilities that legOS alone can offer on the RCX platform through the extensive use of math and large arrays. Even if you don't write a program as ambitious as the one used for Trailerbot, these strengths can be used with virtually any RCX robot to make it more flexible and powerful.

Going Further with LegOS—"Use the Source, Luke!"

I hope that these two chapters and the examples I have presented cover everything the average user might want to know about legOS. If you still want to learn more—perhaps to find the one feature that you know "must be there" or to add one that you'd really like to use—there is one last resource you already have at your fingertips: the source code to legOS itself.

Because legOS is an Open Source program, when you download legOS you get all the source code for it. Similarly, because the project began more than two years ago, thousands of other people have downloaded and used the legOS source. Many of them have written patches that have been incorporated into the source you are now using. More have likely been written between the writing of this book and the time you start to use legOS. Because of this constant change and breadth of features, one of the best things you can do to enrich your knowledge of legOS (after reading this book, of course) is to read the source code of the OS itself.

While "read the source" may sound intimidating for a beginning C programmer (or someone who hasn't had an Operating Systems course in a while) the legOS source code has many virtues that makes it fairly easy to read. Chief among these is brevity—there really isn't much source to look through. In this sense, legOS is quite efficient. If you are an experienced programmer and want to dedicate an evening or two, you can basically understand the entire OS from top to bottom. More importantly, for less experienced programmers, once you find the file you are looking for, legOS source is generally well commented and cleanly laid out. With the help of these comments you can quickly become a more proficient legOS programmer, even if you are just starting to learn C and are unfamiliar with the internals of operating systems.

> **NOTE** *I use the phrase Open Source here as a reasonably unambiguous way to define the terms under which legOS is developed and distributed. However, the phrase I prefer to use is Free Software—meaning you have the freedom to use, modify, and share the source of legOS, not just to obtain it without cost. To know more about Free Software (a type of software that includes Linux and the Gnu C Compiler legOS depends on), check out the homepage of the Free Software Foundation at* `http://www.fsf.org/` *or their definition of Free Software at* `http://www.fsf.org/philosophy/free-sw.html`.

The "include" Directory

The include directory is the logical place to start for legOS newbies. This is where the various .h files live that you've been #including. It is also home to several interesting files I haven't yet covered. For example, one particularly useful file is time.h. This file includes the value sys_time, which is essentially an interface to the system clock. It starts at zero and is incremented in milliseconds to let you know how long a program (or more usefully, a function in a program) has been running. For example, I used it to time the efficiency of the floating point emulation mentioned in the "Math in LegOS" section earlier in this chapter. Similarly, the OS uses this value for many things, including sleep() and msleep().

There are also interesting sub-directories in include. For example, the directory include/c++ contains the start of a C++ interface for sensors. c++.cpp in the demo directory uses this interface and demonstrates how you can write and build a C++ program for your RCX. include/rom and include/sys contain some interesting low-level information and many hardware-related functions, such as ones that can turn off your RCX and check the RCX's batteries.

The LegOS Kernel

Once you've browsed through include, don't shy away from the kernel itself. While legOS is not a "real" operating system, poking around in its innards might help you better understand the behavior of your legOS programs. If you feel this bold, kernel/kmain.c is the logical place to start because it is what is first called by the hardware and must be the starting point for any attempt to trace the complete behavior of the OS.

Perhaps more relevant to most users is boot/config.h. Editing config.h allows you to directly control what functions are included in the kernel through the use of #define statements, which control #ifdef switches in the heart of the kernel. If you don't want a feature, just comment it out, type make in the legOS directory, and the system will attempt to build a kernel without those features. Be aware that "attempt" is the key word here—commenting out some of these options will prevent the kernel from being built properly. However, some other options are quite useful. For example, I find the little running man pretty irritating, so commenting out CONF_VIS gets rid of him. More seriously, the standard legOS kernel is 18KB, and judicious removal of options (particularly sound, which uses a large table of notes) can remove 3 or 4 KB. This could conceivably help a project squeezed for memory. Additionally, if you want to use LNP with more than one RCX, you'll want to look here because each robot's LNP address must be configured with CONF_LNP_HOSTADDR.

What about the Rest?

This section was not intended to be comprehensive of the legOS code base. Hopefully, though, it has covered the starting points for exploring the source and has made legOS easier to use for you. Who knows? You might be the next person to figure out something useful that legOS can do. You might even be the one who makes it more useful to others.

Homebrew Sensors

Michael Gasperi

Part Four

Homebrew Passive Sensors

RCX SENSORS CAN BE DIVIDED into two main types: passive and powered. *Passive sensors* include Touch and Temperature while Light and Rotation are examples of *Powered sensors*. Making homebrew Passive sensors is relatively easy. Only a minimal understanding of electronics is necessary to build new and useful sensors for your RCX. Powered sensors are more complex, but they open up the RCX to practically unlimited sensing possibilities. Because of their simplicity, passive sensors will be discussed first while powered sensors will be covered in the next chapter.

The RCX is an extremely well designed product and the projects described in this book are unlikely to damage your RCX even if you do something wrong. If you have trouble making or understanding the sensor projects, there are many places to get help. You should be able to find help from teachers or people that work in electronics stores and repair shops. Your local library and bookstores should have beginner's books on electricity too.

> **CAUTION** *You should follow some simple precautions to ensure your safety. First, never attach anything connected to your RCX to household electricity. This includes soldering wires while the sensor is connected to the RCX. Second, do not apply too much pressure when cutting things—you might slip.*

Getting Parts

In the United States there are hundreds of Radio Shack retail stores that carry small electronic parts as well as complete electronic products. Their prices and selection are not the best, but because of the convenience and relative omnipresence of the stores, parts available at these stores will be used whenever possible. They also sell a number of books and electronic kits that can fill the gaps in electrical knowledge needed to understand and build the projects in this book. Throughout these two homebrew sensor chapters, the Radio Shack catalog number (RS#) will follow the first mention of a part or tool available from them. These catalog numbers will also be given in the bill of materials that go with more advanced projects.

There are many other suppliers available for electronic parts and the contact information for a few of them is listed in Appendix A. These suppliers have printed catalogs and Web pages that make ordering easy. Because they have the largest selection, Mouser Electronics catalog numbers (ME#) will be listed for parts not available from Radio Shack. . Mail order suppliers tend to have minimum order size requirements. Make sure you plan ahead before ordering so you get not only the parts you need for the project you're working on today, but also in the future.

Making homebrew sensors may also require additional LEGO parts not provided with the MINDSTORMS Robotics Invention System (RIS). These can be purchased from several sources, including LEGO Shop-At-Home and Pitsco LEGO Dacta. As with the electronic parts, we will follow the first mention of a LEGO part you can get from LEGO Shop-At-Home with its catalog number (S@H#). Contact information for both sources is provided in Appendix A.

Alligator Clip Quickie

You probably want to get started right away. Fortunately, the *alligator clips* shown in Figure 9-1 provide you with a quick and easy way to get experience with homebrew sensors, although the results are not very rugged or permanent. Alligator clips are metal clothespin like devices used to create electrical connections. You can buy jumper test leads that are a short wire with an alligator clip on each end. These test leads allow you to create temporary electrical circuits without tools. Sets come in a variety of colors and sizes, and for our purposes the miniature size is the best (RS#278-1156).

Figure 9-1. An alligator clip and a jumper test lead

To begin, we need to study the LEGO electrical connector shown in Figure 9-2. From the top, the connector looks like a normal 2 x 2 LEGO brick. However, on closer examination you can see exposed metal partly around the circumference of the stud sides. It appears there are four separate electrical connections, but there are really only two. Pairs of the studs are connected together internally. Holding the RCX so you can read the display or holding a LEGO wire so the cord is coming out toward you, the pairs are on the left and right. This connector design allows the flexibility of building with the wire in any direction.

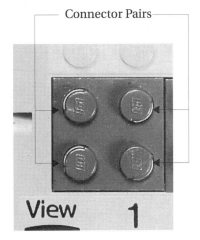

Figure 9-2. LEGO electrical connectors on the top of the RCX

On the bottom of the LEGO electrical connector, there are areas of exposed metal on the inside walls (see Figure 9-3). It appears there are four separate electrical connections, but, again, there are only two here. With the wire coming out toward you, the pairs are, again, on the left and right. The easiest way to make connections is to plug a LEGO wire onto the RCX, then attach two test leads to the bottom of the connector on the other end of the LEGO wire. Make sure the teeth of the clip are pinching against the metal. The plastic may be slightly scratched by this process, but no real damage is done.

Now it is time for the first experiment. First, you need to set the RCX input port 1 to expect a Touch sensor. There are many ways to do this, but the easi-

Figure 9-3. Alligator clips on the bottom of the LEGO connector

est is to run the built in RCX program number 2. You could also write a RCX Code program that has a Touch Sensor Watcher on port 1. Once the program has been run, the input port will remain as a Touch type whether or not the program is still running and even if the RCX is turned off and back on again.

Using the display on the RCX, push the **View** button once to select input port number 1 (see Figure 9-4). A small arrow will be pointing to the 1 and the display will read 0. If you accidentally push the **View** button too many times, just keep pushing it until the display comes around to input port 1 again. Now if you connect the two alligator clips on the free ends of the test leads together, the display reading will change to a 1 and the arrow will fill in. Congratulations, you just built your first homebrew sensor.

Figure 9-4. Alligator clips and the RCX display

Coin Detector

Touching two alligator clips together probably does not seem like a very useful sensor. To make things more interesting, let's add some aluminum foil and make a coin detector like the one you see in Figure 9-5. Take two one stud wide sloped roof bricks and cover them with a single layer of household aluminum foil. Leave a little extra foil on each brick so the alligator clips can be attached later. Now assemble the roof bricks facing each other with a single stud gap between them. Attach an alligator clip to the aluminum foil of each brick, and you now have a coin detector. When a coin is placed upright between the bricks it completes the electrical circuit and the RCX will read 1. This could trigger the RCX to perform a task such as dispensing candy from a vending machine, or counting money in an elaborate piggy bank.

Figure 9-5. The coin detector

Cut Wire Connector

You could go through life only using the alligator clip method, but you would find that your projects kept popping apart and didn't look very professional. The simplest and most attractive way to make permanent homebrew sensors is to cut the longer LEGO wires in half. This gives you two connectors with plenty of wire to connect the sensor. Extra wires are available from LEGO Shop-At-Home (S@H#5111) and are not very expensive, especially when compared to factory-made sensors. The only problem is that the LEGO wire can be a bit tricky to cut and strip.

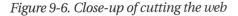

The LEGO wire combines a tough rubber insulator with a fine-stranded wire conductor. Cutting the wire in half is not much of a challenge, but you will find that you can not "unzip" or separate the two conductors the way you can with speaker wire or lamp cord. They must be cut apart by carefully cutting the web of rubber between them with sharp scissors or a knife. Usually cutting about 1.5 inches (4 cm) is enough to work with, but you may need more depending on the sensor. Figure 9-6 shows you the detail of this procedure.

Figure 9-6. Close-up of cutting the web

The next challenge is to strip the insulation off the ends of the two wires (see Figure 9-7). With normal wire you can take wire strippers (RS#64-2129), bite down into the insulation about 1/2 inch (1 cm) from the end, and pull. For this wire, you will need to be much more careful. The rubber insulation is so tough that even if a tiny piece remains uncut, the end will not pull

Cut Remaining Insulation

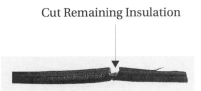

Figure 9-7. Close-up of wire before stripping

off. You must bite down using strippers, then tug gently at the insulation around the bite and determine that you can see down to the strands of wire all the way around. Any remaining rubber must be cut with a sharp knife before you try to pull the piece of insulation off. Sometimes is it easier to do the whole job with a sharp knife and skip the stripper all together. Once the ends are stripped, twist the stranded wire to keep the ends from fraying.

There are several other homebrew methods for making your own LEGO-compatible connectors from scratch. They depend primarily upon replacing a brick's studs with brass screws or tubes. These techniques are not as reliable as the cut wire method and should be considered only if you are shipwrecked on a desert island. Another excellent method for making connectors will be covered in "The Cut Electric Plate Connector," later in this chapter.

Stick-In-Ring Switch

The stick-in-ring switch lets you to create a non-directional touch sensor for mobile robots. Its use for obstacle avoidance dates back over fifty years to the robotics pioneer W. Grey Walter. In 1948, he started making turtle-like robots with both light and touch sensitivity. The turtle shell was connected to a stick-in-ring switch that gave the robot 360° touch sensitivity. The switch consists of a metal stick centered inside a metal ring. The bottom of the stick and the ring are rigidly attached to the body of the robot while the top of the stick supports the shell that covers the robot. The stick and the ring are also electrically connected to form a switch. Any disturbance of the shell bends the stick to come in contact with the ring and closes the circuit.

A good ring can be made with a ¼-inch (6.4 mm) ring lug. Radio Shack sells an assortment package that includes this size (RS#63-3120), but you should be able to find these in most hardware stores (see Figure 9-8). Along with the ring lug you need a 1 inch (2.54 cm) long 6-32 round head machine screw and two nuts. First, you tighten one nut all the way to the head of the screw to form a terminal for one stripped LEGO wire. Then the screw is secured to a TECHNIC beam with the second nut. The ring lug is designed to be crimped onto a #10 gauge wire, but if you just slightly deform the collar, it can be threaded like a nut onto the end of the screw. The stick part of the switch is made from a cross axle with aluminum foil wrapped around it at the same height as the ring. Wrap one layer of foil, then add the stripped LEGO wire, and then wrap two more layers of foil. A loop of cellophane tape at the top will hold the whole thing together.

Figure 9-8. Stick-in-ring switch parts

Final assembly depends upon your particular robot. In Figure 9-9 you can see the stick secured vertically with a 2 x 1 cross-axle beam. The ring is mounted three studs higher. The ring position around the stick is adjusted by removing the stick and screwing the ring on or off the screw to move it back and forth. The robot shell is mounted on the end of the stick and any contact with the shell will bend the stick enough to touch the ring (see Figure 9-10).

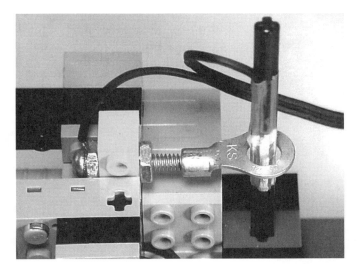

Figure 9-9. An assembled stick-in-ring switch

Figure 9-10. The finished turtle robot

Terminal Block Temperature Sensor

Probably the quickest way to create a sturdy homebrew sensor is to attach the sensor to the stripped wire with a dual row terminal block. A dual row terminal block has two screws per position, which allows you to make permanent circuits easily with only a screwdriver. A two-position dual row terminal block (RS#274-656) can be used to attach the cut wire on one side and the sensor on the other. The result is not particularly compact or attractive, but it works quite well.

The LEGO temperature sensor contains a device called a *thermistor*. We will go into the details of how it works in "The RCX Input," later in this chapter. Radio Shack sells a thermistor (RS#271-110) similar to the one in the LEGO temperature sensor (see Figure 9-11). It looks like a small blue blob with two wires coming out of it. If you carefully bend the wires apart without putting stress on the sensor itself you can then attach it to the terminal block.

> **NOTE** *Be careful to keep the exposed wires around the thermistor dry because if they get wet the temperature reading will be thrown off.*

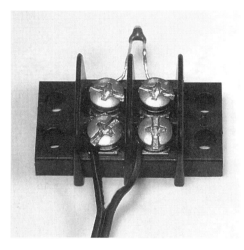

Figure 9-11. Radio Shack thermistor in terminal block

The RCX needs to be programmed to expect a temperature sensor on the input port. If you are using RCX Code, you can either use the Test Panel to select Temperature on the input, or simply write a program that has a Temperature Sensor Watcher, on port 2, for example, and run it. You can select either Fahrenheit or Celsius. However, Celsius is the default. Now you should be able to read the temperature on the RCX display by using the **View** button to select the proper input. Recall that the Radio Shack thermistor is not an exact replacement for the LEGO part and you will find that it reads about 9°F (5°C) high over a wide range of temperatures. Later in this chapter we will find ways to make more accurate temperature sensors.

The temperature value the RCX reads in an alternative language like NQC or Visual Basic is scaled to be ten times bigger than the one you see on the display. That is, 56.7 degrees on the display will be the value 567 internal to the RCX. This is because the RCX uses only whole numbers or integers when it computes. Despite the apparent resolution of one-tenth of a degree, the measured temperature is seldom more accurate than one degree.

RCX Input

Let's play with a device that will help us understand how the RCX reads passive sensors. A *potentiometer* is a variable resistor, and a *resistor* is an electrical device that restricts the flow of electricity. Think of electricity as flowing, like water in a hose, and a resistor as a place in the hose pinched to limit the flow. A potentiometer is equivalent to a valve with a knob you turn to adjust the flow of electricity. They are found in computer joysticks and the controls in your home stereo.

Resistance is measured in Ohms and typical values can range from zero (a short circuit) up to tens of millions (practically not connected). Because people get tired of writing zeros, there is a short way to write something like 50,000 Ohm as simply 50K Ohm or 1,000,000 as 1M Ohm (see Figure 9-12) where K stands for thousands and M stands for millions. We will encounter fixed resistors in "More Accurate Temperature Sensors," later in this chapter, but for now, we need a 50K Ohm linear taper potentiometer (RS#271-1716).

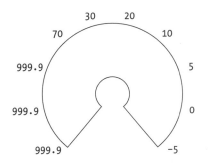

Figure 9-12. The 50K Ohm potentiometer

The device has three terminals, and the electrical resistance between the center terminal and the outer two varies as the shaft is turned. For example, if the shaft is turned fully counterclockwise, the resistance between the left terminal and the center is 0 Ohm, but if the shaft is turned fully clockwise, the resistance increases to 50K Ohm. When the shaft is directly in the middle of its travel, the resistance will be 25K Ohm. The resistance is always 50K Ohms between the outer terminals, which is why it is called a 50K Ohm potentiometer.

When we hook up the left and center terminals of the potentiometer to the RCX, we create a kind of fake temperature sensor. As you turn the potentiometer shaft you will find that the RCX is not always happy with the resistance values it sees. The real thermistor is never expected to create a resistance as low as the potentiometer creates when it is rotated fully counterclockwise and when the RCX reads 999.9 instead of a real temperature. You will also see the reading 999.9 if nothing is hooked up to the input. As the shaft is rotated clockwise, the temperature will range from +70°C (158°F) to about −5°C (23°F); see Figure 9-13. If you add this dial and a knob to your 50K Ohm potentiometer, then you can set any temperature you want.

Figure 9-13. The 50K potentiometer Celsius temperature dial

227

If you are only using the RIS software, you are limited to Touch and Temperature for passive sensors. However, alternative languages like NQC or Visual Basic allow control of the RCX inputs in another way. You can set an input to a type described in the LEGO Technical Reference Manual as "None" (NQC sensor type SENSOR_TYPE_NONE). Despite its uninspiring name, this sensor is actually the most useful passive type of all because it allows direct access to the analog to digital (A/D) converter inside the RCX. You can also set the input to either Switch (Touch) or Temperature, and then set the sensor mode to the (equally uninspiring) mode called "Raw" to get the same effect. The A/D converter converts an analog voltage across the input port into a digital value. The values from the converter range from 0 to 1,023, and from now on we will call this the Raw input mode. For example, the following line of NQC sets sensor port 1 to Raw input mode:

```
SetSensorType(SENSOR_1, SENSOR_TYPE_NONE);
```

If the RCX is reading a voltage across the input port, where is the voltage coming from? The answer is, from itself. You can prove this by measuring the voltage with a DC voltmeter if you have one. On the RCX input connector, touch the voltmeter positive (red) probe to the exposed metal of one of the studs on the left, and touch the negative (black) probe to one on the right. A good voltmeter will measure something close to 5 volts, while a cheap meter will probably read something slightly less. If you hook the probes up backwards, you will measure a negative voltage.

Assuming you have an alternative language and can set an input port to read Raw values, you can use the values to understand what's going on inside the RCX. With nothing hooked up to the input, the Raw reading is 1,023. As soon as we hook up the 50K Ohm potentiometer, the Raw value drops to around 853 with the shaft rotated fully clockwise. This tells us there is a resistor inside the RCX in series with the supplied voltage. By knowing the resistance value of the potentiometer (50K Ohm) and the reading with (853) and without it (1,023), we can determine the internal resistor is a 10K Ohm. In "The 50K Ohm Potentiometer Angle Sensor," later in this chapter we will use this fact and a little algebra to turn a potentiometer into a precise angle sensor.

More Accurate Temperature Sensors

The LEGO temperature sensor can be duplicated by adding a 2.2K Ohm fixed resistor (RS#271-1325) in series with the Radio Shack thermistor. The combination doesn't match exactly, and the hotter or colder the temperature is from 25°C (77°F), the greater the difference becomes. The error can be over 6°C (11°F), but it can be easily corrected with a little software. In the next equations, T is the internal temperature reading in the RCX and is ten times larger than the actual temperature. Tfixed is the corrected temperature, but it will still be ten times larger.

$$\text{Tfixed} = \frac{7}{6} \times T - 40 \ \text{ for } {}^\circ C$$

$$\text{Tfixed} = \frac{7}{6} \times T - 120 \ \text{ for } {}^\circ F$$

The Visual Basic code to carry out the correction in Fahrenheit is shown next:

```
.MulVar 1, 2, 7        'With T in Var1 multiply by 7
.DivVar 1, 2, 6        'Now divide by 6
.SubVar 1, 2, 120      'Subtract 120, now Var1 = fixed temperature
```

> **NOTE** *The Visual Basic code appearing in this book uses SPIRIT.OCX (part of the RIS 1.0 and 1.5 software) to provide RCX APIs from within Visual Basic. Consult the Software Development Kit (SDK) for RIS 1.0/1.5 for more information on programming with SPIRIT.OCX.*

In NQC, the conversion could be done like this:

```
// convert temperature to Fahrenheit in variable named t
t = t * 7 / 6 - 120;
```

You can buy thermistors from Mouser Electronics that are accurate to within a few degrees all by themselves. You have two choices: a miniature one (ME#527-0503-10K), and a larger one (ME#334-42103). The larger unit is about a third the cost of the miniature one and is much easier to work with. The fixed resistor should be a 2.2K Ohm 1% and will need to be ordered from Mouser Electronics as well (ME#271-2.2K).

The graph you see in Figure 9-14 shows how much error to expect throughout the -20°C to 70°C (-4°F to 158°F) range of the RCX. Positive error means the RCX reads a temperature that is too high and negative error means it reads too low. The miniature Mouser Electronics thermistor with a 2.2K Ohm resistor is the most accurate with less than 3°C (5°F) error. The large Mouser Electronics thermistor has a little more error, and the Radio Shack thermistor is significantly off at the extremes and will need the correction software to be useful. The plot also shows the error you get with Radio Shack thermistor used without a resistor. By the time you get to 40°C (104°F) it is off the chart.

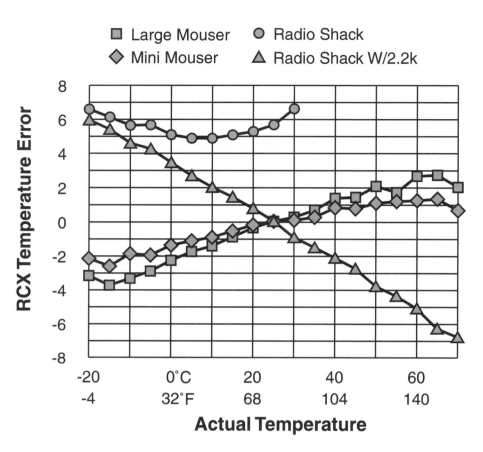

Figure 9-14. Plot of temperature error

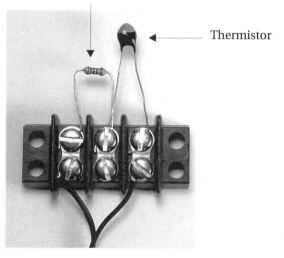

2.2K Resistor

Thermistor

Figure 9-15. A more accurate temperature sensor on the terminal block

While you are ordering parts, you might as well get a three position dual row terminal block to hook it all together (ME#538-3140). In Figure 9-15, a thermistor lead and a resistor lead are both under the same screw just to make the connections easier to see. You could just as easily connect the resistor diagonally between the screw on the upper left and the screw centered between the LEGO wires.

Waterproof Temperature Sensor

One drawback to assembling the temperature sensor on a terminal block is that it isn't waterproof. Water conducts electricity about as well as the thermistor, so the reading will be thrown off if it gets wet. One simple solution is to connect the thermistor and resistor directly together and then enclose them inside a balloon. The thin long type used to make balloon animals is perfect.

Twist together one of the resistors and one of the thermistor leads. Then twist the two LEGO wires to the remaining resistor and thermistor leads. I recommend soldering the connections to make them stronger, but if you are careful, you can skip this step. The exposed wires need to be insulated so they don't touch. Because the voltages are so low, this can be done with regular cellophane tape. Figure 9-16 shows the waterproof temperature sensor parts.

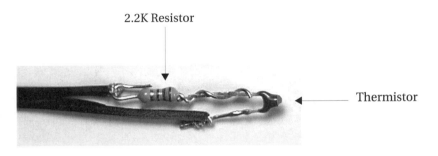

Figure 9-16. Waterproof temperature sensor parts

Now slip a balloon over the assembly like a sock and secure at the top with a rubber band as shown in Figure 9-17. The sensor is not very rugged so you need to be careful not to damage it.

Figure 9-17. Waterproof temperature sensor using a balloon

A sturdier solution is to enclose the large Mouser Electronics thermistor and the resistor inside a short piece of Silicone or PVC plastic tubing measuring $3/16$- inch (4.8 mm) on the inside diameter. This is the standard size sold for air-line tubing in aquariums (see Figure 9-18). The tubing's natural inside diameter is slightly smaller than the thermistor outside diameter so the tubing seals tightly when the thermistor is pressed inside. First, you need to feed a short piece of tubing about 2.5 inches (7 cm) long onto the cut and stripped LEGO wires. Don't forget this step, because you can't get the tube on after you connect the rest of the parts. Connect everything up like before, insulate with tape, and slowly slide the tube over the wires and resistor up to the thermistor. You only need to press the thermistor into the tube ¼-inch (5 mm) to make a good seal. The other end of the tube can be sealed with silicon or other waterproof glue. You might want to seal the thermistor end too, just in case.

Figure 9-18. Waterproof temperature sensor using aquarium tubing

A Relative Humidity Sensor

A *psychrometer* is an instrument made with two thermometers, which measures relative humidity. The end of one thermometer is kept wet (the wet bulb) so that the cooling that results from evaporation makes it register a lower temperature than the dry (dry bulb) thermometer. When readings are taken at the same time, it is possible to determine the relative humidity of air. The relative humidity is usually found by looking it up on a table using the difference between the two temperatures. This process can be automated by programming the RCX to do all the work.

To make your psychrometer you need two accurate temperature sensors. You can use either the software corrected Radio Shack thermistor or one of the Mouser Electronics thermistors with a 2.2K Ohm resistor. The dry bulb thermometer doesn't need to be waterproof, but the wet bulb obviously does (see Figure 9-19). Wrap the end of the wet bulb thermometer with a short length of paper towel and secure it with a rubber band. Now arrange the paper towel to hang over a small container of water. Make sure the temperature sensor is well above the water level in the jar so that it picks up the cooler temperature of the water evaporating from the paper towel. The dryer the air is, the cooler the wet bulb will be. You need to wait about an hour after setting up the psychrometer for the temperatures to stabilize.

Figure 9-19. The wet bulb temperature sensor

To program the RCX, we need an equation that will convert the wet and dry bulb temperatures to relative humidity. The following equation works over a reasonable range of household temperature and humidity conditions where DRY and WET are the temperatures in Fahrenheit:

$$H = \frac{310 \times (WET - DRY)}{DRY} + 100$$

However, before we write the program, we need to take into account that the temperature readings within the RCX are scaled by ten times and you can only compute numbers that lie between –32,768 and +32,767. A temperature difference of 19.2°F would be 192 inside the RCX. If you multiply 192 by 310, you get a number much bigger than +32,767. For that reason we need to divide the DRY and WET values by ten. That way they will not only the correct temperature values, but will also keep the arithmetic in range.

Listing 9-1 is a simple example program written in Visual Basic that sets up two temperature inputs, reads them, corrects them if necessary, and converts the readings into relative humidity.

Listing 9-1. Visual Basic program listing for humidity sensor

```
.SetSensorType 0, 2     'Sensor 1 is Temperature Type
.SetSensorType 1, 2     'Sensor 2 is Temperature Type
.SetSensorMode 0, 6, 0  'Sensor 1 Degrees F Mode
.SetSensorMode 1, 6, 0  'Sensor 2 Degrees F Mode
.SetVar 1, 9, 0         'Read Sensor 1 into Var1
.SetVar 2, 9, 1         'Read Sensor 2 into Var2
'The next 6 lines are needed if you are using the Radio Shack
'thermistor with a 2.2K Ohm resistor. Omit for Mouser thermistors
.MulVar 1, 2, 7         'With T in Var1 multiply by 7
.DivVar 1, 2, 6         'Now divide by 6
.SubVar 1, 2, 120       'Subtract 120, now Var1 = fixed temp
.MulVar 2, 2, 7         'With T in Var2 multiply by 7
.DivVar 2, 2, 6         'Now divide by 6
.SubVar 2, 2, 120       'Subtract 120, now Var2 = fixed temp
'
.DivVar 1, 2, 10        'Var1 = Var1 / 10 = DRY
.DivVar 2, 2, 10        'Var2 = Var2 / 10 = WET
.SubVar 2, 0, 1         'Var2 = Var2 - Var1
.MulVar 2, 2, 310       'Var2 = Var2 * 310
.DivVar 2, 0, 1         'Var2 = Var2 / Var1
.SumVar 2, 2, 100       'Var2 = Var2 + 100 = Relative Humidity
```

Listing 9-2 is a complete NQC program that does the same thing:

Listing 9-2. humidity.nqc – NQC program listing for humidity sensor

```
// humidity.nqc

#define DRY     SENSOR_1
#define WET     SENSOR_2

// uncomment this line for Radio Shack adjustmet
// #define RADIO_SHACK_ADJUST

task main()
{
    int wet, dry, hum;

    // configure the sensors
    SetSensor(DRY, SENSOR_FAHRENHEIT);
    SetSensor(WET, SENSOR_FAHRENHEIT);

    // read the sensors
    #ifdef RADIO_SHACK_ADJUST
        dry = DRY * 7 / 6 - 120;
        wet = WET * 7 / 6 - 120;
    #else
        dry = DRY;
        wet = WET;
    #endif

    // compute humidity
    wet /= 10;
    dry /= 10;
    hum = (wet - dry) * 310 / dry + 100;
}
```

50K Ohm Potentiometer Angle Sensor

It's hard to use a normal size 50K Ohm potentiometer in LEGO creations. Fortunately, there are rugged miniature potentiometers available from Mouser Electronics (ME#594-149-1503). The threaded mounting shank of the potentiometer is ¼-inch (6.35 mm) in diameter, which is a little bigger than a TECHNIC axle hole so you will need do a little drilling to mount it. LEGO plastic is so soft you can drill it simply by twisting a drill bit held with locking pliers. The shaft of the potentiometer is

¹/₈-inch (3.18 mm) in diameter and several sizes of LEGO gears can be pressed onto it with enough friction that they won't slip during normal operation. If the gear is accidentally rotated beyond the stops of the potentiometer, it will slip to prevent any damage. Electrical connections are made to the center and—if you want a clockwise increasing angle—to the top potentiometer leads. If you need counter-clockwise angles, attach wires to the center and bottom leads. A simple mounting example is shown in Figure 9-20.

Figure 9-20. The mounted miniature potentiometer with gear

You would like the sensor to read angle in degrees, but you will find that the Raw values don't exactly track the shaft angle. A little math will show us how to fix this problem in software. First of all, the RCX Raw reading is related to the sensor resistance by the following equation, where X is the reading and R is the sensor resistance in Ohms.

$$X = \frac{1,023 \times R}{10,000 + R}$$

The 1,023 is the maximum Raw value and the 10,000 comes from the internal 10K Ohm pullup resistor in the RCX. What we really want is an equation for sensor resistance, so we solve for R.

$$R = \frac{10,000 \times X}{1,023 - X}$$

The potentiometer resistance is linear with angle A, hence the term "linear taper." The following equation shows how at 0 resistance the pot is at 0 degrees, and at 50,000 (50K Ohms) the pot is at 270 degrees.

$$A = \frac{270 \times R}{50,000}$$

We can substitute the equation for R in the previous example and get an equation for angle A in terms of the Raw value X.

$$A = \frac{54 \times X}{1,023 - X}$$

It might look like we are done, but there is a problem. If you coded this with the integer math the RCX uses, when X gets larger than 607, the result will be larger than 32,767 and there would be an overflow. Instead of the previous equation, we will use the following one. It breaks up the multiply into two steps and prevents the overflow.

$$A = 2 \times \frac{27 \times X}{1,023 - X}$$

The following Visual Basic code fragment implements the previous equation with nice results.

```
.SetSensorType 0, 0      'Sensor 1 is None or Raw
.SetVar 1, 9, 0          'Var1 = Input with potentiometer
.SetVar 2, 2, 27         'Var2 = 27
.MulVar 2, 0, 1          'Var2 = Var2 * Var1
.SetVar 3, 2, 1023       'Var3 = 1023
.SubVar 3, 0, 1          'Var3 = Var3 - Var1
.DivVar 2, 0, 3          'Var2 = Var2/Var3
.MulVar 2, 2, 2          'Var2 = Var2 * 2 = Angle in degrees
```

A similar calculation could be done in NQC like this (assuming variables a and x were already declared):

```
a = (27 * x) / (1023 - X) * 2;
```

Cut Electric Plate Connector

An excellent electrical connector can be made from LEGO electric plates (S@H#5037), (see Figure 9-21) as was discovered by Dean Husby. These plates resemble regular building plates except they have the electrical characteristics of the LEGO connector. The only problem is, they don't come in the 2 x 2 size you really want. Longer electric plates need to be cut down to the right size.

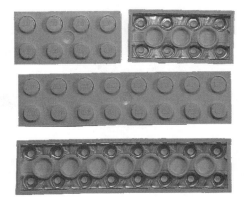

To cut an electric plate, you need to put together a guide first. The guide is made from two 2 x 4 plates and two 2 x 1 plates assembled around the electric plate like a collar. Using a single edge razorblade or similar sharp knife, push the blade into the sides of the electric plate as far as possible. Then cut the tube and other plastic on the bottom of the plate. Now carefully score the plastic top of the plate as deeply as possible. After

Figure 9-21. The top and bottom of the LEGO electric plates

removing the cutting guide you should be able to bend the electric plate back and forth at the cut until it breaks. Sensor connections to the electric plate are made on the bottom and need to be soldered to insure reliable operation. Figure 9-22 shows you the steps involved in cutting an electric plate.

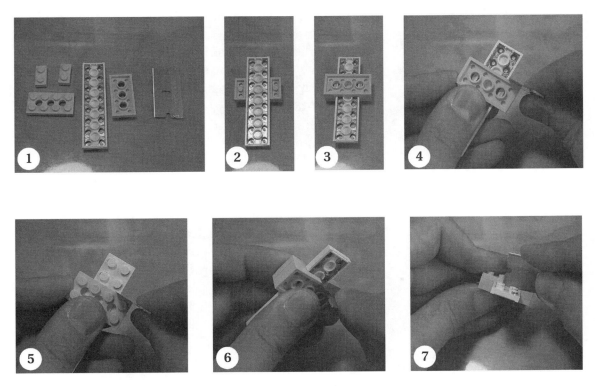

Figure 9-22. Cutting the electric plate step-by-step (Continues)

Chapter 9

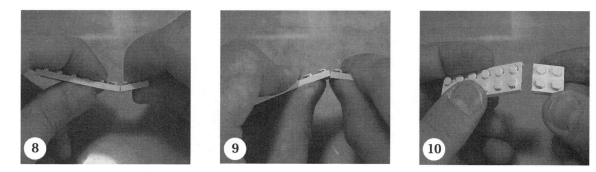

Figure 9-22. Cutting the electric plate step-by-step (Continued)

CdS Photocell Sensor

A sensor that works nicely with the cut electric plate connector is the Cadmium Sulfide (CdS) photocell. Sometimes Photocells are also called Light Dependant Resistors or LDRs because they have a resistance that varies with the amount of light falling on them. The Radio Shack package (RS#276-1657) has five photocells, which is sometimes an assortment of slightly different styles. Mouser Electronics sells photocells individually in several sizes (ME#338-76C348 or 338-54C348). The sensor should be used with the RCX Raw type input mode discussed already.

Figure 9-23. The CdS photocell soldered to the cut electric plate

The CdS photocell leads need to be trimmed to about $3/8$-inch (10 mm) in length. Soldering must be done quickly or you will melt the electric plate plastic (see Figure 9-23). Load the tip of a pencil type soldering iron with solder so that a small drop starts to form. While holding the lead of the sensor against the metal of the electric plate, bring the drop of solder down and let it flow over the joint. Only hold the iron there for a second. Repeat for the other lead. Even if you melt the plate a little, you will probably still be able to use it.

After you solder both leads of the CdS sensor, you can glue a regular 2 x 2 plate to the bottom. You will probably need to trim away some of the studs of the plate before it will fit flush because the solder and wires take up too much room. Connection to the sensor is made just like the LEGO Touch sensor. Figure 9-24 displays the completed CdS photocell sensor.

Figure 9-24. The finished CdS photocell sensor

The finished CdS light sensor will pick up light in all directions. If you want more directional sensitivity, you need to focus the light on the sensor with a lens. LEGO has a magnifying glass lens that comes with Adventurers Sets. It can be purchased in an accessories kit (S@H#5381). It needs to be placed about three and one-half stud lengths away from the CdS to focus light from a distance. A crude camera can be constructed by mounting the CdS sensor and lens handle on a 2 x 1 cross-axle beam as shown in Figure 9-25. A complete enclosure should be built, which shields all other light from hitting the CdS sensor.

Figure 9-25. The basic elements of a crude camera

One advantage of the CdS light sensor is that it operates over a much wider range (0 to 1,023) than the LEGO Light sensor, which only goes from about 20 to 100. However, the main advantage of the CdS photocell is that it is more responsive to the colors of light we see. The LEGO Light sensor uses a Silicon phototransistor that is sensitive mostly to red and infrared light. The plot in Figure 9-26 shows the light sensitivity of a Silicon phototransistor and a CdS photocell, along with the sensitivity of the human eye. With red, green, and blue transparent filters, you could build a robot that searched for a specific color object like a green plant. This could be done with three separate CdS photocells, or by rotating the filters in front of a single sensor.

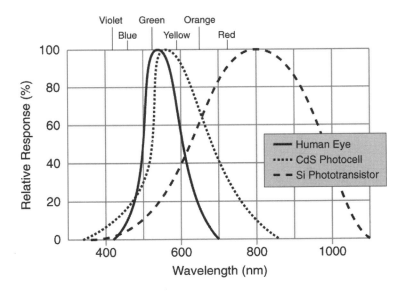

Figure 9-26. Relative photo sensor sensitivities

Galvanic Skin Response

Galvanic Skin Response (GSR) is used in lie detectors and in biofeedback training. In theory, you can judge the emotional state of a person by measuring their GSR. The more you sweat, the lower the resistance of your skin. People who are under stress sweat more and their skin resistance goes down, while people who are at ease show a high skin resistance. You could put together a science project where you related the GSR of a person while they were playing a challenging video game versus relaxing.

Figure 9-27. A simple way to measure galvanic skin response

The easiest place to measure GSR is between two fingers on the same hand as shown in Figure 9-27. Make two rings from aluminum foil and cellophane tape. Attach each ring to a wire of a stripped LEGO wire. Wear the rings on two adjacent fingers, but make sure they don't touch each other directly. When the RCX is programmed for a Raw type sensor, the readings vary around 850. Lower numbers indicate more stress while higher numbers indicate a more relaxed state.

> **NOTE** *Only use electronic devices attached to your body that are powered batteries. Never use household electricity.*

Listing 9-3 is a simple Visual Basic program for biofeedback training. It takes a reading every five seconds and compares the new reading to the old one. If the new reading is higher, it indicates that the subject is becoming more relaxed and a low tone is produced. If the reading is lower, the subject is less relaxed and a high tone is produced. If the readings are the same, a medium tone is produced. The objective is to try to make the RCX produce mostly low tones.

Listing 9-3. Visual Basic program listing for biofeedback training

```
.SetSensorType 2, 0     'Set Input 3 to Raw
.SetVar 1, 9, 2         'Var1 = Old = Input 3
.Loop 2, 0              'Loop Forever
 .SetVar 2, 9, 2        'Var2 = New = Input 3
 .If 0, 2, 2, 0, 1      'If New = Old play mid tone
   .PlayTone 110, 500   'Indicates no change
 .EndIf
 .If 0, 2, 1, 0, 1      'If New < Old play high tone
   .PlayTone 220, 500   'Indicates less relaxed
 .EndIf
```

```
.If 0, 2, 0, 0, 1     'If New > Old play low tone
  .PlayTone 55, 500   'Indicates more relaxed
.EndIf
.SetVar 1, 0, 2       'Old = New
.Wait 2, 300          'Wait a short while
.EndLoop
```

A similar program written in NQC appears in Listing 9-4.

Listing 9-4. galvanic.nqc – NQC program listing for biofeedback training

```
// galvanic.nqc

#define GALV SENSOR_1
#define DURATION 500
#define DELAY 300

task main()
{
    int new, old;

    SetSensorType(GALV, SENSOR_TYPE_NONE);

    old = GALV;

    while(true)
    {
        new = GALV;
        if (new > old)
            PlayTone(55, DURATION); // lower stress
        else if (new < old)
            PlayTone(220, DURATION); // higher stress
        else
            PlayTone(110, DURATION); // same stress

        old = new;
        Wait(DELAY);
    }
}
```

The program is just a starting point for biofeedback training. You will probably want to play with the time between readings and the tone frequencies to make it more comfortable for your own use.

Voltage Input Sensor

All of the sensors presented up to this point have changed electrical resistance in reaction to a change in the sensed condition. Even a switch is an extreme example of a change in resistance with a change in position. Occasionally, we want to sense voltage. As we already know, the RCX really reads the voltage on the sensor input. The fact that there is a voltage present at the input just makes some sensors easier to use. You could apply a voltage of your own to the input and the RCX would read that instead.

The problem with blindly connecting a voltage to the input is that it can damage the RCX. The RCX circuitry cannot tolerate a negative input voltage. Although it has some internal protection, it is not wise to push things like this. The voltage the RCX applies to the input is 5 V in series with a 10K Ohm resistor. If you only apply voltage in series with a 10K Ohm resistor and you don't exceed 5 V, you can't damage the RCX. In fact, the voltage can range from –5 V to +5 V, and with the RCX in Raw mode, the plot in Figure 9-28 shows the values you should see.

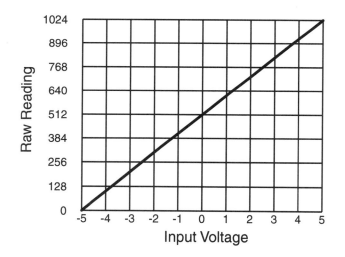

Figure 9-28. A plot of Raw value vs. voltage input

Here is a simple equation that will give you the Raw value for a given input voltage where X is the Raw value and V is the voltage:

$$X = 512 \times \left(\frac{V}{5} + 1\right)$$

You can use a three position terminal block and a 10K Ohm resistor (RS#271-1355) to make a voltage input sensor like the one you see in Figure 9-29. It is built just like the accurate temperature sensor, except the voltage is applied where the thermistor used to be. Two short lengths of wire provide connections to a source of voltage like a battery. If the two wires are connected to each other, then the reading will be near 512 (0 V). A new AA alkaline battery will read 230 (-1.6 V) when hooked in one direction and 730 (+1.6 V) in the other.

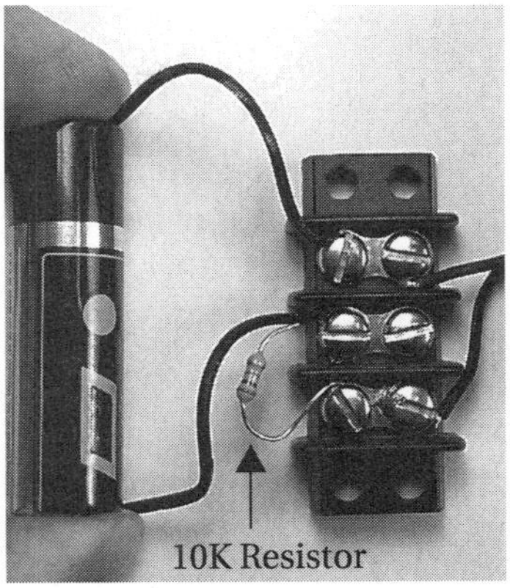

10K Resistor

Battery Tester

Figure 9-29. The voltage input sensor

A battery tester is a useful application of voltage sensing for the RCX. A good AA battery has a voltage greater than 1.5 V, a poor AA battery is between 1.5 V and 1.25 V, and a dead AA battery is below 1.25 V. Let's make the RCX produce the 'increasing frequency sweep' system-sound for good batteries, the 'beep beep' for poor, and the 'buhhh' for dead batteries. However, there are a few things to consider before writing the program.

It would be nice if it didn't matter how the battery was connected to the input so that the voltage could be either positive or negative. Also, if no battery is connected, the RCX will pull the input to 5 V all by itself. Because no battery would generate more than 1.75 V, any readings greater than that should be made to look like 0 V. These features can be created by subtracting 512 from the Raw reading and then taking the absolute value of the result. Now the value will range from 0 (0 V) to 512 (5 V). The three threshold voltages we need are 179 (1.75 V), 154 (1.5 V), and 128 (1.25 V). The finished program appears in Listing 9-5.

Listing 9-5. Visual Basic program listing for an AA battery tester

```
.SetSensorType 0, 0     'Set Input 1 to Raw
.SetVar 1, 9, 0         'Var1 = Input 1
.SubVar 1, 2, 512       'Var1 = Var1 - 512
.AbsVar 1, 0, 1         'Var1 = ABS(Var1)
.If 0, 1, 0, 2, 179     'If Var1 > 1.75V
 .SetVar 1, 2, 0        'Treat it like it was 0V
.EndIf
.If 0, 1, 1, 2, 128     'If Var1 < 1.25V
 .PlaySystemSound 4     'Buhh
.Else                   'Var1 > 1.25V
 .PlaySystemSound 1     'Beep Beep
.EndIf
```

```
.If 0, 1, 0, 2, 154    'If Var1 > 1.5V
 .PlaySystemSound 3    'Increasing Sweep
.EndIf
```

A similar program in NQC appears in Listing 9-6.

> **NOTE**   *The NQC program has slightly different behavior than the Visual Basic version. Specifically, with a good battery, the Visual Basic program plays two sounds (Beep-Beep and Increasing Sweep), while the NQC version plays only one sound.*

Listing 9-6. battery.nqc – NQC program listing for an AA battery tester

```
// battery.nqc

#define BATT SENSOR_1

task main()
{
    int b;
    SetSensorType(BATT, SENSOR_TYPE_NONE);

    b = abs(BATT - 512);

    // treat > 1.75V as 0V
    if (b > 179)
        b = 0;

    if (b < 128)
        PlaySound(SOUND_LOW_BEEP);
    else if (b < 154)
        PlaySound(SOUND_DOUBLE_BEEP);
    else
        PlaySound(SOUND_UP);
}
```

A Tachometer

By themselves, most sensors do not create large enough voltages to use the voltage input. However, there is one that does and it was supplied with your MINDSTORMS kit—the LEGO motor (S@H#5225). A DC motor is normally used by applying a voltage to its terminals, which then causes the motor's shaft to turn. It is also possible to reverse this process: turning the shaft will generate a voltage at the motor's terminals. Turning the shaft faster will result in a higher voltage. . The polarity of the voltage depends on whether you are turning the shaft clockwise or counterclockwise. The only thing we need to make a speed sensor or tachometer is a LEGO wire with a 10K Ohm resistor in series with one of the wires.

If you are careful, you can splice the 10K Ohm resistor inline with a LEGO connector wire, as you can see in Figure 9-30. Cut through only one of the two wires and then cut the web in both directions about 1/2 inch (1 cm). Now strip both ends and attach the 10K resistor in the middle. You can wrap tape around the whole thing to make it look nice and to electrically insulate it. If you accidentally cut both wires, simply reconnect the second wire and cover the joint with tape. Soldering the connections will make them more reliable.

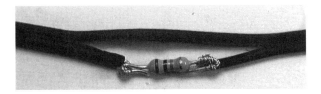

Figure 9-30. The tachometer connector wire

A Potpourri of Passive Sensors

By now you should have a pretty good idea of how to make your own passive sensors. Here are a few more quick ideas for sensors. We will leave the details to you to figure out.

- **Strain:** If you stretch or compress conductive material, its resistance changes. You can salvage bend sensors or use the conductive foam used to package integrated circuits to show the effect.

- **Salinity:** The more salt dissolved in water, the lower its resistance. By simply hanging the bare ends of cut LEGO wires in a jar of water you can measure the resistance of the water. You could also use this principle to determine the amount of moisture in soil or other absorbent material.

- **Displacement:** Travel up to 4 inches or 10 cm in one direction can be measured using slide potentiometers. This special potentiometer is used in audio equipment to adjust volume by pushing a knob back and forth, rather than by rotating it.

- **Limit Switches:** There are a wide variety of limit switches available. They turn on or off in response to pressure, temperature, tilt, vibration, magnetic fields, proximity, touch, level, or flow. Some pressure switches are so sensitive you only need to blow into them to activate them.

- **Carbon Microphone:** Some older telephones used a carbon microphone that worked by changing resistance with sound vibrations. If you can find one of the old microphone elements, you can connect it to the RCX and it will have a Raw reading of about 200. However, the value will vary significantly when you speak into it.

- **Junk Box:** Computer mice, printers, joysticks, games, stereos, tape players and radios have switches, buttons, and potentiometers that can be made into homebrew passive sensors.

Part Cross-reference List

The following table includes a parts cross-reference list for the products discussed in this chapter.

PART	RADIO SHACK	MOUSER ELECTRONICS
Alligator Test Lead Set	278-1156	548-285
Wire Cutter/Stripper	64-2129	5876-101S
¼" 10-12 Ring Lug	63-3120	571-33458
2 Pos Dual Row Terminal Block	274-656	538-2140
3 Pos Dual Row Terminal Block	N/A	538-3140
Thermistor	271-110	N/A
Large Thermistor	N/A	334-42103
Miniature Thermistor	N/A	527-0503-10K
2.2K Ohm 1% ¼-Watt Resistor	271-1325	271-2.2K
10K Ohm 5% ¼-Watt Resistor	271-1355	271-10K
50K Ohm Linear Taper Pot	271-1716	594-149-1503
CdS Photocells	276-1657	338-76C348 or 338-54C348

Conclusion

Passive sensors are simple to understand and easy to homebrew. Just about anything that changes in resistance as a response to something can be used as a passive sensor. Unfortunately, not everything can be sensed this easily. Now it is time move on to powered sensors.

CHAPTER 10

Homebrew Powered Sensors

POWERED RCX SENSORS are more complicated than the passive type because they require more electronic parts and certain new skills to put them together. They are worth learning to build because they are more versatile than passive sensors. They can output beacons, amplify weak signals, and even have a degree of intelligence. This new functionality allows for a wider range of sensing and frees the RCX for more important control duties. Examples of powered LEGO sensors include the Light and Rotation sensors. In this chapter we give instructions to build a specialized light sensor, a sound sensor, an optointerrupter, and two general purpose interface circuits that hook up to the RCX just like the LEGO Light sensor. The LEGO Rotation sensor interface is very specialized and will not be covered in this book.

Getting Parts and Tools

As with the passive sensors, every effort has been made to use parts that are available from Radio Shack retail stores. Because there are so many more parts, most of the catalog numbers will only be listed in the "Bill of Materials for Powered Sensors" section. If you don't live near a Radio Shack retail store, you can purchase items from their 800 number service, and even online. Mouser Electronics part numbers will be also given as a second source. The names and contact information of these and other suppliers are listed in Appendix A.

In addition to electronic parts, you might need a few new tools. The most important being an electronic breadboard, and if you intend to make your powered sensors permanent, a soldering iron. More information about these tools and instructions on how to use them will be covered throughout the chapter. Diagonal cutters are also necessary for cutting extra component leads after soldering. Other tools that will make building easier are needle-nose pliers, a multimeter, and a small screwdriver set.

Getting Started

Because you may have had minimal experience with building electronics projects like these, we will cover the topic from a fairly basic level. In addition to understanding electronics, there is a certain art to constructing electronic projects that involves skills such as reading schematics, soldering, and packaging. We will go step-by-step in detail through the building process so that hopefully everyone can build the projects with success.

As with the passive sensors, if you have trouble making or understanding the sensor projects, there are many places to get help. You should be able to find help from teachers or people that work in electronics stores and repair shops. Your local library and bookstores should have beginner's books on electricity too.

We will use a two-step process in building the projects. The first step is to build and test the complete circuit on an electronic breadboard. The breadboard allows you to construct electronic circuits without soldering, which makes correcting mistakes easy. The second step is to transfer the parts from the breadboard to a printed circuit board with the same layout as the breadboard and solder them in place to make the project permanent.

RCX Powered Interface

The RCX powered interface must supply power to the sensor and read its value using the same pair of wires. It accomplishes this by rapidly alternating between these two functions. First, the RCX applies about 8 volts to the sensor port, much like it applies voltage to the motor outputs. It does this for a short 3 milliseconds or a 0.003-second time period. It then measures the sensor value the same way it does for a passive sensor —for an even shorter 0.1 millisecond or 0.0001-second time period. After that, it repeats the process over again. The challenge in building a powered sensor is to separate these two functions. On top of that, it would be nice if it didn't matter which direction the LEGO connector wire was attached to the RCX.

Sensor Power Circuit

The circuit shown in Figure 10-1 gets power to the sensor. The parts labeled D1 to D4 are called *switching diodes.* They act as one-way valves for electricity and their industry standard part number is 1N4148. The diode symbol looks like an arrow pointing at a line, and the electric current can only flow through the diode in the direction of the arrow. The real diode has one end with a painted stripe, which corresponds to the side with the line in the diode's symbol. The 1N4148 is similar to another diode called the 1N914 and either can be used for these projects.

> **NOTE** *On a circuit diagram, dots represent electrical connections. For example, the vertical wire connected to both D1 and D2 is NOT connected to the horizontal wire that goes to the RCX.*

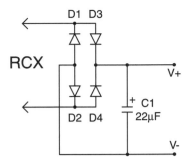

Figure 10-1. A power circuit diagram

The arrangement of four diodes is called a *bridge rectifier,* which is normally used to convert alternating current (AC) into direct current (DC). This may seem confusing because the RCX does not produce AC. The circuit is used here only so that the sensor will work regardless of how the LEGO connector wire is attached to the RCX. Imagine the positive terminal of the RCX attached to the top connector on the circuit diagram and the negative terminal attached to the lower, as shown on the left in Figure 10-2. Electrical current cannot flow into D1 because it is not oriented correctly, but it can flow into D3. The current then flows into whatever sensor circuitry you have and out through D2. If the RCX polarity is reversed, D4 and D1 pass the current.

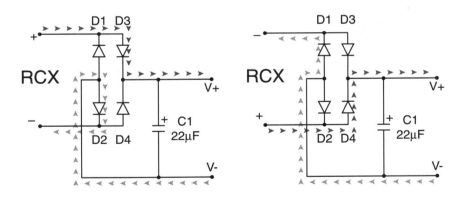

Figure 10-2. Current flow through the power circuit

The part labeled C1 is an aluminum electrolytic capacitor. It acts like a small rechargeable battery and, just like a battery, it has positive and negative terminals. On the real capacitor only the negative end is usually marked. Two things are needed to specify a capacitor like this. Its capacity of 22 microfarads (abbreviated μF) defines the size of the capacitor, much like AA, C, and D define the size of a battery. The rated voltage of 35 V defines the maximum voltage the capacitor can be charged without damage. For this circuit, the capacitor will never be charged over 10 V, however, 35 V is the lowest value Radio Shack retail stores carry. You can always use a part with a higher voltage than you need.

Now let's put these parts on the electronic breadboard. As you can see in Figure 10-3, the breadboard has several vertical columns of five electrically con-nected holes (labeled A-E and F-J), along with two long rows of connected holes (labeled X and Y) at the top and bottom. If your breadboard is not labeled like this, make your own labels and stick them to the edge of the board. The columns are numbered starting from 1, but we skip column 1 to make the eventual layout on the printed circuit board easier. Inside the holes are spring contacts that pinch the component leads or wires to make the electrical connections.

Figure 10-3. Labels on the electronic breadboard

Poke the part leads into the breadboard until they hit bottom. The lead will extend about ¼-inch or 6 mm below the surface of the board. Look at Figure 10-4 and Table 10-1, which gives the hole locations to determine the placement of each part. It helps to trim the length of the part leads so they don't stand too high off the breadboard. The RCX wires need to be attached to short pieces of solid #22 gauge hookup wire so they can be plugged into the breadboard too. Strip enough insula-tion from the wire so that it can be inserted fully into the breadboard.

NOTE *Occasionally, parts are so close that their leads bump together and create a short circuit. To prevent this, strip insulation from hookup wire and slip the insulation over the part leads. For example, in Figure 10-4 insulation is used on the negative lead of C1.*

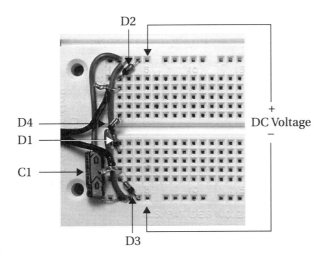

Figure 10-4. The power circuit on the breadboard

Table 10-1. Power Circuit Part Placement Table

PART	COLUMN	ROW
D1 stripe 1N4148	2	G
D1 plain	3	X
D2 stripe1N4148	2	A
D2 plain	4	X
D3 stripe1N4148	4	Y
D3 plain	2	J
D4 stripe1N4148	3	Y
D4 plain	2	E
C1 + 22µF	2	Y
C1 -	2	X
RCX 1	2	B
RCX 2	2	I

To test the circuit, we need an input port of the RCX to be configured for a powered sensor. The easiest way to do this is to run the built-in program number 3. This program sets input port 2 to expect a Light sensor. You could also write and run your own program to do the same thing or use the test panel. Make sure the port is actually set to Light type by plugging in your LEGO Light sensor and confirming that the red LED lights up.

Now disconnect the LEGO Light sensor and hook your circuit to the RCX input port. You should use a voltmeter to measure a DC voltage between 5 V to 8 V across X to Y. The exact voltage depends on the condition of the batteries in the RCX. Remember that the negative connection is on the top and the positive is on the bottom. If you measure less than 5 V DC, you probably have one of the diodes or the capacitor backwards. Make sure the circuit works with the LEGO wire connected to the RCX in all four directions. It is a good idea to disconnect the LEGO wire from the RCX while you are building the circuit or making corrections to prevent accidental damage to the RCX.

Sensor Measurement Circuit

Only two more diodes and a resistor are needed to provide a way for the RCX to measure the sensor's value. Diodes D5 and D6 are the same type of diodes we have already been using. The zigzag-shaped symbol in Figure 10-5 is a resistor. It is labeled R1 and has 1K Ohm value. You also need to know that it has 5% tolerance and is the ¼-watt size. The 5% number indicates how close to the 1K Ohm value the part was made.

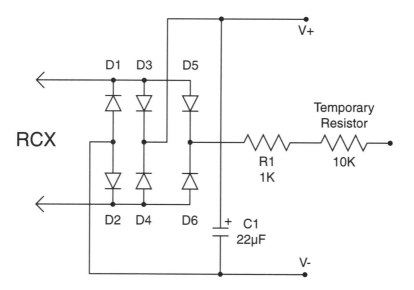

Figure 10-5. The sensor measurement circuit

The actual part is a small cylinder with four colored bands painted on it. The first three bands specify the value of the resistor and the fourth specifies the tolerance. You can find the color code printed on the resistor packaging or in many books on electronics. Unlike the diode or Aluminum electrolytic capacitor, it doesn't matter which way the resistor is oriented.

Rather than buying many individual value resistors from Radio Shack, I recommend buying one of their 5% ¼W carbon-film assortments (RS#271-308 or 271-312). You can use resistors that are more accurate, such as 1%, but for these circuits we really don't need them. A 10K Ohm resistor will be used to test the circuit and must be later removed.

It is probably not obvious why this circuit works, but it is really quite simple. Remember D3 and D4 are responsible for the positive side of the power supply. You will notice that diodes D5 and D6 are oriented the same way as D3 and D4 in the power circuit. When the RCX applied power for the sensor, capacitor C1 charged up to around 7 V. When the RCX goes to read the sensor, it only applies 5 V. Because C1 has a higher voltage than 5 V, the electricity would like to flow back into the RCX. It can't, because the diodes D3 and D4 are both pointing in the wrong direction. However, either D5 or D6 can conduct, and the RCX reads the sensor measurement through them and through R1.

Assemble the sensor measurement circuit by looking at Figure 10-6 and following along the part placements in Table 10-2. Make sure you orient diodes D5 and D6 properly.

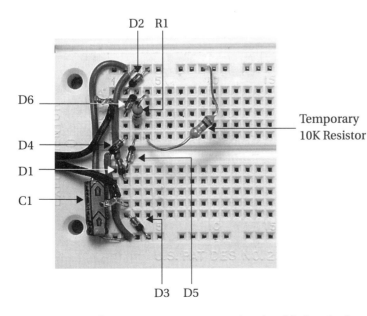

Figure 10-6. The sensor measurement circuit added to the breadboard

Table 10-2. Sensor Measurement Part Placement

PART	COLUMN	ROW
D5 stripe 1N4148	3	E
D5 plain	2	F
D6 stripe1N4148	3	A
D6 plain	2	C
R1 - 1K brown-black-red-gold	3	D
R1	4	A
10K brown-black-orange-gold	4	E
10K	9	X

Turn on the RCX and press the **View** button to see the value read from your partially built sensor. It should be near 61. When you move the 10K Ohm resistor lead from hole 9X to 9Y, the reading should drop to near 0. If this is not what you get, check the direction of the diodes and their placement. After the circuit checks out, remove the 10K Ohm resistor. With a few more parts we can build our first powered sensor.

Optointerrupter Sensor

An *optointerrupter* works by shining light across a short opening to a light detector. If something blocks the path of the light, the detector will register it. This can be used to sense the presence of small objects. The circuit diagram for the optointerrupter is shown in Figure 10-7. A light emitting diode (LED) will be used for the light source and our old friend from Chapter 9, the Cadmium Sulfide (CdS) photocell, will be the photo detector. Ideally the LED should be a bright yellow or green type with a narrow (12°) view angle. This means it will project the light in a narrow beam rather than broad illumination. Many other types of LEDs will work, but they should not be rated for a current greater than 30 mA.

The symbol for an LED is just like the 1N4148 diode, with the addition of two arrows that symbolize the light emitting from the part. In place of the painted stripe on the diode, the LED has one side flat to indicate which lead has the line in the circuit. The LED needs a resistor R2 in series with it to limit the amount of electric current that will flow through it. Photocells are drawn like a resistor with a line through it to symbolize that light can cause the device to change in resistance.

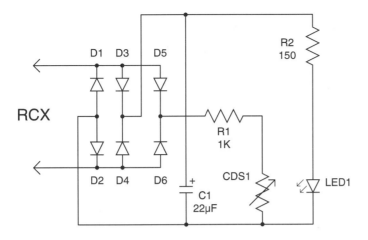

Figure 10-7. Optointerrupter sensor circuit diagram

Add the parts to the breadboard as pictured in Figure 10-8 and listed in Table 10-3. Make sure the CdS photocell and the LED are physically pointed at each other with a small gap between them. To test the completed circuit you will need to shield the photocell from all other light or test it in darkened room. First, the LED should be shining fairly brightly. With nothing blocking the light from hitting the photocell the RCX should read 100. If you slip a thick piece of cardboard between the LED and photocell the reading should drop to less than 90.

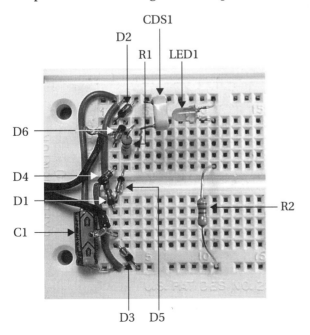

Figure 10-8. Optointerrupter sensor circuit on the breadboard

Table 10-3. Optointerrupter Sensor Part Placement Table

PART	COLUMN	ROW
R2 - 150 brown-green-brown-gold	11	Y
R2	11	E
LED1 Round	11	A
LED1 Flat	11	X
CDS1	4	D
CDS1	5	X

At this point, you may want to commit your optointerrupter to a printed circuit board. However, I suggest you work through the other sensor projects first because they reuse many of the parts you have already placed. You can always rebuild the circuit and transfer it later. If you are moving on, remove R2, LED1, and CDS1, and get ready to add an integrated circuit.

Buffer Circuit

The LM324N is an integrated circuit (IC) with four small amplifiers inside. These amplifiers are a special type called *operational amplifiers.* Explaining the theory behind them is well beyond the scope of this book, but you don't need to fully understand them to use them. While we don't need four amplifiers, the LM324N is the only amplifier Radio Shack retail stores sell that can operate at low power supply voltages—it just happens to have four. All four amplifiers share the same power supply connections on pins 4 and 11.

The symbol for one of the LM324N amplifiers is a triangle with the pin numbers and various internal connections marked like the one in the buffer circuit diagram Figure 10-9. The amplifier output is the connection at the point of the triangle, while the two inputs to the amplifier are marked + and – on the back of the triangle. A signal can be fed into either input, but the polarity of the output signal will be inverted by the - input and not inverted by the + input. The power supply connections are marked V+ and V–. The part number of the LM324N in the circuit is U1.

The N in the LM324N means it comes in a 14-pin dual inline package (DIP). The pins are numbered starting with the pin closest to the dot or dimple in the lower left corner of the part. Some parts are not marked with a dot and have a notch in the center of the left end. The pin numbers increase counterclockwise to the upper left corner, which is pin 14 as seen in Figure 10-10. The pins on the LM324N may be bent outward slightly and you should not try to insert the part into the breadboard without first bending the pins inward to make them stand straight. Lay the

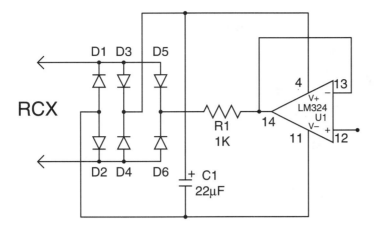

Figure 10-9. The buffer circuit

IC on one of the rows of pins and gently roll it to bend the lower pins into line. Turn the IC over and bend the pins on the other side as well. Inserting the LM324N into the breadboard may take a little pressure, but don't force it. Watch that some of the pins do not get bent under the part.

Figure 10-10. LM324N quad operational amplifier

Pin 1 should be in location 4F as shown in Figure 10-11. Pin 14 will then be in location 4E with one end of R1 already in column 4. If you need to remove the IC, insert a small screwdriver blade into the slot that runs along the middle of the breadboard and gently lever the IC out. Three short pieces of hookup wire, called jumpers, are needed to make the rest of the connections given in Table 10-4. A temporary wire will be connected for testing the circuit only.

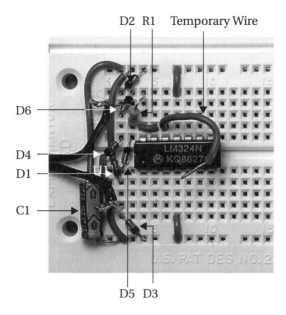

Figure 10-11. Buffer circuit on the breadboard

Table 10-4. Buffer Part Placement Table

PART	COLUMN	ROW
U1 - Pin1 LM324N	4	F
Jumper 1	7	X
Jumper 1	7	A
Jumper 2	7	J
Jumper 2	7	Y
Jumper 3	4	D
Jumper 3	5	D
Temporary Wire	6	D
Temporary Wire	8	X

With the RCX turned on and with the display showing the reading from the partially built sensor, make the following tests:

Attach the free end of the temporary wire to location 8X. The display should read between 90 and 100. Now attach the free end to 8Y. The display should now read between 0 and 10. If you don't get these readings, check that the LM324N has pin 1 in the correct location and recheck the jumpers.

Buffered Voltage Input

At this point, your partially built powered sensor has many practical applications. Any small, positive signal can be connected to the + input through the buffer circuit to the RCX. This particular configuration doesn't amplify the signal, but it does separate the signal source from the RCX. Many laboratory instruments and sensing devices have voltage outputs that are not strong enough to be input directly to the RCX and this circuit provides the needed buffer. The plot in Figure 10-12 shows the RCX reading for different input voltages. The performance of the circuit is partly limited by the RCX battery condition, as can be seen in the plot.

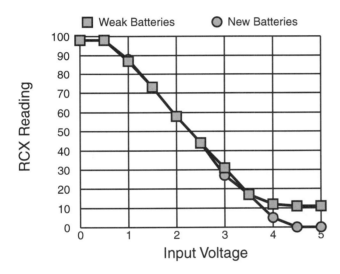

Figure 10-12. Input voltage and RCX reading with buffer circuit

Amplifier Circuit

A more functional use of the LM324N is to amplify input to the signal. This can be accomplished by using two resistors: R2 and R3. In this configuration, the op amp will amplify voltages on the + input by a factor of 1+R2/R3. This factor is called the *gain* of the amplifier and simply means that under normal conditions the voltage of the output pin will be equal to the voltage on the input multiplied by the gain. For this circuit, the gain is 1 + 10 / 4.7 = 3.13. The input signal can now be three times smaller and still create a significant reading on the RCX. Figure 10-13 illustrates an amplifier circuit diagram.

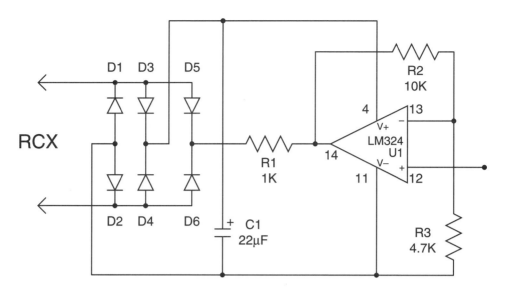

Figure 10-13. An amplifier circuit diagram

To build the circuit we need to remove Jumper 3 from U1 pins 13 and 14. It is replaced with resistor R2. Resistor R3 is also connected to U1 pin 13 and to the negative power supply at the top. Follow Figure 10-14 and Table 10-5 to insert the parts correctly.

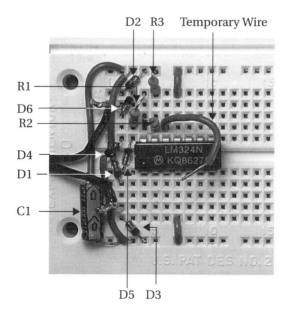

Figure 10-14. Amplifier circuit on the breadboard

Table 10-5. Amplifier Part Placement Table

PART	COLUMN	ROW
R2 -10K brown-black-orange-gold	4	D
R2	5	D
R3 - 4.7K yellow-violet-red-gold	5	A
R3	5	X

Amplified Voltage Input

The plot in Figure 10-15 shows how sensitive the circuit is now that it has gain. This can be useful for sensors that have small signal outputs. The effect of low batteries can be seen in the plot. As the sensor power supply drops, the performance of the LM324N also suffers.

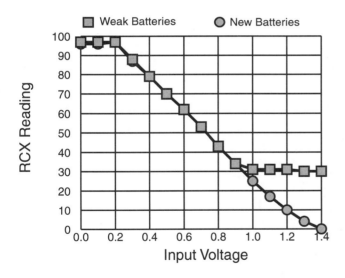

Figure 10-15. Input voltage and RCX reading with amplifier circuit

Differential Light Sensor

It is tricky to track a light source with a single light sensor. With two sensors, it is easy to determine which sensor is receiving more light and to move in that direction. The problem with this method is that the RCX has only three inputs, and you would only have one left to keep track of everything else. What we need is an intelligent light sensor, one that only provides the difference between the two light sensors.

We need only a few new parts to build the differential light sensor shown in Figure 10-16. First, you need to remove the temporary wire. Next, add R4, D8, D9, and the two CdS sensors. Try to use two identical CdS sensors and do not trim the length of their leads. Even ones that look similar may have different resistance with the same amount of light. You will need to slip long pieces of insulation stripped from hookup wire over the leads to prevent them from touching and shorting out. Follow Figure 10-17 and Table 10-6 for part placement to construct the differential light sensor.

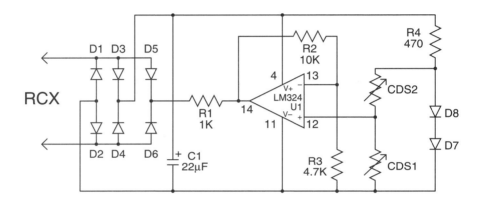

Figure 10-16. Differential light sensor circuit diagram

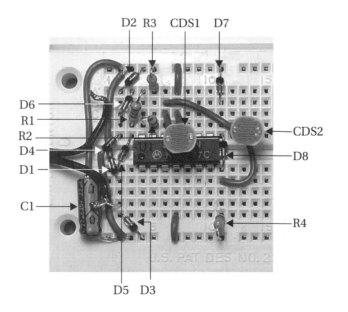

Figure 10-17. Differential light sensor on the breadboard

Table 10-6. Differential Light Sensor Part Placement

PART	COLUMN	ROW
R4 - 470 yellow-violet-brown-gold	11	J
R4	11	Y
D7 Stripe 1N4148	11	X
D7 Plain	11	B
D8 Stripe 1N4148	11	E
D8 Plain	11	F
CDS1	6	C
CDS1	7	C
CDS2	6	B
CDS2	11	G

The voltage on the + input is determined by the two CdS photocells. If there is equal light falling on the photocells, they will have equal resistance and the voltage across them will be equally split. However, if more light is falling on one or the other photocell, the voltage will be pulled up or down accordingly.

Resistor R4 and diodes D7 and D8 are used to create a constant voltage for the photocells to share. Diodes are like one-way valves for electricity, but they don't perform the task perfectly. In the process of passing the electricity, they throw away about 0.7 V. By putting two diodes in series, we end up with 1.4 V for the photocells to share. The remaining power supply voltage is thrown away in resistor R4.

If the two photocells see the same light, the voltage on the + input will be ½ of 1.4 V or 0.7 V. This 0.7 V will be amplified by the LM324N by a factor of 3.13 to become 2.2 V. The RCX should read around 50. The reading will move up or down from 50 depending on which photocell gets more light.

After constructing the circuit on the breadboard, plug it back onto the RCX and turn on the RCX. Check that the voltage on the plain end of D8 is about 1.4 V. Push the **View** button to see the reading from the sensor. With normal room light, the reading should be between 40 and 60. Overall light levels shouldn't affect the reading much, but as you cover CDS1 the value should go way down, and as you cover CDS2 the value should go way up. Due to variations in the CdS photocells and other components, the center value could be different. If your circuit works but you don't get 50, try swapping the CdS photocells.

You may want to commit your differential light sensor to a printed circuit board. However, I suggest you work through the last sensor project first because it reuses many of the parts you have already placed. You can always rebuild the circuit and transfer it later. If you are moving on, remove R2, R3, R4, D7, D8, CDS1, and CDS2, and get ready to give your RCX an ear.

Sound Sensor

A sound sensor for the RCX needs to do more than just interconnect a microphone. First, we need a lot of amplification because the output of a microphone is tiny compared to the voltages the RCX measures. Second, we don't really want to measure the individual waves of the sound—we want to measure the overall amplitude of the sound. For example, when you clap your hands, the sound sensor should indicate the presence of a single loud noise.

The sound sensor circuit makes use of two of the LM324N amplifiers. The first one is the buffer circuit you have already seen earlier in this chapter. The second acts as a high gain amplifier that takes the tiny signal from the microphone and makes it big enough for the RCX to measure. Resistors R4 and R3 set the gain of the amplifier close to 50. Resistor R6 is the power supply resistor for the microphone MIC. Capacitor C3 couples the microphone to the amplifier, while R5 keeps the amplifier + input near 0 V. Diode D7, capacitor C2, and resistor R2 make up a circuit that will only detect the peaks of the sound waves. Figure 10-18 illustrates the circuit diagram for the sound sensor.

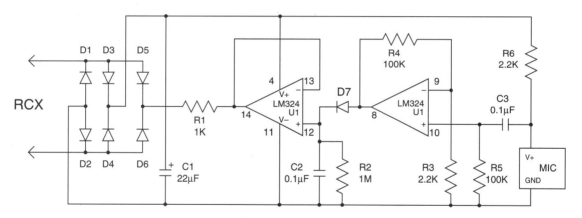

Figure 10-18. Sound sensor circuit diagram

Capacitors C2 and C3 are very different than capacitor C1. They are monolithic or ceramic s and look like small pancakes with two wires coming out of the edge. They have significantly less capacity than C1, and if C1 were an AA battery then these would be watch batteries. Unlike C1, they don't care which polarity the voltage is applied to them so they don't need the + indication on their symbol.

The microphone MIC is an electret condenser microphone. It contains a small amplifier of its own, and it gets power by feeding a voltage through resistor R6. The method is very similar to the RCX passive sensor interface. The output signal appears as a small voltage variation on the resistor, which must be coupled through a capacitor C3 to be further amplified. Power must be applied to the microphone in the correct polarity. You will notice that the negative lead of the microphone element connects to the metal body of the microphone.

Assemble the sound sensor circuit by looking at Figure 10-19 and following along the part placements in Table 10-7. Make sure you properly orient diode D7 and the microphone leads.

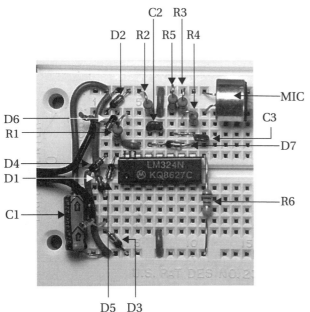

Figure 10-19. Sound sensor on the breadboard

Table 10-7. Sound Sensor Part Placement Table

PART	COLUMN	ROW
Jumper 3	4	D
Jumper 3	5	D
R2 - 1M brown-black-green-gold	5	X
R2	6	A
R3 - 2.2K red-red-red-gold	9	X
R3	9	A
R4 - 100K brown-black-yellow-gold	9	B
R4	10	B

Table 10-7. Sound Sensor Part Placement Table (Continued)

PART	COLUMN	ROW
R5 - 100K brown-black-yellow-gold	8	X
R5	8	A
R6 - 2.2K red-red-red-gold	11	Y
R6	11	E
C2 - 0.1µF	6	C
C2	7	C
C3 - 0.1µF	11	C
C3	8	C
MIC +	11	A
MIC -	11	X
D7 Stripe 1N4148	6	D
D7 Plain	10	D

It will be easier to understand how the circuit works with a few illustrations. Figure 10-20 shows the signals inside the circuit over a very short period of time. Each vertical division is only $1/1000$-second or 1 ms wide. At that speed, each wave of a 1 kHz signal is visible. The first trace shows that the microphone converts the sound wave into a small electronic wave with amplitude of only $1/10$ volt (or 100 mV). Actually, this signal is measured at the input to the amplifier at pin 10.

The output of the amplifier is in the middle trace. The first thing you will notice is that the scale is in volts because the signal is now about fifty times bigger. You might also notice that the output does not go negative even when the input signal is telling it to. That is because there is only a single, positive power supply in the sensor. So the signal out of the amplifier is larger and only represents the positive part of the original sound wave.

The last trace shows how the peak detector made from C2, R2, and D7 works. Diode D7 charges C2 whenever the output voltage of the amplifier is higher than the voltage C2 already has. However, when the output voltage is less, the diode will not let electrical current flow out of C2 and it holds the voltage. Only R2 slowly discharges C2. The buffer amplifier part of the circuit prevents the RCX measurement voltages from messing up the peak detector.

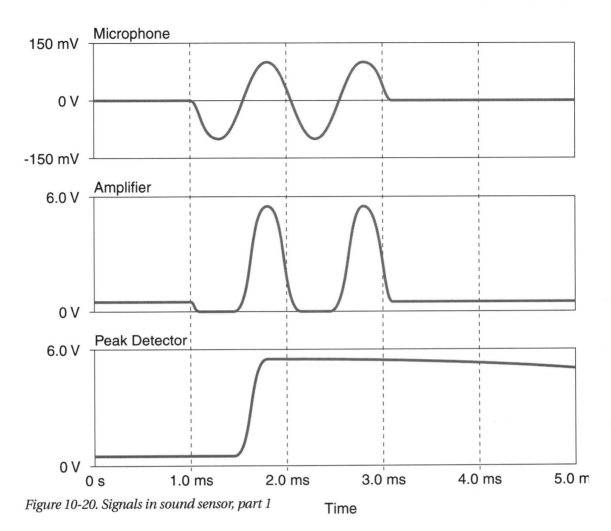

Figure 10-20. Signals in sound sensor, part 1

Figure 10-21 shows signals on a longer timescale. The width of the whole plot is half a second. Near time zero, the microphone picks up a loud clap. It is amplified and the peak detector value jumps up. After the clap sound is over, the peak detector slowly returns to 0 V. The RCX reads 0 V as a number near 100 and 5 V as a number near 0. When things are quiet, the RCX will read near 100 and when a loud sound is heard, the value will momentarily drop proportionally to the loudness of the sound.

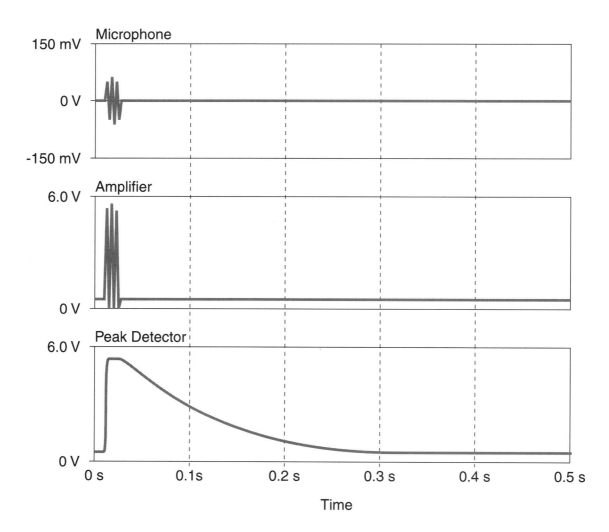

Figure 10-21. Signals in sound sensor part 2

Printed Circuit Board

The Global Specialties™ Experimenter PC Board (see Figure 10-22) matches the layout of the electronic breadboard exactly. It has the same row and column markings as the breadboard so it should be easy to transfer the parts from the breadboard to the PC board. The only problem with the PC board is that it is too long. We only need ten columns of connections to make even the most complex project in this book. This means that one Experimenter PC Board could be the source for four powered sensors.

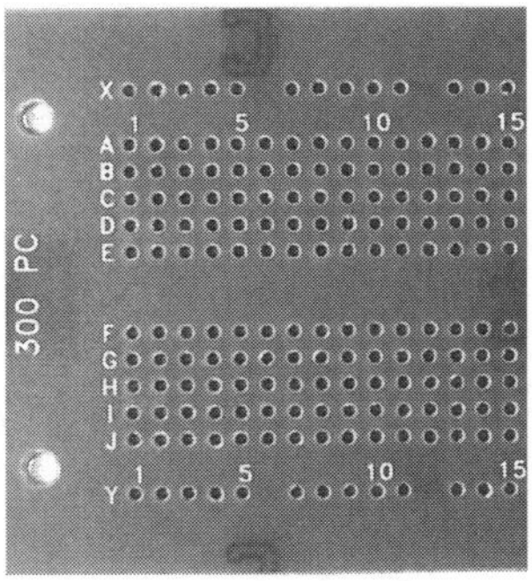

   Cutting the PC board (see Figure 10-23) is easier than you might think. A straightedge ruler and a sharp knife are all that is required. Score the board by creating a shallow groove in the top and bottom of the board along a column of holes where you want to cut it. Once the board has been scored, it will snap by bending it at the groove.

   Start by laying the straightedge ruler along column 1 of the top of PC board. Take a sharp knife and run it along the straightedge the entire width of the board. The knife will bump along from hole to hole. At first don't use very much pressure, just keep running the knife along the same path over and over until a groove develops. It usually takes about ten passes. Repeat the process on the bottom side of the board.

   Bracing your thumbs at the groove, gently bend the board down on both sides with your fingers. It should snap with a reasonable amount of force (see Figure 10-24). If it doesn't snap, continue to cut at the grooves to make them a little deeper and try again. Repeat the process cutting along column 12. You will be left with a small PC board with ten columns of holes.

   We skipped column 1 when putting the parts on the breadboard. That column is now the jagged edge of your PC board. As you cut away additional small PC boards you will notice that the printed column numbers won't match anymore. The original painted numbers are easily scratched off and you can remark

Figure 10-22. Close-up of the left end of the experimenter 300PC board

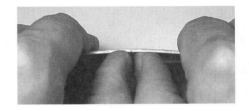

Figure 10-23. Cutting grooves in the PC board

Figure 10-24. Snapping the PC board at the groove

them with permanent marker. Figure 10-25 shows what the bottom of the PC board should look like.

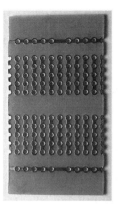

Figure 10-25. The finished bottom of a small PC board

Soldering

Soldering the parts to the PC board is perhaps the scariest part of building homebrew sensors. It requires a certain amount of skill, but after a few connections you'll find that it really isn't difficult. Making good solder connections requires following a few basic rules:

- The soldering iron should be a 25 to 40 watt pencil type with a $^1/_8$ to $^3/_{16}$ inch chisel or cone-shaped tip.

- Always wait at least five minutes for the soldering iron to come up to temperature.

- The solder should be rosin core 60/40 Tin-Lead content with a .062-inch diameter. NEVER use acid core or the type used for plumbing.

> **CAUTION** *Lead is a poison and has been proven to cause health problems especially for young children. Never leave solder around where people may handle or eat it.*

- When first using a new tip, coat the tip with a good coat of solder and wipe off the excess with a damp sponge.

- The soldering iron must be kept clean by quickly wiping it on a damp sponge each time before making a connection.

CAUTION *Remember to unplug the soldering iron when you're finished using it.*

The first step in soldering a component to the PC board is to make absolutely sure that you have the component leads in the right holes and that the part is properly oriented (see Figure 10-26). If you built the circuit on the breadboard first, it is a simple matter of pulling parts off the breadboard and placing them one by one onto the PC board. Push leads of a component through the holes and spread the leads apart to keep the component from falling out when you turn the PC board over to solder. You can work one part at a time but the job will go faster if you place several parts close together at the same time and then solder.

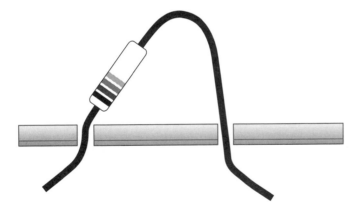

Figure 10-26. Placement of the component on the PC board

To make a solder joint, touch the soldering iron tip to both the PC board copper pad and the component wire at the same time and allow the connection to heat for a second (see Figure 10-27).

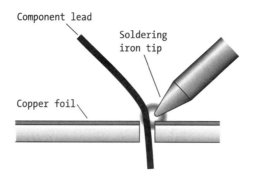

Component lead

Soldering
iron tip

Copper foil

Figure 10-27. The heating connection

Now bring the solder to the hot connection, not the iron tip, and allow enough solder to flow around the connection (see Figure 10-28). You might think that the high temperature of soldering would instantly damage the components. However, they are designed to tolerate the heat for awhile and you should not be afraid to take the time to make a good joint.

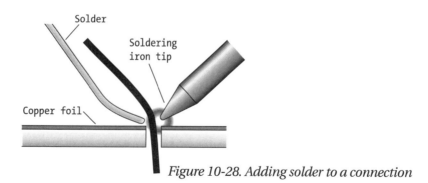

Solder

Soldering
iron tip

Copper foil

Figure 10-28. Adding solder to a connection

Remove the solder and iron and allow the connection to cool for a few seconds before you move anything (see Figure 10-29). The solder should be shiny and look almost wet when it first cools.

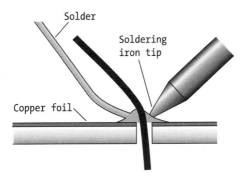

Figure 10-29. Let solder flow around the connection.

Poor solder joints, such as those shown in Figure 10-30, are usually the result of insufficiently heating the joint. The joint may have voids, like the first example, or have a blob-like appearance, as in the second example. Bad joints may also look dull. Just reheat the joint and add solder if necessary.

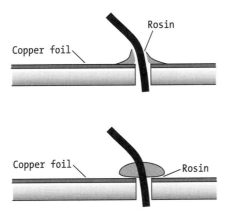

Figure 10-30. Examples of bad solder joints

Cut off the excess component lead close to the connection with diagonal cutters as shown in Figure 10-31.

NOTE   *Clip the leads so the ends will not fly into your eyes.*

Figure 10-31. Cut excess component lead flush with the joint.

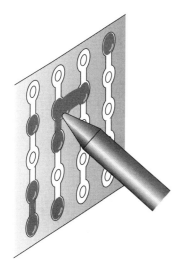

Figure 10-32. How to remove a solder bridge

Solder bridges are a common problem when soldering this type of PC board. A little too much solder gets into the joint and flows over onto the next trace. Don't panic! Hold the PC board vertically in one hand and bring the soldering iron tip up to the bridge from below. The excess solder should flow back onto the tip where you can wipe it off on the damp sponge. Desoldering tools are available that can be used to vacuum practically all the solder from a joint. Figure 10-32 shows you how to get rid of a solder bridge.

Another problem is solder covering a hole where you need to insert a part. Usually a technique similar to the bridge removal will work to clear the hole. Just coax the solder down the copper track away from the blocked hole with the soldering iron. You can also melt the solder while pushing the component lead into the hole. Because all of the holes in a column are connected anyway, you can relocate a part into a nearby hole (within the same column) that is not blocked. There is also a product called *desoldering braid* that, when heated along with the solder, will wick up extra solder.

Figure 10-33 shows how the sound sensor should look after it has been constructed on the PC board. Because many of the parts in the power circuit are close together, they have had insulation added to their leads. You may also notice that the unused pins of the LM324N have not been soldered at all. You may solder these pins if you want to, but this step is unnecessary and you are more likely to create solder bridges.

Figure 10-33. The sound circuit on a PC board

Packaging

Putting your sensor into an enclosure is not absolutely necessary, but this procedure does give the sensor a finished appearance and makes it less prone to damage. There are many ways to enclose your sensor. The simplest is to build a small box out of LEGO beams and plates. Some LEGO parts are large and hollow like the 9 V battery box (S&H#5391), which allows the entire sensor to be put inside with little modification. Another method that often horrifies LEGO fanatics is to cut, hollow out, and glue together LEGO bricks to accommodate the sensor electronics. Finally, the sensor can be enclosed in any small box that happens to be the right size and then fastened to a LEGO plate with glue, double-sided tape, or rubber bands.

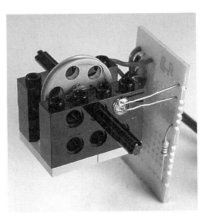

The packaging example shown in Figure 10-34 is a minimalist approach. A rotation detector has been built using the optointerrupter. The LED fits nicely into the hole of a TECHNIC beam, and the CdS photocell can be glued to another beam with epoxy. A one-stud wide space between the LED and photocell will accommodate the pulley element. Each time a hole

Figure 10-34. The Optointerrupter built with LEGO parts

comes into alignment with the LED and photocell, the RCX will read near 100, but the RCX reads near 0 when the spoke blocks the light.

Figure 10-35 is an example of how to build boxes out of LEGO bricks. A 4 x 6-stud box was made from LEGO beams, which provided holes for the cord and the CdS photocells to pass through. The nose is not just cosmetic. It will help to exaggerate the difference in light striking the two photocells. The top and bottom are made up of 4×6 plates while the smile piece adds a bit of whimsy to the project. Figure 10-36 is an inside view of the sensor.

Figure 10-35. Differential light sensor mounted in a LEGO box

Figure 10-36. The inside of a LEGO box from above

One easily obtained enclosure is the Tic Tac® breath mints candy box shown in Figure 10-37. They are available at most convenience store checkout counters. The PC board will easily fit inside and the lid has a large hole for the LEGO connector wire to fit through. The CdS photocells can see through the clear plastic, and the microphone can hear out of the hole in the lid. You don't need to remove the original label entirely, simply cut around the top so you can pull the lid off to fit the sensor inside.

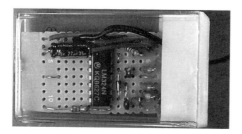

Figure 10-37. The sound sensor in a Tic Tac® box

Going Further

You can find practically everything known about homebrew RCX sensors on my Web page at http://www.plazaearth.com/usr/gasperi/lego.htm. I've been documenting the homebrew sensors that I have developed, as well as providing links to many other experimenter's projects since the LEGO Mindstorms kit first came out in October 1998. This information is the result of the many individuals working cooperatively over the Internet through the LUGNET newsgroup and e-mail. There is useful information about the LEGO sensors there as well. You will find that the topics are not covered in as much detail as this book, but after working through these two chapters, you should be able to grasp the concepts more easily.

Bill of Materials for Powered Sensors

In Tables 10-8 through 10-13 we have compiled lists of all of the components you need to make the various projects in this chapter. Part numbers for both Radio Shack and Mouser Electronics are given along with descriptions, which should allow you to locate equivalent parts from other suppliers.

Table 10-8. All Projects

PART DESCRIPTION	COMPONENT VALUE	RADIO SHACK	MOUSER ELECTRONICS
Resistor Assortment	All the resistors needed for all the projects in one package.	271-308 or 271-312	Buy Individual Resistors
Breadboard	Solderless Electronic Breadboard from Global Specialties.	276-175 or 276-174	510-103-1350 or 510-103-2304
PC Board	Experimenter PC Board from Global Specialties.	276-170	510-EXP-300PC
Hookup Wire	#22 Gauge Solid Insulated	278-1221	Purchase Locally
Test Resistor	10K Ohm 5% ¼W	271-1335	291-10K
LEGO Wire	Longer Type		

Table 10-9. Optointerrupter Sensor

PART NUMBER	COMPONENT VALUE	RADIO SHACK	MOUSER ELECTRONICS
D1 - D6	1N4148 or 1N914 Switching Diode	276-1122 or 276-1620	625-1N4148
C1	22µF Aluminum Electrolytic rated at least 16V	272-1014 or 272-1026	140-XAL16V22
R1	1K Ohm 5% ¼W	276-1321	291-1K
R2	150 Ohm 5% ¼W	271-1312	291-150
CDS1	Cadmium Sulfide Photocell	276-1657	338-76C348 or 338-54C348
LED1	Bright Yellow or Green, 12 Degree View Angle LED	276-301 or 276-304	592-SLA580MT3

Table 10-10. Buffered Voltage Input

PART NUMBER	COMPONENT VALUE	RADIO SHACK	MOUSER ELECTRONICS
D1 - D6	1N4148 or 1N914 Switching Diode	276-1122 or 276-1620	625-1N4148
C1	22µF Aluminum Electrolytic rated at least 16V	272-1014 or 272-1026	140-XAL16V22
R1	1K Ohm 5% ¼W	276-1321	291-1K
U1	LM324N Quad Opamp	276-1711	511-LM324N

Table 10-11. Amplified Voltage Input

PART NUMBER	COMPONENT VALUE	RADIO SHACK	MOUSER ELECTRONICS
D1 - D6	1N4148 or 1N914 Switching Diode	276-1122 or 276-1620	625-1N4148
C1	22µF Aluminum Electrolytic rated at least 16V	272-1014 or 272-1026	140-XAL16V22
R1	1K Ohm 5% ¼W	276-1321	291-1K
R2	10K Ohm 5% ¼W	271-1335	291-10K
R3	4.7K Ohm 5% ¼W	271-1330	291-4.7K
U1	LM324N Quad Opamp	276-1711	511-LM324N

Table 10-12. Differential Light Sensor

PART NUMBER	COMPONENT VALUE	RADIO SHACK	MOUSER ELECTRONICS
D1 - D8	1N4148 or 1N914 Switching Diode	276-1122 or 276-1620	625-1N4148
C1	22µF Aluminum Electrolytic rated at least 16V	272-1014 or 272-1026	140-XAL16V22
R1	1K Ohm 5% ¼W	276-1321	291-1K
R2	10K Ohm 5% ¼W	271-1335	291-10K
R3	4.7K Ohm 5% ¼W	271-1330	291-4.7K
R4	470 Ohm 5% ¼W	271-1317	291-470
CDS1 & CDS2	Cadmium Sulfide Photocell	276-1657	338-76C348 or 338-54C348
U1	LM324N Quad Opamp	276-1711	511-LM324N

Table 10-13. Sound Sensor

PART NUMBER	COMPONENT VALUE	RADIO SHACK	MOUSER ELECTRONICS
D1 - D7	1N4148 or 1N914 Switching Diode	276-1122 or 276-1620	625-1N4148
C1	22µF Aluminum Electrolytic rated at least 16V	272-1014 or 272-1026	140-XAL16V22
R1	1K Ohm 5% ¼W	276-1321	291-1K
R2	1MOhm 5% ¼W	271-1356	291-1M
R3 & R6	2.2K Ohm 5% ¼W	271-1325	291-2.2K
R4 & R5	100K Ohm 5% ¼W	271-1347	291-100K
C2 & C3	0.1 µF 50V Monolithic or Ceramic Capacitor	272-109 or 271-135	581-UDZ104K1
MIC	Electret Condenser Microphone Element Two Wire Type	270-090	252LM049
U1	LM324N Quad Opamp	276-1711	511-LM324N

Conclusion

Even the simplest powered sensors require more effort than any passive sensor. However, it is worth it to be able to build sensors that can perform more complex functions. This chapter is only the starting point for this subject. The general purpose interfaces can be used to create sensors that measure just about anything you can think of. Sensors for air pressure, magnetic field direction, and object distance have already been built and used in LEGO robots.

APPENDIX A

Internet Resources

THERE IS A WEALTH of Internet resources for LEGO MINDSTORMS. A brief list of a few such Web sites is presented below. Since the printed page moves somewhat slower than the Internet, some of the links below may have changed or moved by the time you read this.

Your first stop should be this book's own page on the Apress Web site on `http://www.apress.com`. Here you will find additional information about the topics and robots in this book including links to other MINDSTORMS sites. All of the sample programs in the book can also be downloaded from this site.

General Information

`http://www.legomindstorms.com`: The official LEGO MINDSTORMS site. On it you will find tips from LEGO's master builders, product announcements, creations from other MINDSTORMS users, and several discussion groups.

`http://www.lugnet.com`: LUGNET is a fixture in the online LEGO community that combines extensive reference material with discussion groups on a variety of LEGO-related topics. The robotics discussion group (and its subgroups) are of particular interest to MINDSTORMS users.

`http://www.crynwr.com/lego-robotics`: A repository for information and links about the internal operation of the RCX, alternative development tools, creating custom sensors, and many other advanced topics.

NQC

`http://www.enteract.com/~dbaum/nqc`: The homepage for NQC. This site contains the latest version of NQC, along with associated documentation, links to other NQC sites, and interesting robots powered by NQC.

`http://www.cs.uu.nl/people/markov/lego`: The homepage for RcxCC, an easy-to-use development environment based on NQC.

`http://www.lugnet.com/robotics/rcx/nqc/`: An area of LUGNET dedicated to discussion of NQC. This is the best place to ask questions about NQC.

pbForth

`http://www.hempeldesigngroup.com/lego/pbForth`: The homepage for pbForth. Visit this site to download the latest version of pbForth and related documentation.

`http://www.lugnet.com/robotics/rcx/pbforth/`: Area of LUGNET dedicated to discussion of pbForth. This is the best place to ask questions about pbForth.

`http://www.forth.org`: A good place to look for general Forth resources.

`http://www.forth.com`: A commercial Forth vendor's site with a nice history of Forth.

`ftp://ftp.taygeta.com/pub/Forth/Literature/rtfv5.pdf`: A shareware book on Forth details.

LegOS

`http://legOS.sourceforge.net`: The current home for legOS. This site includes the latest source tree (via anonymous CVS), documentation, and archived releases of legOS and related tools.

`http://www.noga.de/legOS`: Markus Noga's original legOS site. As of version 0.2.4, development and maintenance have been migrated to the source-forge site listed above.

`http://www.lugnet.com/robotics/rcx/legos/`: An area of LUGNET dedicated to discussion of legOS. This is the best place to ask questions about legOS.

Homebrew Sensors

`http://www.plazaearth.com/usr/gasperi/lego.htm`: The Homebrew sensors homepage. This site contains a wealth of information about how to build sensors.

Suppliers

LEGO Shop-At-Home is a mail-order source for extra LEGO parts. They do not presently have a Web site. Orders and catalog requests may be placed by calling (800) 453-4652.

`http://www.pitsco-legodacta.com`: The homepage for Pitsco LEGO Dacta, the U.S. distributor for LEGO's educational line of products, and a good source for extra MINDSTORMS parts. Phone: (800) 362-4308.

`http://www.radioshack.com`: The homepage for Radio Shack, a good source for the parts used in this book's homebrew sensor projects. Phone: (800) 843-7422.

`http://www.mouser.com`: The homepage for Mouser Electronics, another source for homebrew sensor parts. Phone: (800) 346-6873.

`http://www.digikey.com`: The homepage for Digi-Key, another source for homebrew sensor parts. Phone: (800) 344-4539.

`http://www.jameco.com`: The homepage for Jameco Electronics, another source for homebrew sensor parts. Phone: (800) 831-4242.

NQC API Reference

THE NQC API CONSISTS OF functions, values, and constants. A function is something that can be called as a statement and generally causes some action to be taken. A value is something that gets evaluated by the program and can be used in a calculation, a condition, or an argument to a function. A constant is a symbolic name of a certain number that has a special meaning. In the following example, On() is a function, Timer(0) is a value, and OUT_A is a constant.

```
if (Timer(0) > 10)
    On(OUT_A);
```

The NQC API contains many different functions, values, and constants, which are summarized below by category (such as "sensors" "outputs," etcetera). NQC presently understands four different targets: the original RCX, CyberMaster, Scout, and RCX 2.0 (an RCX running the 2.0 firmware). Since some calls are only available on certain targets, the API reference also includes a column that specifies which target(s) the API is valid for. The codes are as follows:

R: RCX (original or 2.0)

C: CyberMaster

S: Scout

R2: RCX 2.0

Sensors

This portion of the API handles the configuration and reading of sensors. Note that in some cases a sensor's value can be read several different ways (for example, a raw value, a boolean value, or a processed value).

FUNCTION	DESCRIPTION	TARGETS
SetSensor(sensor, config)	set sensor's type and mode	R
SetSensorType(sensor, type)	set sensor's type	R
SetSensorMode(sensor, mode)	set sensor's mode	R,C

(Continued)

FUNCTION	DESCRIPTION	TARGETS
ClearSensor(sensor)	clear a sensor's value	all
CalibrateSensor()	calibrate the light sensor	S
SetSensorHysteresis(x)	set light sensor hysteresis	S
SetSensorLowerLimit(x)	set light sensor lower limit	S
SetSensorUpperLimit(x)	set light sensor upper limit	S

VALUE	DESCRIPTION (RANGE)	TARGETS
SensorValue(n)	sensor's current value (0-2)	all
SensorType(n)	sensor's type (0-2)	all
SensorMode(n)	sensor's mode (0-2)	R,C
SensorValueBool(n)	sensor's boolean value (0-2)	R
SensorValueRaw(n)	sensor's raw value (0-2)	R,S
SENSOR_1, SENSOR_2, SENSOR_3	alternatives for SensorValue(n)	all

CONSTANT	DESCRIPTION	TARGETS
SENSOR_MODE_RAW, SENSOR_MODE_BOOL, SENSOR_MODE_EDGE, SENSOR_MODE_PULSE, SENSOR_MODE_PERCENT	modes for SetSensorMode()	R,C
SENSOR_MODE_CELSIUS, SENSOR_MODE_FAHRENHEIT, SENSOR_MODE_ROTATION	modes for SetSensorMode()	R
SENSOR_TYPE_NONE, SENSOR_TYPE_TOUCH, SENSOR_TYPE_TEMPERATURE, SENSOR_TYPE_LIGHT, SENSOR_TYPE_ROTATION	types for SetSensorType()	R
SENSOR_TOUCH, SENSOR_LIGHT, SENSOR_ROTATION, SENSOR_CELSIUS, SENSOR_FAHRENHEIT, SENSOR_PULSE, SENSOR_EDGE	configurations for SetSensor()	R

Outputs

This section of the API handles control of the outputs, which generally are used for motors but can also be used for lights. In the case of the Scout, there is an additional function to control its built-in light.

FUNCTION	DESCRIPTION	TARGETS
SetOutput(outputs, mode)	set mode of outputs	all
SetDirection(outputs, dir)	set direction of outputs	all
SetPower(outputs, power)	set power level for outputs	all
On(outputs)	turn outputs on	all
Off(outputs)	turn outputs off	all
Float(outputs)	make outputs float	all
Fwd(outputs)	set outputs to forward direction	all
Rev(outputs)	set outputs to reverse direction	all
Toggle(outputs)	flip direction of outputs	all
OnFwd(outputs)	set outputs to forward and turn on	all
OnRev(outputs)	set outputs to reverse and turn on	all
OnFor(outputs, time)	turn on outputs for specified time	all
SetGlobalOutput(outputs, mode)	set global mode for outputs	R2,S
SetGlobalDirection(outputs, dir)	set global direction for outputs	R2,S
SetMaxPower(outputs, power)	set maximum power for outputs	R2,S

VALUE	DESCRIPTION (RANGE)	TARGETS
OutputStatus(n)	current status of output (0-2)	all
GlobalOutputStatus(n)	global status of output (0-2)	R2,S

CONSTANT	DESCRIPTION	TARGETS
OUT_A, OUT_B, OUT_C	outputs	all
OUT_ON, OUT_OFF, OUT_FLOAT	modes for SetOutput()	all
OUT_FWD, OUT_REV, OUT_TOGGLE	directions for SetDirection()	all
OUT_LOW, OUT_HALF, OUT_FULL	values for SetPower()	all

Sound

This section of the API handles the playing of sounds and notes.

FUNCTION	DESCRIPTION	TARGETS
PlaySound(sound)	play a system sound	all
PlayTone(freq, duration)	play a note of given frequency and duration. Scout and RCX2 can use a variable for frequency	all
MuteSound()	mute all sounds	R2,S
UnmuteSound()	unmute all sounds	R2,S
ClearSound()	clear any buffered sounds	R2
SelectSounds(group)	select a different group of sounds	S

CONSTANT	DESCRIPTION	TARGETS
SOUND_CLICK, SOUND_DOUBLE_BEEP, SOUND_DOWN, SOUND_UP, SOUND_LOW_BEEP, SOUND_FAST_UP	values for PlaySound()	all

Display

This section of the API manages the LCD display—it is only valid for the RCX.

FUNCTION	DESCRIPTION	TARGETS
SelectDisplay(mode)	select a display mode	R
SetUserDisplay(value, precision)	display any value	R2

CONSTANT	DESCRIPTION	TARGETS
DISPLAY_WATCH	display mode for system clock	R
DISPLAY_SENSOR_1, DISPLAY_SENSOR_2, DISPLAY_SENSOR_3	display modes for sensors	R
DISPLAY_OUT_A, DISPLAY_OUT_B, DISPLAY_OUT_C	display modes for outputs	R
DISPLAY_USER	mode for SelectDisplay()	R2

Communication

There are a variety of communication mechanisms including simple IR messages, the Visible Light Link (VLL), and general serial communication.

FUNCTION	DESCRIPTION	TARGETS
SendMessage(message)	send an IR message	R,S
ClearMessage()	clear the IR receive buffer	R,S
SetTxPower()	set power level for IR	R,S
SendVLL(value)	send value using VLL	S
InternalMessage(message)	place message in receive buffer	R2
SetSerialPacket(value)	set serial packet format	R2
SetSerialComm(value)	set serial communication settings	R2
SetSerialData(n, value)	set serial tx data (n = 0-15)	R2
SendSerial(first, count)	send specified serial data	R2

VALUE	DESCRIPTION (RANGE)	TARGETS
Message()	check IR receive buffer	R,S
SerialPacket()	serial packet format	R2
SerialComm()	serial communication settings	R2
SerialData(n)	serial tx data (0-15)	R2

CONSTANT	DESCRIPTION	TARGETS
TX_POWER_LO, TX_POWER_HI	values for SetTxPower()	R,S
SERIAL_PACKET_DEFAULT	raw packets	R2
SERIAL_PACKET_PREAMBLE	use preamble for packets	R2
SERIAL_PACKET_NEGATED	use negated bytes for packets	R2
SERIAL_PACKET_CHECKSUM	use checksum for packets	R2
SERIAL_PACKET_RCX	RCX-style packets	R2
SERIAL_COMM_DEFAULT	normal comm settings	R2
SERIAL_COMM_4800	use 4800 baud communication	R2
SERIAL_COMM_76KHZ	use 76KHz carrier	R2
SERIAL_COMM_DUTY25	use 25% duty cycle	R2

Timers and Counters

All of the targets contain timers with 100 ms resolution. The Scout features three of these timers while the other targets all have four. With the RCX 2, the timers can also be read with a 10 ms resolution. The Scout and RCX 2 also provide counters (the Scout has two while the RCX 2 has three). In the case of the RCX 2, these counters overlap with global storage locations 0, 1, and 2).

FUNCTION	DESCRIPTION	TARGETS
ClearTimer(timer)	clear a timer (timer = 0-3*)	all
SetTimer(timer, value)	set timer to value	R2
IncCounter(counter)	increment counter by 1	R2,S
DecCounter(counter)	decrement counter by 1	R2,S
ClearCounter(counter)	reset counter to 0	R2,S
Value	Description (Range)	Targets
Timer(n)	value of timer in 100ms (0-3*)	all
FastTimer(n)	value of timer in 10ms (0-3)	R2
Counter(n)	value of counter (0-2*)	R2,S

*Scout only has three timers (0-2) and two counters (0-1).

VALUE	DESCRIPTION (RANGE)	TARGETS
Timer(n)	value of timer in 100ms (0-3*)	all
FastTimer(n)	value of timer in 10ms (0-3)	R2
Counter(n)	value of counter (0-2*)	R2,S

*Scout only has three timers (0-2) and two counters (0-1).

Access Control

The Scout and the RCX 2 provide an access control mechanism, which is supported using NQC's acquire statement.

FUNCTION	DESCRIPTION	TARGETS
SetPriority(p)	set a task's priority	R2,S

CONSTANT	DESCRIPTION	TARGETS
ACQUIRE_OUT_A, ACQUIRE_OUT_B, ACQUIRE_OUT_C	acquire codes for outputs	R2,S
ACQUIRE_SOUND	acquire code for sound	R2,S
ACQUIRE_USER_1, ACQUIRE_USER_2, ACQUIRE_USER_3, ACQUIRE_USER_4	user definable acquire codes	R2

Events

The Scout and the RCX 2 support event monitoring. In the case of the Scout, the event codes are hardwired to certain stimuli (such as a timer or counter) and constants are provided for each event code. The limits at which the timers or counters should trigger an event are set using specific functions.

In the RCX 2, each event can be assigned to any event source and type. Parameters for the event, such as limits and hysteresis, may also be set. When configuring an RCX 2 event its number (between 0 and 15) is used. When specifying lists of events (such as for Event() or a monitor statement), each event number must be converted into an event mask, and the masks may then be added together. The macro EVENT_MASK() takes an event number and computes its event mask.

FUNCTION	DESCRIPTION	TARGETS
SetEvent(event, source, type)	configure event for specified source and type	R2
ClearEvent(event)	clear event configuration	R2
ClearAllEvents()	clear configuration of all events	R2
CalibrateEvent(event, low, high, hyst)	calibrate event	R2
Event(events)	post specified events	R2,S
SetLowerLimit(event, limit)	set lower limit for event	R2
SetUpperLimit(event, limit)	set upper limit for event	R2
SetHysteresis(event ,hyst)	set hysteresis for event	R2
SetClickTime(event, time)	set click time for event	R2
SetClickCounter(event, count)	set event click counter	R2
SetTimerLimit(timer, limit)	set limit for timer	S
SetCounterLimit(counter, limit)	set limit for counter	S
SetSensorClickTime(time)	set click time for light sensor	S

VALUE	DESCRIPTION (RANGE)	TARGETS
ActiveEvents(task)	events active for given task	R2,S
EventState(event)	state of an event	R2
LowerLimit(event)	lower limit for event	R2
UpperLimit(event)	upper limit for event	R2
Hysteresit(event)	hysteresis for event	R2
ClickTime(event)	click time for event	R2
ClickCounter(event)	number of clicks for event	R2

CONSTANT	DESCRIPTION	TARGETS
EVENT_TYPE_PRESSED, EVENT_TYPE_RELEASED, EVENT_TYPE_PULSE, EVENT_TYPE_EDGE, EVENT_TYPE_FASTCHANGE	event types for boolean sensors	R2
EVENT_TYPE_LOW, EVENT_TYPE_NORMAL, EVENT_TYPE_HIGH, EVENT_TYPE_CLICK, EVENT_TYPE_DOUBLECLICK	event types for any source	R2
EVENT_TYPE_MESSAGE	event type for messages	R2
EVENT_1_PRESSED, EVENT_1_RELEASED, EVENT_2_PRESSED, EVENT_2_RELEASED	Scout event codes for touch sensors	S
EVENT_LIGHT_HIGH, EVENT_LIGHT_NORMAL, EVENT_LIGHT_LOW, EVENT_LIGHT_CLICK, EVENT_LIGHT_DOUBLECLICK	Scout event codes for the light sensor	S
EVENT_COUNTER_0, EVENT_COUNTER_1	Scout event codes for counters	S
EVENT_TIMER_0, EVENT_TIMER_1, EVENT_TIMER_2	Scout event codes for timers	S
EVENT_MESSAGE	Scout event code for an IR message	S

Miscellaneous

FUNCTION	DESCRIPTION	TARGETS
Wait(time)	wait specified time (in 10ms)	all
StopAllTasks()	stop all tasks	all
SetRandomSeed(seed)	set seed for random numbers	R2
SetSleepTime(minute)	set minutes before auto-sleep	all
SleepNow()	go to sleep	all

VALUE	DESCRIPTION (RANGE)	TARGETS
Random(n)	random number between 0 and n	all

Special Features–RCX

The following functions and values are valid when writing programs for the RCX.

FUNCTION	DESCRIPTION	TARGETS
CreateDatalog(size)	create the datalog	R
AddToDatalog(value)	add value to the datalog	R
UploadDatalog(start, count)	upload datalog values	R
SetWatch(hours, minutes)	set the system clock	R
SelectProgram(program)	select and run the specified program	R2

VALUE	DESCRIPTION (RANGE)	TARGETS
Program()	current program number	R
Watch()	value of system clock	R
BatteryLevel()	voltage level of battery	R2
FirmwareVersion()	firmware version number	R2

Special Features—Scout

The following functions, values, and constants are valid when writing programs for the Scout.

FUNCTION	DESCRIPTION	TARGETS
SetLight(x)	turn light on/off	S
Set-ScoutRules(m,t,l,tm,fx)	set the Scout's rules	S
SetScoutMode(mode)	set the Scout's mode	S
SetEventFeedback(x)	set which events result in audible feedback	S

VALUE	DESCRIPTION (RANGE)	TARGETS
ScoutRules(n)	current rules settings (0-4)	S
TimerLimit(n)	limit for a timer (0-3)	S
CounterLimit(n)	limit for a counter (0-1)	S
EventFeedback()	which events have audio feedback	S

CONSTANT	DESCRIPTION	TARGETS
LIGHT_ON, LIGHT_OFF	values for SetLight()	S
SCOUT_MODE_STANDALONE, SCOUT_MODE_POWER	modes for SetScoutMode()	S

Special Features—CyberMaster

The following functions, values, and constants are valid when writing programs
for the CyberMaster.

FUNCTION	DESCRIPTION	TARGETS
Drive(motor0, motor1)	fully control both motors	C
OnWait(motors, n, time)	set direction and speed (n) of motors for specified time	C
OnWaitDifferent(motors, n0, n1, n2, time)	set direction and speed (n0-n2) of motors for specified time	C
ClearTachoCounter(motors)	reset tacho counters for motors	C

VALUE	DESCRIPTION (RANGE)	TARGETS
SENSOR_L, SENSOR_M, SENSOR_R	alternatives for SensorValue(n)	C
TachoCount(n)	tacho counter for motor (0-1)	C
TachoSpeed(n)	speed for motor (0-1)	C
ExternalMotorRunning()	status of external motor	C
AGC()	value of automatic gain control	C

CONSTANT	DESCRIPTION	TARGETS
OUT_L, OUT_R, OUT_X	alternative names of outputs	C

APPENDIX C

Frequently Used Forth Words

THIS IS A REFERENCE FOR the most frequently used Forth words, the ones that you can find in just about every pbForth script. The RCX-specific words are also included. These definitions are adapted from the Draft ANSI Standard for Forth. Each definition includes a preferred pronunciation, if necessary, as well as an indication of membership in the CORE or optional EXTENSION word set.

Rather than quote directly from the Standard, I have rephrased the important aspects of the definition of each word. The result is a simple description suitable for most purposes. For more detailed information, consult the Standard directly, available online in the Forth Literature section at `http://www.forth.org/`.

If you want details specific to this implementation of Forth, you can get more information online from `http://www.hempeldesigngroup.com/lego/pbForth`. The pbForth implementation may change from time to time, so be sure to check back once in a while to see if anything has been modified.

Table C-1 is the key to understanding the stack parameters.

Table C-1. Stack Parameters

PARAMETER	DESCRIPTION
n	Signed cell value
u	Unsigned cell value
x	Any cell value
a-addr	Address in memory
d	Double precision value, which is 2 cells wide
f	Boolean flag
"string"	Whitespace delimited string, not including the quotes

It should also be noted that you may see a stack parameter that looks like "u1|n1". This means that the parameter can be either unsigned or signed. In fact, any time you see parameter types separated by a "|", it means any of the types is valid.

Stack Words

DUP   *"dupe"*   CORE

(x -- x x)

Duplicates the topmost element x on the stack.

DROP   CORE

(x --)

Removes the topmost element x from the stack.

2DROP   *"two-drop"*   CORE

(d --)

Removes the topmost element d from the stack. This is a double-precision parameter, so the top *two* cells are removed. It has exactly the same effect as DROP DROP.

SWAP   CORE

(x1 x2 -- x2 x1)

Exchanges the top two stack items.

OVER   CORE

(x1 x2 -- x1 x2 x1)

Copies x1 to the top of the stack.

ROT   *"rote"*   CORE

(x1 x2 x3 -- x2 x3 x1)

Rotates the value x1 to the top of the stack.

PICK   CORE

(... x1 n -- x1 x2)

Picks the nth item from the stack and copies it to the top. 0 PICK is the same as DUP, and 1 PICK is the same as OVER. Very useful for grabbing a number way down the stack without jumping through hoops.

Math Words

+   *"plus"*   **CORE**

(n1|u1 n2|u2 n3|u3)

The value n2|u2 is added to n1|u1 and returned as n3|u3.

-   *"minus"*   **CORE**

(n1|u1 n2|u2 n3|u3)

The value n2|u2 is subtracted from n1|u1 and returned as n3|u3.

*   *"star"*   **CORE**

(n1|u1 n2|u2 n3|u3)

Returns n3|u3 as the product of n1|u1 and n2|u2. Note that the result is limited to the range of signed 16-bit numbers.

/   *"slash"*   **CORE**

(n1 n2 n3)

Divides n1 by n2 returning the quotient n3. Note that this is fixed-point math, so the result is simply an integer.

MOD   **CORE**

(n1 n2 -- n3)

Divides n1 by n2 and returns the remainder as n3.

/MOD   *"slash-mod"*   **CORE**

(n1 n2 n3 -- n4)

Divides n1 by n2, returning the remainder n3 and the quotient n4.

*/   *"star-slash"*   **CORE**

(n1 n2 n3 -- n4)

Multiplies n1 by n2 and holds the result in a temporary 32-bit signed number. Then divides the result by n3 and returns the quotient. This is most useful in scaling operations where there is a risk of overflow after the first multiplication.

MIN   **CORE**

(n1 n2 -- n3)

Returns on the stack as n3 the smallest of the signed numbers n1 and n2.

MAX   CORE

(n1 n2 -- n3)

Returns on the stack as n3 the largest of the signed numbers n1 and n2.

ABS   *"abs"*   CORE

(n u)

Returns as u the absolute value of the signed number n.

NEGATE   CORE

(n1 -- n2)

Returns n2 as the negative of n1.

1+   *"one-plus"*   CORE

(x1 -- x1+1)

Adds one to the value on the top of the stack. This is just a short form for 1 +.

2*   *"two-star"*   CORE

(x1 -- x1*2)

Multiplies the value on the top of the stack by two. This is just a short form for 2 *.

Logical Words

AND   CORE

(x1 x2 -- x3)

The result of the bitwise AND of x1 and x2 is left on the stack as x3.

OR   CORE

(x1 x2 -- x3)

The result of the bitwise OR of x1 and x2 is left on the stack as x3.

XOR   *"x-or"*   CORE

(x1 x2 -- x3)

The result of the bitwise XOR of x1 and x2 is left on the stack as x3.

INVERT CORE

(x1 -- x2)
The bitwise inverse of x1 is returned to the stack as x2.

Conditional Words

= *"equals"* CORE

(x1 x2 -- f)
If x1 and x2 are bit-for-bit equal, then f is true.

< *"less-than"* CORE

(n1 n2 -- f)
If n1 is less than n2 using signed arithmetic, then f is true.

> *"greater-than"* CORE

(n1 n2 -- f)
If n1 is greater than n2 using signed arithmetic, then f is true.

0= *"zero-equals"* CORE

(x -- f)
The value of f is true only if all bits in x are zero.

0< *"zero-less"* CORE

(n -- f)
The value of f is true if and only if n is less than zero.

Compiler and Memory Words

: *"colon"* CORE

This is the basic defining word. It uses the next whitespace-delimited string as the name for the new word. When that name is later invoked, the code inside the definition is executed.

;   *"semicolon"*   **CORE**

Terminates a colon definition.

CREATE   **CORE**

```
Compile Time: ( " name" -- )
Run Time: ( -- a-addr )
```

This is a defining word. It uses the next whitespace-delimited string as the name for the new word. When that name is later invoked, the address of the data space for that word is returned. This is used mostly with `ALLOT` to make data structures.

The following example creates a new word called `TEST` and allocates sixteen cells of storage:

```
CREATE TEST 16 CELLS ALLOT
```

This example creates a new word called `TEST1` and sets four consecutive cells to known values:

```
CREATE TEST1 1 , 2 , 3 , 4 ,
```

,   *"comma"*   **CORE**

(x --)

This word allocates a cell in the data space and copies x into it.

ALLOT   **CORE**

(n --)

The data space pointer is moved by the number of bytes indicated by the signed value n. Normally, it is only moved a positive amount to reserve space for a data structure made with `CREATE`.

CELLS   **CORE**

(n1 -- n2)

Calculates the number of address units occupied by n1 cells. On the RCX, a cell is 2 bytes, and memory is byte addressable. So 4 `CELLS` will return 8.

CELL+   *"cell-plus"*   **CORE**

(n1 -- n2)

Returns the next cell-aligned address. On the RCX, a cell is 2 bytes, so this word always returns n1 + 2.

VARIABLE   CORE

Compile Time: (" name" --)

Run Time: (-- a-addr)

This is a defining word. It uses the next whitespace-delimited string as the name for the new word. The contents of the data field are undefined. When that name is later invoked, the address of the data field is returned.

Skip leading space delimiters. Parse name delimited by a space. Create a definition for name with the execution semantics defined next. Reserve one cell of data space at an aligned address. Name is referred to as a "variable".

name Execution: (a-addr)

a-addr is the address of the reserved cell. The program is responsible for initializing the contents of the reserved cell.

CONSTANT   CORE

Compile Time: (x " name" --)

Run Time: (-- x)

This is a defining word. It uses the next whitespace-delimited string as the name for the new word and copies x into its data field. When that name is later invoked, x is copied back onto the stack.

VALUE   CORE EXT

Compile Time: (x " name" --)

Run Time: (-- x)

This is a defining word. It uses the next whitespace-delimited string as the name for the new word and copies x into its data field. When that name is later invoked, x is copied back onto the stack. The word TO can be used to change this value, which is what makes it different from a CONSTANT.

TO   CORE EXT

(x " name" --)

This uses the next whitespace-delimited string as the target for storing the value x. The target word must have been previously defined as a VALUE.

@   *"fetch"*   CORE

(a-addr -- x)

Retrieves the cell value that is stored at a-addr and puts it on the stack as x.

!	*"store"*	CORE

(x a-addr --)

Store the value x into the cell at address a-addr.

Control Structure Words

IF		CORE

Run Time: (f --)

This word must be used inside a definition.

The code between the IF and ELSE is executed if the condition being evaluated is true. If the conditional does not use ELSE, the code between the IF and THEN is executed.

The following example will print "Non-Zero" or "Zero" depending upon the parameter passed as input to TEST.

```
: TEST IF ." Non-Zero" ELSE ." Zero" THEN ;
```

ELSE		CORE

This word must be used inside a definition

The code between ELSE and THEN is executed if the condition being evaluated by IF is false.

THEN		CORE

This word must be used inside a definition

Terminates an IF or an ELSE clause.

BEGIN		CORE

This word must be used inside a definition.

The code between BEGIN and UNTIL is executed as long as the value on the stack just before UNTIL is zero.

The following example will loop until the parameter passed as input to TEST is zero:

```
: TEST BEGIN 1 - 0= UNTIL ;
```

UNTIL   CORE

Run Time: (f --)

This word must be used inside a definition.

Terminates a REPEAT loop if the value on the stack is non-zero. Note that this word consumes a stack item.

DO   CORE

Run Time: (n1|u1 n2|u2 --)

This word must be used inside a definition.

The code between DO and LOOP is executed until n2|u2 is equal to n1|u1.

The following example will print the value of the looping index from 0 to 9:

```
: TEST 10 0 DO I . LOOP ;
```

LOOP   CORE

This word must be used inside a definition.

This word adds one to the loop index and checks it against the loop limit. If they are equal, then the loop is terminated.

I   CORE

Run Time: (-- n|u)

This word must be used inside a definition.
The current loop control value is copied to the stack. This is most often used inside a DO loop to get the loop index onto the stack.

Input and Output Formatting Words

DECIMAL   CORE

(--)

Sets the base for numeric conversion to decimal, or 10.

HEX   CORE EXT

(--)

Sets the base for numeric conversion to hexadecimal, or base 16.

.   *"dot"*   CORE

(n --)

Prints n as a signed number at the terminal depending upon the current numeric conversion base.

U.   *"u-dot"*   CORE

(u --)

Prints u as an unsigned number at the terminal depending upon the current numeric conversion base.

RCX Extension Words

RCX_INIT   *"r-c-x-init"*   RCX EXT

(--)

This function is the master startup of the RCX, it sets up all of the internal structures and allows the OC1A interrupt service routine to do its thing.

RCX_ECHO   *"r-c-x-echo"*   RCX EXT

(-- a-addr)

Returns the address of a variable, which you can use to control the operation of RCX_EMIT. The value is initially FALSE.

RCX_EMIT   *"r-c-x-emit"*   RCX EXT

(x --)

Sends a character to the output device using EMIT if RCX_ECHO is non-zero. If RCX_ECHO is zero characters are not sent back to the output port when uploading scripts. This helps to eliminate the double-echo during ASCII downloads.

It should be noted that only the least significant 8 bits are used to form the ASCII character.

POWER_INIT   RCX EXT

(--)

Sets up the power management system of the RCX. This must be called before POWER_OFF to ensure that the RCX wakes up properly.

POWER_OFF   RCX EXT

(--)

This word shuts down the RCX systems and puts it into a sleep mode. When you press the **On-Off** switch again, it wakes up exactly where you left off. It is *vital* that POWER_INIT is called before POWER_OFF or the RCX will hang.

RCX_POWER   *"r-c-x-power"*   RCX EXT

(-- a-addr)

Returns the address of a buffer to store the result of power queries in. More importantly, after doing a POWER_GET, the results can be saved in this variable.

The following example shows how to use the RCX_POWER word to read the battery voltage and return it on the stack:

```
HEX RCX_POWER DUP 4001 POWER_GET @
```

POWER_GET   RCX EXT

(a-addr code --)

Here's the word you need when you want to figure out the raw battery voltage or if the **On-Off** switch is pressed. The results are placed in the buffer pointed to by a-addr. The allowable hex values for code are

```
0x4000 On/Off button state - 0 if pressed
0x4001 Raw battery voltage
```

LCD_SHOW   *"l-c-d-show"*   RCX EXT

(segment --)

Turns on the selected LCD segment. You must use LCD_REFRESH to actually update the display. The following table shows the correspondence between segments and the numerical codes:

```
0x3006 standing figure
0x3007 walking figure
0x3008 sensor 0 view selected
0x3009 sensor 0 active
0x300a sensor 1 view selected
0x300b sensor 1 active
0x300c sensor 2 view selected
0x300d sensor 2 active
0x300e motor 0 view selected
0x300f motor 0 backward arrow
```

```
0x3010 motor 0 forward arrow
0x3011 motor 1 view selected
0x3012 motor 1 backward arrow
0x3013 motor 1 forward arrow
0x3014 motor 2 view selected
0x3015 motor 2 backward arrow
0x3016 motor 2 forward arrow
0x3018 datalog indicator
0x3019 progress indicator
0x301a progress indicator
0x301b battery low indicator
0x301c IR activity
0x301d IR activity
```

LCD_HIDE   *"l-c-d-hide"*   RCX EXT

(segment --)

Turns off the selected LCD segment. You must use LCD_REFRESH to actually update
the display. See the table in the description of LCD_SHOW for the correspondence
between segments and numerical codes.

LCD_NUMBER   *"l-c-d-number"*   RCX EXT

(comma value format --)

This is the routine used to format values in the LCD. The hex-valued comma
parameter has the following possibilities:

```
0x0000 Single digit to right of display, use with format = 0x3017
0x3002 No decimal point
0x3003 10th's decimal point
0x3004 100th's decimal point
0x3005 1000th's decimal point
```

The hex-valued format parameter is used to determine where and how the value
parameter is displayed:

```
0x3017 Single digit on right of display, use with comma = 0x0000
0x3001 Signed with no leading zeros
0x301F Unsigned with leading zeros
```

LCD_4TH   *"l-c-d-forth"*   RCX EXT

(--)

Puts "4th" on the LCD display. Remember to call LCD_REFRESH.

LCD_CLEAR　　　　　　　　*"l-c-d-clear"*　　　　　　　RCX EXT

(--)

Quickly clears the entire display.

LCD_REFRESH　　　　　　　*"l-c-d-refresh"*　　　　　　RCX EXT

(--)

Updates the display. This *must* be called before you will see any changes due to LCD_NUMBER or LCD_SHOW or LCD_HIDE words being used. It is probably a good idea to call this only as often as necessary.

SOUND_PLAY　　　　　　　　　　　　　　　　　　　　RCX EXT

(sound code --)

Plays one of the seven predefined system sounds. The legal hex values for code are

```
0x4003 Sound is queued
0x4004 Sound is unqueued
```

The legal values for sound are

```
0x0000 Blip
0x0001 Beep Beep
0x0002 Downward Tones
0x0003 Upward Tones
0x0004 Low Buzz
0x0005 Fast Upward Tones
0x0006 Low Buzz
```

RCX_SOUND　　　　　　　　*"r-c-x-sound"*　　　　　　RCX EXT

(-- a-addr)

Returns the address of the buffer to use when figuring out the state of the RCX sound system.

The following example shows how to use the RCX_SOUND word to read the sound system state and return it on the stack:

```
RCX_SOUND DUP SOUND_GET @
```

SOUND_GET   RCX EXT

(a-addr --)

Grabs the current state of the sound system and places the result in the buffer pointed to by a-addr. The result is zero if the system is idle (no sound is playing), or a non-zero value if it is busy.

BUTTON_INIT   RCX EXT

(--)

Initializes the button reading system.

RCX_BUTTON   *"r-c-x-button"*   RCX EXT

(-- a-addr)

Returns the address of the buffer to use when figuring out the state of the RCX buttons.

The following example shows how to use the RCX_BUTTON word to read the button state and return it on the stack:

```
RCX_BUTTON DUP BUTTON_GET @
```

BUTTON_GET   RCX EXT

(a-addr --)

Returns the current state of the buttons in the buffer pointed to by a-addr on the RCX front panel according to the following flags:

```
0x0001 Run
0x0002 View
0x0004 Prgm
```

MOTOR_SET   RCX EXT

(power mode idx --)

Sets the motor specified by an index of 0-2 to a power between 0-7. The allowed modes are

```
0x0001 forward
0x0002 backward
0x0003 stop
0x0004 float
```

SERVO_INIT   RCX EXT

(--)

Updates the OC1A and OC1B interrupt handlers to allow them to generate servo-compatible waveforms. This word must be called before SERVO_SET is used.

SERVO_SET   RCX EXT

(level mode idx --)

This sets up the servo pulse width handler to generate the proper pulse widths. The servo driver circuit can be made polarity sensitive, which allows up to two servos to be controlled from one RCX output port. The output port is specified by an index of 0-2.

The mode specifies the direction of the signal polarity. If you are using the unipolar version of the servo signal converter, you can control two servos at once from one output port. The allowed modes are

```
0x0001 forward
0x0002 backward
```

This level may range from 0 to 255. Smaller levels correspond to shorter pulse widths. The pulse widths range from 0.50 ms to a 2.50 ms. maximum. It should be noted that the servos I tested use this as a practical range for 180 degrees of travel on the servo arm. Test your servos with an initial level of 128, which gives a 1.50 ms pulse and will center the servo arm.

SENSOR_INIT   RCX EXT

(--)

Initializes the sensor subsystem. For all calls to sensor functions, the idx is a value between 0 and 2.

SENSOR_ACTIVE   RCX EXT

(idx --)

Sets the specified sensor to be an active type. The light and rotation sensors are active.

SENSOR_PASSIVE   RCX EXT

(idx --)

Sets the specified sensor to be a passive type. The touch and temperature sensors are passive.

SENSOR_TYPE   RCX EXT

(type idx --)

Sets the sensor type to one of the following:

```
0x0000 Raw sensor (useful for custom devices)
0x0001 Touch sensor
0x0002 Temperature sensor
0x0003 Light sensor
0x0004 Rotation sensor
```

SENSOR_MODE   RCX EXT

(mode idx --)

Sets the specified sensor to one of the following modes. Use your common sense when combining different modes and types.

```
0x0000 Raw mode
0x0020 Boolean mode
0x0040 Edge detection - every transition counts
0x0060 Pulse detection - only negative transitions count
0x0080 Percent of scale
0x00A0 Degrees Celsius
0x00C0 Degrees Fahrenheit
0x00E0 Angle detection
```

SENSOR_READ   RCX EXT

(idx -- code)

Reads the specified sensor and returns a flag indicating success (0) or busy (other values).

SENSOR_CLEAR   RCX EXT

(idx --)

Clears the sensor's current raw, value, and boolean fields. The type and mode are left unchanged.

SENSOR_RAW   RCX EXT

(idx -- value)

Retrieves the sensors current raw data field. Note that this item will not change unless you first call SENSOR_READ.

SENSOR_BOOL   RCX EXT

(idx -- value)

Retrieves the sensors current boolean data field. Note that this item will not change unless you first call the SENSOR_READ.

SENSOR_VALUE   RCX EXT

(idx -- value)

Retrieves the sensors current value data field. Note that this item will not change unless you first call the SENSOR_READ.

TIMER_SET   RCX EXT

(value -- idx)

Sets the specified internal low-resolution firmware timer to the desired value (0-3). Note that these timers handle 0.1-second increments up to 0x7FFF, and that they are count UP and WRAP timers. Also note that timer numbers beyond 3 will scribble over memory.

TIMER_GET   RCX EXT

(idx -- value)

Retrieves the current value of the low-resolution timer specified by idx.

timer_SET   RCX EXT

(value idx --)

Sets the specified internal high-resolution firmware timer (0-9) to the desired value. Note that these timers handle 0.01-second increments up to 0xFFFF, and that they are count DOWN and STOP timers. Also note that timer numbers beyond 9 will scribble over memory.

LegOS API Reference

THIS FUNCTION REFERENCE is intended as a quick guide to legOS's functionality. It is not exhaustive, but it covers all of the functions commonly used in legOS programs. The format is reasonably straightforward: function name (with accepted arguments); description of functionality; and required .h file. The most frequently used function appears first within each section.

> **NOTE** *Most of the #include files can be found in the legOS/include/ directory if you want to look at them in more detail.*

LCD Functions

FUNCTION NAME	DESCRIPTION	#INCLUDE
void lcd_clear(void)	Deletes everything from the LCD, including walking man.	<rom/lcd.h>
void lcd_int(int i)	Prints the integer i to the LCD.	<rom/lcd.h>
void cputw(unsigned word)	Prints the word (a value in hex) to the LCD.	<conio.h>
void cputc(char c, int pos)	Prints a character c to the LCD in position pos.	<conio.h>
void cputs(char *s)	Prints a string s to the LCD. String should have no more than 5 characters, not including the terminator.	<conio.h>
void cls(void)	Similar to lcd_clear(void), but does not effect walking man or other non-character portions of LCD.	<conio.h>
void dlcd_show(segment a)	Turns on the segment a. dlcd.h contains a complete listing of segment names.	<dlcd.h>
void dlcd_hide(segment a)	Like dlcd_show, turns off the segment a	<dlcd.h>

Motor Functions

`MAX_SPEED` is a handy constant defined to the maximum speed of the motors. Currently, it is set to 255. The `motor_x_dir` functions takes one of the values of the MotorDirection enum shown here:

```
typedef enum {
    off = 0,            //!< freewheel
    fwd = 1,            //!< forward
    rev = 2,            //!< reverse
    brake = 3           //!< hold current position
```

FUNCTION NAME	DESCRIPTION	#INCLUDE
`void motor_a_dir(MotorDirection dir)`, `void motor_b_dir(MotorDirection dir)`, `void motor_c_dir(MotorDirection dir)`	Changes the direction of the appropriate motor to dir.	<dmotor.h>
`void motor_a_speed(unsigned char speed)`, `void motor_b_speed(unsigned char speed)`, `void motor_c_speed(unsigned char speed)`	Changes the speed of the appropriate motor to a value 0-MAX_SPEED.	<dmotor.h>

Sensor Functions

The dsensor.h file uses a number of #defines to provide the values of the various sensors. `SENSOR_1`, `SENSOR_2`, and `SENSOR_3` each contain the raw value (best displayed in hex) of the respective sensor. `TOUCH_1`, `TOUCH_2`, and `TOUCH_3` interpret the sensors as a touch sensor. `LIGHT_1`, `LIGHT_2`, and `LIGHT_3` interpret the sensors as light sensors. `ROTATION_1`, `ROTATION_2`, and `ROTATION_3` return the stored values of the rotation sensors, but won't be meaningful unless the relevant `ds_rotation` functions are called first, as described in the following table.

FUNCTION NAME	DESCRIPTION	#INCLUDE
void ds_active(volatile unsigned *sensor)	Puts the sensor pointed to by *sensor into active or powered mode.	<dsensor.h>
void ds_passive(volatile unsigned *sensor)	Cuts power to *sensor, presumably previously turned on by ds_active().	<dsensor.h>
void ds_rotation_on(volatile unsigned *sensor)	Turns on a rotation sensor pointed at by *sensor. *sensor must be activated with ds_active() first.	<dsensor.h>
void ds_rotation_off(volatile unsigned *sensor)	Turns off the rotation sensor *sensor.	<dsensor.h>
void ds_rotation_set(volatile unsigned *sensor, int position)	Sets the rotation sensor *sensor to position. Can be called repeatedly once ds_rotation_on() is called, but should have msleep(100) called afterward each time.	<dsensor.h>

Math Functions

Floating point emulation is compiled in by default.

FUNCTION NAME	DESCRIPTION	#INCLUDE
void srandom(unsigned int seed)	seeds the random number generator	<stdlib.h>
long int random()	get a random number in range 0-2^{31}-1. Unlike the standard Unix random() implementation, srandom() *must* be called prior to the first call to random().	<stdlib.h>

Program Control

The behaviors of most of these functions are roughly analogous to their Unix cousins. There are a few useful constants: DEFAULT_STACK_SIZE (defined as 512) is usually passed as the last argument of execi(), and PRIO_NORMAL, PRIO_HIGHEST, and PRIO_LOWEST (10, 20, and 1, respectively) can be passed as the fourth argument to execi().

FUNCTION NAME	DESCRIPTION	#INCLUDE
pid_t execi(int (*code_start) (int, char **), int argc, char **argv, priority_t priority, size_t stack_size)	Starts a new thread with the function *code_start, passing to it argc and argv, and giving it assigned priority and stack size. Returns a process id.	<unistd.h>
void kill(pid_t procid)	Kills the process identified by procid.	<unistd.h>
void yield(void)	Returns control to the legOS scheduler.	<unistd.h>
wakeup_t wait_event(wakeup_t(*wakeup) (wakeup_t), wakeup_t data)	Suspends the current thread, passes data to function *wakeup, and resumes the current thread when *wakeup returns true.	<unistd h>

Time Control

FUNCTION NAME	DESCRIPTION	#INCLUDE
int msleep(unsigned int mseconds)	Sleeps the current thread for the specified number of milli-seconds. The return value is currently meaningless.	<unistd.h>
int sleep(unsigned int seconds)	Like msleep, but with seconds. the return value is currently meaningless.	<unistd.h>
time_t sys_time	Variable that stores the current value of the system clock in ms.	<time.h>

Hardware Control

FUNCTION NAME	DESCRIPTION	#INCLUDE
void power_off(void)	Powers down the hardware without erasing legOS or programs in memory.	<rom/system.h>
void reset(void)	Resets the RCX completely.	<rom/system.h>

Music

The struct note_t is defined as follows:

```
typedef struct {
  unsigned char pitch;     //!< note pitch, 0 ^= A_0 (~55 Hz)
  unsigned char length;    //!< note length in 1/16ths
} note_t;
```

One copy of a struct basically represents one note of the length specified in the second member of the struct. For convenience, there is also a long list of pitches #defined in dsound.h, which are of the form PITCH_A0 and can be passed as the first member of the note_t struct.

FUNCTION NAME	DESCRIPTION	#INCLUDE
void dsound_play(const note_t *notes)	This plays all the notes in the array notes. Note that it returns immediately and does not wait for the sounds to be played.	<dsound.h>
void dsound_set_duration(unsigned duration)	Sets the length of a 16th note to duration. This is 200ms by default.	<dsound.h>
void dsound_set_internote(unsigned duration)	Sets the wait in between notes to duration. This is 15ms by default.	<dsound.h>
void dsound_stop(void)	Stops the last call of dsound_play().	<dsound.h>
int dsound_playing(void)	Returns non-zero if a sound is playing, zero otherwise.	<dsound.h>

Buttons

Despite commentary here and in the code, with the standard kernel, these functions will work only with the **View** and **Program** keys.

FUNCTION NAME	DESCRIPTION	#INCLUDE
`int getchar()`	Waits until a button is pressed, and then returns the value of the button that was pressed: 0x01 for On/Off, 0x02 for Run, 0x04 for View, 0x08 for Program.	<dkey.h>
`wakeup_t dkey_pressed(` ` wakeup_t data)`	Data contains one or more keys (using the same values as `getchar()`) and the function returns when at least one is pressed.	<dkey.h>
`wakeup_t dkey_released(` ` wakeup_t data)`	Data contains one or more keys (using the same values as `getchar()`) and the function returns when all have been released.	<dkey.h>
`unsigned char dkey_multi`	This variable contains the keys that are pressed, using the same values as `getchar()`.	<dkey.h>

Semaphores

Return values for all of these functions should be 0 on success and –1 on failure. Also, they are basically POSIX compliant. For more detail, see the appropriate Linux man pages.

FUNCTION NAME	DESCRIPTION	#INCLUDE
`int sem_init(sem_t * sem,` ` int pshared, unsigned int value)`	Initializes the semaphore sem to the value of 'value'. pshared is ignored.	<semaphore.h>
`int sem_wait(sem_t * sem)`	Suspends the current thread until sem is non-zero.	<semaphore.h>
`int sem_post(sem_t * sem)`	Increments the value of sem.	<semaphore.h>

LNP functions

LNP includes only robot-side functions, since PC-side functions may vary by implementation. Also, the LNP functionality is not very robust yet: this is about all it can currently handle.

FUNCTION NAME	DESCRIPTION	#INCLUDE
lnp_logical_write(const void *buf,size_t len)	Writes a string of length len from *buf to the IR channel.	<lnp/lnp-logical.h>

Standard C Library Functions

These are fairly generic C functions. If you want more detail, refer to the standard Linux man pages for the functions.

FUNCTION NAME	DESCRIPTION	#INCLUDE
void *calloc(size_t nmemb, size_t size)	Standard memory allocation for array with nmemb elements each with size bytes and return a pointer to the first memory location.	<stdlib.h>
void *malloc(size_t size)	Allocates size bytes of memory and return a pointer to the first memory location.	<stdlib.h>
void free(void *ptr)	Frees the memory space pointed at by *ptr.	<stdlib.h>
void *memcpy(void *dest, const void *src, size_t size)	Copies size bytes from *src to *dest and returns a pointer to dest.	<string.h>
void *memset(void *s, int c, size_t n)	Starting with *s, fills n bytes with the value c. Returns a pointer to s.	<string.h>

(Continued)

FUNCTION NAME	DESCRIPTION	#INCLUDE
`char *strcpy(char *dest, const char *src)`	copies a string from *src to *dest. Returns a pointer to *dest.	<string.h>
`size_t strlen(const char *s)`	Returns the length of the string *s in bytes	<string.h>
`int strcmp(const char *s1, const char *s2)`	Compares the strings s1 and s2, and returns zero if they are equal, otherwise, negative or positive values if string s1 is less than or greater than string s2 .	<string.h>

APPENDIX E

Installing LegOS

INSTALLING LEGOS IS A two-step process. First, the compilers and the other tools for building legOS must be installed. Second, the legOS source itself must be installed and built. Ironically, it's the first part of this process (installing the tools) that tends to be the most problematic. Once the proper tools have been installed, building the legOS kernel and the libraries is quite simple. Originally, the only way to install the tools was to download the sources, configure them, and build the tools yourself. Today things are a bit easier; pre-built binaries are available for some of the most popular systems. This appendix contains detailed step-by-step instructions for installing legOS using pre-built binaries for the following operating systems:

- Debian Linux

- Red Hat Linux

- Microsoft Windows (95, 98, 2000, NT)

> **NOTE** *The instructions are the most recent available for each of these platforms. In all three cases, the general instructions have been the same for nearly a year, and we've taken great pains to ensure that they will continue to be valid for some time. However, legOS is always a work in progress: legOS 0.2.5 is already in the planning stages, and it is always possible that a new upgrade or bug fix from the gcc maintainers may convince the legOS community to modify the instructions that these have been based on. To see if the instructions have been changed, just check the book's page on the Apress Web site at* http://www.apress.com.

Installing legOS is not always an easy task. So don't get too frustrated if your installation doesn't go exactly to plan. These instructions have been tested pretty thoroughly, but might not cover every possible Windows or Linux setup. Luckily, even if I haven't had your problem, odds are someone else has. So, the best solution is to try the newsgroup at http://lugnet.com/robotics/rcx/legos/. Just post there with a detailed description of the error messages that your problem has generated and what you tried to do to solve it, and you should very quickly get an answer.

If you wish to use legOS on a different system, you will need to build the tools directly from the original sources (unless you are fortunate enough to find someone who has already done this work for you). This can be a long and tricky process requiring lots of time, patience, and bandwidth. Your first step should be to browse the legOS HOWTO at `http://legOS.sourceforge.net/HOWTO`.

LegOS Installation for Debian Linux

Unfortunately, as of this writing there are no .deb packages for legOS. However, there is a tarball with a current cross-compiler that was built against the libraries for Debian 2.2. This tarball should also work with the Debian unstable tree and also with Debian 2.1, though it has not been extensively tested with the latter.

> **NOTE**   *NOTE In order to install legOS, the basic GNU development tools* (make, gcc, *etc.) need to already be installed on your system. In many cases, these tools have already been installed but sometimes they are not. If you have* apt-get *configured, the tools can be installed by running the following command as root:* "apt-get install gcc binutils make". *If you don't have* apt-get *configured, just find the* .deb *files for* gcc *and* make *on your Debian CD. Become root and run* dpkg -i *on each of those files. (The exact file names will vary based on the version of Debian that you have but they should be of the form* gcc_X.Y.deb *and* makeX.Y.deb.*)*

To get and install legOS on any of these three platforms, try the following:

1. Download the following files:

    http://legOS.sourceforge.net/files/linux/debian/rcx-debian2.1.tgz

    http://legOS.sourceforge.net/files/common/legOS-0.2.4.tar.gz

2. Untar the `rcx-debian2.1.tgz` file into a directory by copying it to that directory and then typing `tar xvzf rcx-debian2.1.tgz`. I keep mine in `/usr/local/crossgcc`, but `/usr` is just as "correct" (though it will be harder to remove there). You will need to become root to put it in these locations. You can use the `su` command to do this. If you don't want to become root, or cannot do so, then they will work fine if this is done somewhere in your home directory, like `/home/luis/crossgcc`.

3. Find the directory in which you'd like to install legOS itself. In my case, this is `/home/luis/projects`. Use `cp` to copy `legOS-0.2.4.tar.gz` into that directory, and then type `tar xvzf legOS-0.2.4.tar.gz` to untar the file. It will create a `legOS` directory and copy itself into there. It is important to note that while this directory can be located anywhere, it must be named legOS because of the way the `Makefile` determines the path to the files.

4. Use your favorite text editor to open up the new file legOS/Makefile.common. Find the line that starts with TOOLPREFIX, which should look something like this:

```
# Linux
TOOLPREFIX=/usr/local/bin/h8300-hitachi-hms-
```

Edit it so that it points to the location of your cross-compiler. In my case, that means /usr/local/crossgcc/rcx-debian2.1/bin/h8300-hitachi-hms- your exact location may vary.

```
# Linux
TOOLPREFIX=/usr/local/crossgcc/rcx-debian2.1/bin/h8300-hitachi-hms-
```

5. Change to the legOS directory using cd, and type make. Everything will build (this might take anywhere from ten seconds to a few minutes depending upon your system). LegOS is now ready to be used.

> **NOTE** *The most up-to-date version of these instructions can be found at* http://legOS.sourceforge.net/files/linux/debian. *Alternatively, you can check the book's page on the Apress Web site at* http://www.apress.com *for announcements of any instruction changes.*

LegOS Installation for Red Hat Linux

Red Hat installation, thanks to the work of James Henstridge, who packaged these rpm files, is a pretty smooth procedure. It should work with any Red Hat version of 6.0 or higher.

> **NOTE** *In order to install legOS, the basic GNU development tools* (make, gcc, *etc.) need to already be installed on your system. In many cases these tools have already been installed, but sometimes cases they are not. To install the tools, get your Redhat CD and find the* .rpm *files for* gcc, cpp, *and* make. *Become root and run "*rpm -ivh*" on each of those files. (The exact file names will vary based on the version of Redhat you have but they should be of the form* gcc-X.Y.rpm, cpp-X.Y.rpm, *and* make-X.Y.rpm.)

To get and install legOS under Red Hat Linux, try the following:

1. Download the following files:

   ```
   http://legOS.sourceforge.net/files/linux/redhat/rcx-binutils-
   2.9.5.0.22-1.i386.rpm
   ```

   ```
   http://legOS.sourceforge.net/files/linux/redhat/rcx-egcs-1.1.2-
   1.i386.rpm
   ```

   ```
   http://legOS.sourceforge.net/files/common/legOS-0.2.4.tar.gz
   ```

   Additionally, if you plan on using C++, get the last file:

   ```
   http://legOS.sourceforge.net/files/linux/redhat/rcx-egcs-c++-1.1.2-
   1.i386.rpm
   ```

2. Become the root user by using su and entering the root password. As root, change into the directory in which you placed all of the above files. Once there, (assuming that there are no other .rpm files in the directory) you can type rpm -ivh *.rpm. This will install the necessary packages in the correct places. You can now type exit to leave su and become your normal user again.

3. Now, find the directory in which you'd like to install legOS itself. In my case, this is /home/luis/projects. Use cp to copy legOS-0.2.4.tar.gz into that directory and then type tar xvzf legOS-0.2.4.tar.gz to untar the file. It will create a legOS directory and copy itself into there. It is important to note that while this directory can be located anywhere you want, it must be named legOS because of the way the Makefile determines the path to the files.

4. Use your favorite text editor to open up the new file legOS/Makefile.common. Find the line that starts with TOOLPREFIX, which should look something like:

   ```
   # Linux
   TOOLPREFIX=/usr/local/bin/h8300-hitachi-hms-
   ```

   Edit it by removing the "local" so that it looks like this:

   ```
   # Linux
   TOOLPREFIX=/usr/bin/h8300-hitachi-hms-
   ```

5. Change to the `legOS` directory using `cd` and type `make`. Everything will build (this might take anywhere from 10 seconds to a few minutes depending upon your system). LegOS is now ready to be used.

   If you didn't install the c++ rpm, you'll get a small error during this final step, which looks like this:

   ```
   make: *** [c++.o] Error 127
   ```

   Assuming you don't plan to use legOS's C++ support, you can safely ignore it.

NOTE   *The most up-to-date version of these instructions can be found at* `http:/ /legOS.sourceforge.net/files/linux/redhat`. *Alternatively, you can check the book's page on the Apress Web site at* `http://www.apress.com` *for announcements of any instruction changes.*

LegOS Installation for Windows

If you want to use legOS under Windows, you must first set up a Unix-link environment for legOS to run in and then install legOS itself. The best way to do this presently is by installing the Cygwin environment, a free set of tools developed by Cygnus, Inc. The following instructions will show you how to get up and running with Cygwin and legOS.

NOTE   *There is another option for Windows users: using DJ's Gnu Programming Project (better known as DJGPP) to provide the Unix functionality necessary for legOS. Unfortunately, at the time of this writing legOS 0.2.4 does not work cleanly with the DJGPP tools. Hopefully, this situation will be fixed soon. In the meantime, check up on the situation at* `http://legOS.sourceforge.net/files/ windows/DJGPP`.

One other thing that you'll need is a text editor to write code and, in a worst-case scenario, to get the system running. While NotePad may suffice, a number of coding-oriented free text editors are available on the Web. You may avoid problems (not to mention save yourself time while writing code) if you get one of those. You may want to look at `http://directory.google.com/Top/Computers/Software/Editors` for a reasonably complete and well-sorted list of options.

To get and install legOS under Windows using CygWin, try the following:

1.   Download the following files:

> •LegOS-0.2.4.tar.gz from http://legOS.sourceforge.net/files/common/
> legOS-0.2.4.tar.gz. Save this to your C:\ directory to access easily later.

> •Cygwin (version b20) from http://legOS.sourceforge.net/files/windows/
> cygwin/cygwin.exe. The current version of Cygwin (1.1.0) will not work,
> because the cross-compiler is dependent on the older libraries and no
> newer cross-compiler has been built. If you want to take that challenge
> on, feel free! Your contribution will be welcomed by the rest of the legOS
> community.

> •H8 cross-compiler for Cygwin b20 from http://legOS.sourceforge.net/
> files/windows/cygwin/win-h8-egcs-1.1.2.zip.

2.   Install Cygwin by double-clicking the cygwin.exe program and following
all of the default prompts. If you install the program to someplace other
than c:\cygnus (the default), make sure you remember the location where
you installed it.

3.   Use winzip or a similar program to extract the contents of win-h8-egcs-
1.1.2.zip into c:\cygnus\cygwin-B20\H-i586-cygwin32. If you installed Cygwin
into someplace other than c:\cygnus, make sure you extract win-h8-egcs-
1.1.2.zip into the same directory you have already installed Cygwin into.
You may get a warning about copying cygwin1.dll on top of an older version while you are unzipping the files. You can safely ignore this.

4.   In your Start menu click on Cygnus Solutions->Cygwin B20. This will open
up a Cygwin window. In that window, type cd / (note the direction of the /.)
Then type tar xvzf legOS-0.2.4.tar.gz . This will create a c:\legOS directory and all the files within it. You can now type exit to close this window.
It is important to note that while these files can be placed into directories
other than c:\, if the directory tree in which they are placed does not end
in legOS, you will be unable to build legOS programs without making several changes to a few different makefiles.

> **NOTE** *The first time you open up a Cygwin window, a few small quirks may surprise you. First, you may see an error that says "bash.exe: warning: could not find /tmp, please create!". To avoid this error in the future, type **mkdir /tmp** . Also, when you are done with Cygwin, you'll have to type **exit** and hit the close button in the upper right-hand corner of the window in order to make the window close. This is because Cygwin runs in a DOS window (which is pretty unusual in this day and age, I know.)*

5. Go back to the Start menu and click Run. When the Run prompt comes up, type `sysedit` and hit Enter. This will bring up the System Editor menu. Look for the window that shows the Autoexec.bat file and click it. Now look through this file for a line that says "set path =". If such a line exists, add `;c:\cygnus\cygwin-B20\H-i586-cygwin32\;c:\cygnus\cygwin-B20\H-i586-cygwin32\bin;c:\legOS\util;c:\legOS\util\firmdl` to the end of what is already there. (Make sure you add the first semicolon as a separator!) If the line doesn't already exist, add the complete line `set path = c:\cygnus\cygwin-B20\H-i586-cygwin32\;c:\cygnus\cygwin-B20\H-i586-cygwin32\bin;c:\legOS\util;c:\legOS\util\firmdl;%path%` to the end of the file. When this is done, use the File menu to save your changes and then restart the computer.

6. If you can't do step 5 because you are on an NT or W2K machine and lack administrative rights on your computer, you'll need to set the path manually within legOS. Using your text editor of choice, open `c:\legOS\Makefile.common`, and find the following lines:

```
#NT
TOOLPREFIX=h8300-hms-
```

7. Edit the second line to read:

```
TOOLPREFIX=/cygnus/cygwin32/H-i586-cygwin32/bin/h8300-hms-
```

Be careful of the direction of the slashes.

Once you've done step 5 or 6 (whichever is appropriate), use the Start menu to open another Cygwin console like you did in step 4. Now type the following commands to test the system and build a kernel:

```
cd /legOS
make realclean
make depend
make
```

Barring errors, you should now have a kernel (stored in boot/legOS.srec) and the rest of the legOS tools. LegOS is now ready to be used.

> **NOTE** *The most up-to-date version of these instructions can be found at* http:/ /legOS.sourceforge.net/files/windows/cygwin. *Alternatively, you can check the book's page on the Apress Web site at* http://www.apress.com *for announcements of any instruction changes.*

Index

Symbols

– (minus) math expression in pbForth, 96
' (tick) Forth word, 125, 139
! (store) Forth word, 89–90
* (star) math expression in pbForth, 96
*/ (star-slash) math expression in pbForth, 96, 100
. (dot) Forth word, 90
." (dot-quote) Forth word, 90
/ (slash) math expression in pbForth, 96
: (colon) preceding Forth word definitions, 101
? (question mark) following Forth words, 131
@ (fetch) Forth word, 89–90
+ (plus) math expression in pbForth, 96
< (less than) operator in Forth, 106
= (equal) operator in Forth, 106
> (greater than) operator in Forth, 106
0< (zero—less-than) operator in Forth, 107
0= (zero equal) operator in Forth, 106
10K ohm 5% ¼-watt resistor, part cross-reference list, 246
16-bit signed integer math in pbForth, 97
1N4148 and 1N914 diodes, 250
2DROP Forth word, 103
2DUP Forth word, 103, 126–127

A

AA battery tester for passive sensors, 243–244
AC (alternating current), means of converting to DC (direct current), 251
access control feature in RCX 2.0 Firmware, 64–67
acquire keyword in NQC, 65–66
active sensors. *See* powered sensors
addition (+) math expression in Forth, 96
alligator clips, using with passive sensors, 220–222
alligator test lead set, part cross-reference list for, 246
ALPHA constant, using to move Trailerbot, 208
amplified voltage input
    bill of materials for, 280
    for powered sensors, 263
amplifier circuit for powered sensors, 261–263
amplifiers
    in LM324N IC (integrated circuit), 258–259
    output in sound powered sensors, 268–270
    using with sound powered sensors, 266
AND Forth word, 105–107
angle passive sensor, 234–236
ANGLES constant, using with Trailerbot, 203

API (Application Programming Interface), managing RCX pushbuttons with, 113–117
arrays
    defining Trailerbot's world with, 202–204
    enhancements in RCX 2.0 Firmware, 60–63
ASCII characters, sending from Forth, 90
Automatic Binding Bricks, 3
average.nqc program, 61–62
averaging light sensor for Seeker robot, 134–138

B

back-and-spin obstacle detection strategy for Seeker robot, 38, 40–41, 50
balloons, using with waterproof temperature sensors, 231
BASE system variable, using with base conversion in Forth, 99
baseline value for Seeker robot, 46
battery consumption and pbForth, 84
battery power for RCX, 16
battery testers, using with passive sensors, 243–244
battery voltage in RCX, converting raw battery value to, 100
Beep Beep sound in RCX, 26
begin-until Forth word, 109
bell, ringing in Forth, 90
biofeedback training program in Visual Basic, 240–241
bit position values in pbForth, 97
bitwise operators and conditionals in pbForth, 104–107
Boolean sensor mode, 23–24
boolean value events in RCX 2.0 Firmware, 70
boolean value for sensors, 19–23
boot/config.h file in legOS, 214
BOT_MOTOR_SET and BOT_xyz Forth words, 122
boxes, building for powered sensors, 278
BRAKE state, setting for Seeker robot, 123
brake string versus off string in legOS, 156
bridge rectifier, 251
buffer circuits, using with powered sensors, 258–260
buffer part placement table, 260
buffered voltage input
    bill of materials for, 280
    for powered sensors, 261
buffers in RCX, 29
bump behavior for Seeker robot, 44, 50

bumper of Seeker robot
completing construction of, 36
constructing initial support for, 34
using, 36–41
bump.nqc light-seeking program for Seeker robot, 41–42
bump.nqc program for Seeker robot, 39
bumper program for Seeker robot in RCX Code, 38
BUMPER.TXT pbForth program, 146
bumping and seeking with Seeker robot, 44–50
bumping, creating event for detection of, 75–76
button.c legOS program, 165–166
BUTTON_GET Forth word, 93
BUTTON1.TXT pbForth program, 112–113
BUTTONAPI.TXT pbForth program, 115–116
buttons, using with legOS, 164–166
BUTTONTEST.TXT pbForth program, 116–117
bytecode interpreter in standard firmware, advantages of, 27
bytecodes, role in RCX, 12

C

C
online tutorials, 152
programming, reference books about, 152
C and C++, treatment of bitwise operators by, 105
calculations, printing results in Forth, 90
calibration process, setting thresholds for Seeker robot with, 46–50
camera, constructing crude type of, 239
capacitors
on sound powered sensors, 266
specifying on sensor powered circuit, 252
carpet, moving Trailerbot on, 202
carriage returns, sending to output devices in Forth, 90
catch keyword in NQC, 65
CdS (Cadmium Sulfide) photocell passive sensor, 238–239
using with optointerrupter powered sensor, 256
cell addresses on RCX, 89
cell values, retrieving in Forth, 90
cells on pbForth stack, 89
Celsius sensor mode, 23, 25
Christiansen, Godtfred Kirk, 3
circuit diagrams, 251
for amplifiers, 262
for buffers, 259
for differential light powered sensors, 264
for optointerrupter powered sensor, 257
for powered sensor measurement, 254
for sound powered sensor, 266
<conio.h> file, using with legOS LCD functions, 159
clearing sensors, 23
click events in RCX 2.0 Firmware, 73–74
Click sound in RCX, 26
cls() legOS output function, 158

Code Pilot, 6
coin detectors, using with passive sensors, 222
colon (:) preceding Forth word definitions, 101
compiled version of programs, 13
compilers, role in standard firmware on RCX, 12
conditional and logical operators in Forth, 106–107
conditional statements, checking sensors with, 68
conditionals and bitwise operators in pbForth, 104–107
constants in Forth, 142
Cornelius, Martin, 188
counting mode, setting up sensor in (Seeker robot), 132–133
cputs (char *string) legOS output function, 158
cputs legOS output function, 159–160
cputw(unsigned int x) legOS output function, 158
CR Forth word, 90
CUR state, using to track changes in switch state, 113–114
custom firmware versus standard firmware, 13–14
custom sensors, finding extensions for, 81
cut electric plate connector, using with passive sensors, 237–239
cut wire connector, using with passive sensors, 223

D

datalog in standard firmware, 28–29
DC motors, using with passive sensors, 245
DDK (Droid Developer Kit), 6–7
debouncing process in RCX, 24
decimal numbers
interpreting in pbForth, 98
in RCX display, 94
#define
DECIMAL word, using with base conversion in Forth, 99
decimals, converting positive and negative binary numbers to, 98–99
directives, using with bump.nqc program, 38–40
statements, tracking Trailerbot's world with, 202–204
/dev/ttyS0: error messages, 153–154
"Devil with a Blue Dress On" snippet in legOS, 183–185
defining words, 135–136
DELAY Forth word, using with high-resolution timers and Seeker robot, 138
delete firmware failed firmdl3 error message, diagnosing, 154
desensor.h file, using with rotation sensors in legOS, 181
determinate Forth loops, 110
dictionary (Forth), 86–87
adding definitions to, 88
leaving markers in, 129
differential light powered sensor, 263–265

differential light sensors, bill of materials for, 281

DIFFMOTOR.TXT pbForth programs, 121–122, 127–128

diode symbol for sensor power circuit, 250

diodes arranged as bridge rectifier, 251

DIP (dual inline package) for LM324N IC (integrated circuit), 258

direction functions in legOS, 156

display enhancements in RCX 2.0 Firmware, 57–59

division (/) math expression in Forth, 96

division and multiplication, avoiding when adding new values, 137

dlcd_hide(segment) and dlcd_show(segment) legOS output functions, 159

dll programs and legOS, 153

do-loop Forth word, 111

do-plus-loop Forth word, 111

dot (.) Forth word, 90

dot-quote (.") Forth word, 90

dots on circuit diagram, 250

double type, managing in legOS, 187

Download Tones sound in RCX, 26

DROP Forth word, 102

dry bulb temperature passive sensor, 232–233

dsound.h file, using with legOS, 183

DUP Forth word, 102

duty-cycle of signals in PWM (Pulse Width Modulation), 17

E

e transcendental number, approximating, 100–101

Edge Count sensor mode, 23–24

edge event type in RCX 2.0 Firmware, 70

electric plates, cutting for passive sensors, 237–238

electrical connector, creating for passive sensors, 237

electronic breadboard

    adding optointerrupter power sensor circuit to, 257

    adding sensor measurement circuit to, 255

    amplifier circuit on, 262

    bill of materials for, 279

    comparing to Experimenter PC (printed circuit) Board, 271

    differential light powered sensor on, 264

    inserting LM324N IC (integrated circuit) on, 259–260

    labels on, 252

    sensor power circuit on, 253

    sound powered sensor on, 267

elements of arrays, accessing with RCX 2.0 firmware, 60

ELSE clause, using in pbForth, 104

EMIT Forth word, 90

Enter key, using with Forth, 88–89

epsilon value, using to move Trailerbot, 208

equal (=) operator in Forth, 106

error-deleting program .dll error, 155

event configuration in RCX 2.0 Firmware, 69

event monitoring in RCX 2.0 Firmware, 68–69, 72–73

event source parameter, 69

event type parameters, 69

event_click.nqc program, 74

event_high.nqc program, 72–73

event_pressed.nqc program, 70

events

    enhancement in RCX 2.0 Firmware, 68–76

    using with Seeker robot, 74–76

execi() function in legOS, 168–169

execution time, checking with low-resolution timers, 140

Experimenter PC (printed circuit) Board, 271–272

Expert Builder series, 3

Extreme MINDSTORMS, coining of, 5

F

factoring code in Forth, 121, 123

Fast Upward Tones sound in RCX, 26

fetch (@) Forth word, 90

FILTER Forth words, 137

FILTER1.TXT pbForth program, 135–136

filters, slowing down response of, 138

finite response averaging, 63

firmware

Fahrenheit sensor mode, 23, 25

    downloading to RCX, 54

    relationship to ROM, 12

fixed-point math, 137

FLOAT state, setting for Seeker robot, 123

float type, managing in legOS, 187

floating mode for RCX, 16

floating point library, using with legOS, 186–187

floating versus off in legOS, 156

flywheel, role in adjusting power level for RCX, 17–18

FORGET Forth word, 129

Forth. *See also* pbForth

    basic stack manipulation words in, 102–103

    comments in, 87–88

    constants in, 142

    control-flow words in, 111

    factoring code in, 121, 123

    glossaries in, 87

    managing numbers and expressions in, 95–97

    numeric base conversion in, 99

    reference books about, 85

    testing code in, 88

    variables in, 142

    versus pbForth, 85

Forth dictionary, 86–87

    adding definitions to, 88

    leaving markers in, 129

Forth Interest Group Web site, 85
Forth interpreter, 5
Forth stack, 85–86
Forth, evolution of, 85
    deleting top element of, 102
    deleting top two elements of, 103
    diagrams, 86
    duplicating top element of, 102
    duplicating top two elements on, 103
    exchanging top two elements of, 102
    manipulating with Forth words, 102–103
    performing calculations on, 95–96
    printing top as signed and unsigned numbers
        in, 90
    rotating top three elements on, 102
    using for parameter passing, 109
Forth words, 86
    advice about testing of, 141
    for filter creation and manipulation, 135–136
    for manipulating stack, 102–103
    for sensor creation and manipulation,
        133–134
    format for, 132
    formatting for display, 101
    stack-neutral type of, 141
    vectored execution of, 125–129
FORWARD state, setting for Seeker robot, 123
FPU (Floating Point Unit), managing in legOS,
    186–187
frame for Trailerbot, adding skid and hitch to
    (legOS), 192
functions for switching sensor lights in legOS,
    163–164

G

gain of amplifiers, 261, 263
Galvanic Skin Response sensor, 5
Gasperi, Michael, 5
gcc (GNU C Compiler) and legOS, 152
getchar() function, using with buttons in
    legOS, 165
global variables
    declaring in NQC 56–57
    storing in standard firmware, 28
glossaries in Forth, 87
GNU C Compiler (gcc) and legOS, 152–156
greater than (>) operator in Forth, 106
GSR (Galvanic Skin Response), measuring for
    passive sensors, 240–241

H

.h (header) files
    and legOS functions, 158
    locating in legOS, 214
HANDLE_SENSORS Forth word, 109

handler statement in NQC, 65–66
hardware
    for pbForth, 82
    for RCX, 14–15
hardware layer of RCX, 11
heating connection for solder joints on PC (printed
    circuit) boards, 274
heaven concept for rewarding Trailerbot, 211
Hempel, Ralph, 5
HERE word, determining current location of
    dictionary pointer with, 129
HEX Forth word, 99, 101
hex notation, 93
hex numbers, interpreting in pbForth, 98
hex values for LCD Forth words, 92
high values for sensors, 71
high-resolution timers, using with Seeker robot,
    138–139
history arrays in legOS, 180
homebrew sensors. *See* passive sensors, powered
    sensors
hookup wires, bill of materials for, 279
humidity sensor program
humidity, measuring for passive sensors, 232
    in NQC, 234
    in Visual Basic, 233
Husby, Dean, 237
hysteresis, 21, 71–72

I

IDE, specifying targets for RCX 2.0 Firmware
    with, 55
IF statement, using in pbForth, 104
IF structure, nesting in pbForth, 125
if-else-then Forth word, 111
if-then Forth word, 111
include directory in legOS, 214
indeterminate Forth loops, 110
indexes, accessing in arrays using RCX 2.0
    Firmware, 60–61
infix notation for Forth expressions, 95–97
int type, managing in legOS, 187
Integer math, using with Forth, 96
interface words, 136
Interrupt handlers, starting in Forth, 91
INVERT operator in Forth, 107
IR (InfraRed) interface, 15

J

jumper part placement on sound powered
    sensors, 267
jumpers, using to make connections for buffer-
    part connections, 259–260

K

kernel
    checking for loading of, 153
    for legOS, 214
    for pbForth, 83–84

L

LASM bytecode assembler, 7, 8
LCD display for RCX 2.0 Firmware, 57–59
LCD display for RCX, 25–26, 57–59
LCD Forth words, 92–93
LCD legOS output functions, 158–161
LCD segments, 93–94
lcd.c legOS program, 159–160
LCD_4th Forth Word, 93
LCD_CLEAR Forth Word, 93
lcd_clear() legOS output function, 158
LCD_HIDE Forth word, 93
lcd_int(int x) legOS output function, 158
LCD_NUMBER Forth word, 92
LCD_REFRESH Forth word, 91, 124
lcd_refresh() legOS output function, 159
LCD_SHOW Forth word, 92
LDRs (Light Dependant Resistors), 238–239
lead, cutting flush with solder joints, 276
LED (light emitting diode), using as light source for optointerrupter powered sensor, 256–258
LEGO bricks, 3
    building boxes for powered sensors with, 278
    reference books about, 119
LEGO electric plates, 237–238
LEGO electrical connectors, 221
LEGO MINDSTORMS Internals Web site, 4
LEGO Remote Control in Ultimate Accessory Pack for MINDSTORMS, 186
LEGO SDK (Software Development Kit), 7
LEGO sensors, 5
LEGO temperature sensor, 225–227
LEGO wire, bill of materials for, 279
legOS, 7
    .lx files in, 154
    .o files in, 154
    accessing button-related functions in, 166
    accessing control functions for, 167
    accessing sensors in, 161
    and .h (header) files, 158
    and dll program, 153
    and firmdl3 program, 153
    and program control, 167–170
    components of, 152–156
    debouncing buttons in, 165
    debugging, 188–189
    direction functions in, 156
    doing math in, 186–188
    execi() function in, 168–169
    functions for switching sensor lights in, 163–164
    include directory in, 214

    LCD output functions, 158–161
    managing type sizes in, 187
    motor control in, 156–158
    output functions for, 161–166
    output functions in, 156–161
    requirements for use of, 152
    running demo program for, 154–155
    sleep functions in, 167
    speed functions in, 156–157
    support of semaphores by, 170
    threading in, 168–169
    using buttons with, 164–166
    using history arrays with, 180
    using light sensors with, 163–164
    using raw sensors with, 161
    using rotation sensors with, 181–183
    using sound with, 183–186
    using touch sensors with, 162–163
    wait_event function in, 167–169
    wakeup_t function in, 167–168
    Web site for, 151
legOS
    0.2.x, preemptive multi-tasking in, 170
    LCD display, 26
    custom firmware, 14–15
    firmware for RCX, 4–5
    kernel, 214
    Seeker, 154, 170–180. *See also* Seeker robot (NQC)
less than (<) operator in Forth, 104
LibLNP code, 188
light reading, scanning for peak of, 142–144
light sensors, 18, 20
    averaging readings from, 61–63
    averaging for Seeker robot, 134–138
    differential type of, 263–265
    locating wires for (Seeker robot), 32–33, 36
    monitoring, 72–73
    and thresholds for Seeker robot, 141–148
    using with legOS, 163–164
light sources, tracking for powered sensors, 263–265
light.c legOS program, 163–164
LIGHT.TXT pbForth program, 133–134
lights, seeking with Seeker robot, 41–44
linear taper potentiometer, 236
Linux computers, accessing LNP-enabled RCXs from, 188
LM324N IC (integrated circuit), 258
    removing, 259
    using with sound powered sensors, 266
.lx files in legOS, 154–155
LNP (legOS Network Protocol), 187–188, 214
LNPD (LNP Daemon) code, 188
load of motor, 18
local variables, using with RCX 2.0 Firmware, 56–57
long int type, managing in legOS, 187
looping in pbForth, 104–107, 110–111
Low Beep sound in RCX, 26

low values for sensors, 71
lower limit parameter, using with range events in RCX 2.0 Firmware, 71–72
low-resolution timers, using with Seeker robot, 139–141
LUGNET robotics forum, 4, 84

M

/*MOD (star-slash-mod) math expression in pbForth, 96
/MOD (slash-mod) math expression in pbForth, 96
magnifying glass lens, using with CdS photocell passive sensors, 239
MARKER Forth word, 129
ME# (Mouser Electronics) catalog numbers for passive–sensor parts, 220
mechatronics, disciplines involved in, 81–82
message events in RCX 2.0 Firmware, 74
messages, tracking in RCX, 29
MIC (microphone) on sound powered sensors, 266–268
Micro Scout, 6
Mindfest conference, 5
MINDSTORMS Ultimate Accessory Pack, 186
MINDSTORMS Web site, 53
minus (–) math expression in Forth, 96
MIT Media Lab, role in development of programmable bricks, 3, 5
Moore, Charles, 85
motor control
    commands for Trailerbot (legOS), 200–202
    and display words using vectored execution, 127
    in legOS, 156–158
motor direction, changing, 108–109, 120
motor indicators, updating on LCD for Seeker robot, 123–125
motor states, displaying for Seeker robot, 122–130
MOTOR_SET Forth word, 107, 109
MOTOR_SHOW Forth word, 125–126
MOTORDIR.TXT pbForth program, 109
motors
    adding to Seeker robot, 32–33
    adding to Trailerbot (legOS), 193
motors.c program in legOS, 157
move() functions, calling for Trailerbot, 204–208
msleep() call
    managing in legOS, 167
    using with LCD legOS output function, 160
    using with legOS motor control functions, 157
multiplication and division, avoiding when adding new values, 137
music, controlling pace in legOS, 183

N

n notation in Forth glossaries, 106–107
n1, printing ASCII equivalent in Forth, 90

negative binary numbers, converting to decimals, 98–99
negative versus positive numbers in pbForth, 98
Nelson, Russell, 4
no response from RCX firmdl3 error message, diagnosing, 154
Noga, Markus L., 4, 151
non-volatile firmware on RCX, 83
non-zero values, treatment in Forth, 104
norm_random() function, using to move Trailerbot, 204
normal values for sensors, 71
note_t structures for legOS sounds, characterizing, 183
NQC programming language, 4, 7
    AA battery tester program in, 244
    correcting temperature for passive sensors with, 229
    determining version of, 54
    downloading, 54
    humidity sensor program in, 234
    range of priorities for tasks in, 65
    requesting resources with, 65–66
    rules for compiling programs with, 54
    troubleshooting after compiling sample RCX 2.0 Firmware program, 55
    variables, 56–57
numbers, rational approximations for, 100–101

O

.o files in legOS, 154
obstacle detection by Seeker robot, strategies for, 36–41
octaves, specifying for sound in legOS, 183
Off mode for RCX, 16
off string versus brake string in legOS, 156
ok on pbForth lines, 87
OLD state, using to track changes in switch state, 113–114
On mode for RCX, 16
On–Off pushbutton in RCX, 111–112
operational amplifiers in LM324N IC (integrated circuit), 258–259
optointerrupter powered sensors, 258, 277
    bill of materials for, 280
    circuit diagram of, 256–257
    part placements table, 258
OR Forth word, 105, 107
output directions for RCX, 16
output functions in legOS, 156–161
output ports for RCX, 16, 18
OVER Forth word, 102

P

packaging powered sensors, 277–278
parts, acquiring for passive sensors, 219–220, 246
passive sensors, 18. *See also* powered sensors
    AA battery tester for, 243–244

acquiring parts for, 219–220, 246
adjusting raw values for, 235
angle type of, 234–236
CdS (Cadmium Sulfide) photocell type of, 238–239, 246
creating electrical connectors for, 237
cutting electric plates for, 237–238
definition of, 219
dry bulb temperature type of, 232–233
ideas for creation of, 245–246
measuring GSR (Galvanic Skin Response) for, 240–241
measuring humidity for, 232
plotting temperature errors for, 229–230
raw value versus voltage input for, 242
RCX input for passive sensors, 227–228
using 2.2K ohm fixed resistor with, 228
using alligator clips with, 202–222
using battery testers with, 243–244
using coin detectors with, 222
using cut electric plate connector with, 237
using cut wire connector with, 223
using DC motors with, 245
using dual row terminal block with, 225, 230
using NQC to correct temperature for, 229
using potentiometer with, 227
using psychrometers with, 232
using relative humidity sensors as, 232–234
using RIS (Robotics Invention System) software with, 228
using stick-in-ring switches with, 224–225
using Terminal block temperature sensor with, 225–226
using Tfixed corrected temperature with, 229
using thermistors with, 231–232
voltage input type of, 242–244
wire strippers for making of, 223
pbForth, 5, 7. *See also* Forth
and LCD display, 26
battery consumption and, 84
bit position values in, 97
conditionals and bitwise operators in, 104–107
custom firmware, 13–14
defining new words for, 101–104
downloading, 83
extensibility of, 79–80
fundamentals of, 85–88
generating output to, 89–95
installing, 83–84
interactivity of, 79–80
interpreted quality of, 79–80
looping in, 110–111
math expressions in, 96
online support for, 84
RAM allocation in, 83

sending output to IR (InfraRed) port from, 89–90
signed versus unsigned numbers in, 97–101
standard images for, 84
system firmware for, 83
system hardware for, 82
user programs for for, 83
using on RCX, 82
versus Forth, 85
Web site for, 84
pbForth interpreter
case-sensitivity of, 88
storage of, 88
pbForth kernel, 83–84
pbforth.srec and pbmax.srec standard images for pbForth, 84
PC (printed circuit) boards
bill of materials for, 279
placement of components on, 273
removing solder bridges from, 276
snapping, cutting, and finishing, 271–272
soldering parts of, 272–276
pdedu.srec standard image for pbForth, 84
peak light reading
finding, 144–145
scanning for, 142–144
PEEK statements, 89
Percentage sensor mode, 23–24
photo sensor sensitivities, 239
photocell passive sensors, 238–239
physical versus user-defined resources in RCX 2.0 Firmware, managing, 65
pins on LM324N, bending, 258–259
pitches, specifying for sound in legOS, 183
plus (+) math expression in Forth, 96
POKE statements, 89
positive binary numbers, converting to decimals, 98–99
postfix notation for Forth expressions, 95
potentiometer, using with passive sensors, 227
power circuit part placement table, 253
power level, adjusting for RCX output, 17
POWER_GET Forth word, 102
powered sensors, 18, 219. *See also* passive sensors
amplified voltage input for, 263
amplifier circuit for, 261–263, 261–263
amplifier part placement for, 262
bill of materials for, 279–281
buffered voltage input for, 261
building boxes for, 278
differential light type of, 263–265
packaging, 277–278
sound type of, 266–271
using buffer circuits with, 258–260
using R2 and R3 resistors with, 261–263
Web site for, 279

Pressed event type in RCX 2.0 Firmware, 68
PREV state, using to track changes in switch state, 113–114
Prgm button
  in legOS, 164, 165
  in RCX, 111–112
printed circuit boards, 271–272
priorities for tasks, range in NQC, 65
processed value for sensors, 19
programmable bricks, 3
programs, advantages of breaking into small pieces, 49
Proudfoot, Kekoa, 4, 89, 186
psychrometers, using with passive sensors, 232
Pulse Count sensor mode, 23–24
pulse event type in RCX 2.0 Firmware, 70
pushbuttons in RCX, 111–117
PWM (Pulse Width Modulation), using to create power levels for RCX, 17

Q

Q learning algorithm, using with Trailerbot, 197–198
Q scores, using with Trailerbot, 209–211
Q values, using to move Trailerbot, 208
queued sounds in System ROM of RCX, 26–27

R

RAM allocation in pbForth, 83
random walk behavior of Seeker robot, 41, 44
random() function, using with legOS Seeker, 171
range events in RCX 2.0 Firmware, 71–72
range overflow of signed numbers, 100
raw battery value in RCX, converting to battery voltage, 100
raw light sensor, using with Seeker robot, 133–134
Raw sensor mode, 23–24
raw sensor value, determining, 19, 130
raw sensors, using with legOS, 161
raw values
  adjusting for passive sensors, 235
  versus voltage input for passive sensors, 242
RCX
  adding to Seeker robot, 32–33
  adjusting power level of output for, 17–18
  architecture of, 11–14
  basics of, 89–95
  battery power for, 16
  converting raw battery value to battery voltage, 100
  default display mode for, 58
  display system for, 93–94
  firmware on, 83
  hardware for, 14–15
  IR (InfraRed) interface for, 15
  learning details of, 81–83

output directions for, 16
output ports for, 16
positioning for testing, 120
preparing for manual shutdown, 84
programming for wet and dry bulb temperature sensors, 233
running internal drivers for, 120
sensor ports for, 18–19
sound system in, 94–95
system sounds for, 26–27
using pbForth on, 82
RCX 1 and RCX2 part placements on sensor power circuit, 253
RCX 2.0 Firmware, 8, 13
  behavior of timer display in, 58
  boolean value events in, 70
  click events in, 73–74
  display enhancements in, 57–59
  downloading, 53–54
  edge event type in, 70
  enhancements to accessing arrays with, 60–63
  event configuration in, 69
  event monitoring in, 68–69
  events feature in, 68–76
  managing access control of resources with, 64–67
  message events in, 74
  miscellaneous feature enhancements in, 76
  pressed event type in, 70
  pulse event type in, 70
  released event type in, 70
  requirements for, 53
  sample program, 55
  using local variables with, 56–57
RCX Code, 6, 41–42
RCX
  input for passive sensors, 227–228
  Internals Web site, 4
  powered interface, 250
  programmable brick, 3
  pushbuttons, 111–117
  raw readings, adjusting for passive sensors, 235
  reading with buffer circuit, 261
  ROM, disassembly of, 89
  sensors and motors, 107–110
  versus Scout, 6–7
RCX_BUTTON Forth word, 93
RCX_INIT Forth word, 91
RCX_power Forth word, 102
RCX_SOUND Forth word, 91
RDS (Robotics Discovery System), 6–7
relative humidity sensors, using as passive sensors, 232–234
released event type in RCX 2.0 Firmware, 70
resistors
  bill of materials for, 279
  in optointerrupter powered sensors, 256

in sensor measurement circuits, 254–255
using with sound powered sensors, 266
resources, managing access control with RCX 2.0
        Firmware, 64–67
Return key, using with Forth, 88–89
REVERSE state, setting for Seeker robot, 123
rewarding Trailerbot, 210–211
RIS (Robotics Invention System) software
        using with passive sensors, 228
        version 1.0, 3
        version 1.5, 6
        version 2.0, 8
ROT Forth word, 103
rotation, creating for Trailerbot, 198–200
Rotation sensor mode, 23, 25
rotation sensors, 18, 20
        adding to Trailerbot (legOS), 196–197
        building Trailerbot with (legOS), 190197
        locating wires for (Seeker robot), 32–33
        resolution of, 182
        using with legOS, 181–183
rotation.c legOS program, 181–182
RS# (Radio Shack) for passive sensor parts, 219
rubber bands
        tightening for Seeker robot, 40
        using to construct Seeker robot, 34
Run button, 110–112, 117
running man in legOS, removing, 214
run-time of words, testing with low-resolution
        timers, 140–141

S

sampling sensors, 19
SCAN.TXT pbForth programs, 142–145
Scout programmable brick, 6
SDK (Software Development Kit), for RIS 2.0, 8
seek behavior for Seeker robot, 50
seekbump.nqc program, 46–49
seekbump_access.nqc program, tasks in, 66–67
seekbump_event.nqc, main task for, 75–76
Seeker (legOS) versus Seeker (NQC), 179–180
Seeker application, running, starting, and
        stopping, 146–148
Seeker robot (NQC). *See also* legOS Seeker
        adding motors to, 32–33
        adding RCX to, 32–33
        adding wires to, 32–33
        averaging light sensors for, 134–138
        bum.nqc light–seeking program for, 41–42
        bump and seek behaviors of, 50
        bumping and seeking with, 44–50
        constructing initial bumper support for, 34
        construction of, 31–37
        creating event to detect bumping by, 75–76
        detecting bright light with, 36
        determining threshold value for, 43
        displaying motor states for, 122–130
        finding and avoiding obstacles to, 146

identifying normal state of touch sensor for, 40
introduction to, 31
light sensor and thresholds for, 141–148
making it see and feel, 130–138
motor indicator display codes for, 123
moving, 120–122
reinforcing with beams, 36
running bump.nqc program for, 39–40
running bumper program in RCX code, 38
seeking light with, 41–44
sensor indicators for, 40
setting baseline value for, 46
setting states for, 123
sounds emitted by, 44
strategies for detecting and navigating
        around obstacles by, 36–41
testing and troubleshooting, 40–41
updating motor indicators on LCD for, 124–125
using access control to coordinate bump and
        seek behaviors for, 66–67
using calibration process to set thresholds
        for, 46
using events with, 74–76
using low-resolution timers with, 139–141
using raw light sensor with, 133–134
using timers with, 138–141
using touch sensors as counters in, 132–133
using touch sensors as detectors in, 130–132
using touch sensors in boolean mode with, 131
viewing sensor 2 for, 44
seeker.c legOS program, 171–179
semaphores, legOS support for, 170
sensor creation and manipulation of Forth words,
        133–134
sensor indicators for Seeker robot, 40
sensor measurement circuits, 254–256
sensor modes, 19, 21, 23–25
sensor ports for RCX, 18–19
sensor power circuit, 250–254
        current flow through, 251
        testing, 254
sensor slope, 21
sensor types, 19–20
sensor values, determining range for, 71
SENSOR_BOOK Forth word, 108
SENSOR_BOOL_SHOW Forth word, 132
SENSOR_INIT Forth word, 107
SENSOR_MODE Forth word, 108
SENSOR_PASSIVE Forth word, 108
SENSOR_RAW Forth word, 130
SENSOR_READ Forth word, 108
SENSOR_TYPE Forth word, 108
SENSOR_X, using with legOS raw sensors, 161
sensors, 5
        and motors in RCX, 107–110
        sampling, 19
        setting up in counting mode for Seeker robot,
                132–133
servo monitors, finding extensions for, 81

short circuits, avoiding on electronic breadboard, 253
SHOW_CONDITION Forth word, 104–105
SHOW_NUMBER Forth word, testing, 101–102
SHOWMOTOR1.TXT pbForth program, 124–125
signed integer math, 98
signed versus signed numbers in pbForth, 97–101
skid, building for Trailerbot (legOS), 191–192
slash (/) math expression in Forth, 96
sleep functions in legOS, 167
slope parameter for boolean conversions, 21–22
software for pbForth, 83
solder
    adding to connections on PC (printed circuit) boards, 274
    flowing around connections on PC (printed circuit) boards, 275
solder bridges on PC (printed circuit) boards, removing, 276
solder joints
    bad examples of, 275
    making on PC (printed circuit) boards, 274
soldering irons, cleaning, 273
soldering parts of PC (printed circuit) board, 272–276
Sound and System ROM layer of RCX, 26–27
sound powered sensors, 266–271
    bill of materials for, 281
    capacitors on, 266
    completion of, 276–277
    MIC (microphone) on, 266–267
    part placement of, 267–268
    signals in, 268–270
sound, using with legOS, 183–186
sound.c legOS program, 184–185
SOUND_GET Forth word, 91
SOUND_PLAY Forth word, 91
sounds emitted by Seeker robot, 44
SourceForge Web site, 151
speaker, accessing in legOS, 183
speed functions in legOS, 156–157
SPIRIT.OCX component of RIS 1.0 SDK, 8
stack. *See* Forth stack
stack-neutral Forth words, 141
standard firmware, 12–13, 27–29
    communication feature of, 29
    versus custom firmware, 13–14
    and LCD display, 25
star (*) math expression in Forth, 96
star-slash (*/) math expression in Forth, 96
star-slash-mod (*/MOD) math expression in Forth, 96
steering_results array, using with Trailerbot, 203–208
stick-in-ring switches, using with passive sensors, 224–225
store (!) Forth word, 90

strings, printing in Forth, 90
SWAP Forth word, 86–87, 102
switch state, tracking changes in, 113–114
switching diodes in sensor power circuit, 250–251
system firmware for pbForth, 83
system hardware for pbForth, 82
system ROM codes for sensor modes, 23
System ROM layer of RCX, 12, 26–27, 82–83
system software for pbForth, 81
system sounds
    playing in Forth, 91
    for RCX, 26–27, 94–95

T

table lookups, using as alternative to nested IF structures, 125–126
tachometers, 244–245
Target light value for Seeker robot, 44
TECHNIC sets, 3
temperature errors, plotting for passive sensors, 229–230
temperature sensors, 18, 20, 225–232
temporary wire buffer-part placement, 260
Terminal block temperature sensor, using with passive sensors, 227–228
test resistors, bill of materials for, 279
Tfixed corrected temperature, using with passive sensors, 229
thermistors, 225–226, 229
    part cross-reference list for, 246
    using with passive sensors, 231–232
threading in legOS, 168–169
Tic Tac© boxes, packaging powered sensors in, 278
tick (') Forth word, 125, 139
timed delay, using high–resolution timers with, 139
timekeeping in standard firmware, 28
timer display in RCX 2.0 Firmware, behavior of, 58
TIMER.TXT pbForth programs, using with Seeker robot, 139–140
timers, using with Seeker robot, 138–141
tones emitted by Seeker robot, 44
touch sensors, 18, 20
    adding for bumper of Seeker robot, 36
    as counters in Seeker robot, 132–133
    as detectors in Seeker robot, 130–132
    creating non-directional type for mobile robots, 224–225
    identifying normal state for Seeker robot, 40
    setting RCX input port for, 221
    using in boolean mode for Seeker robot, 131
    using with legOS, 162–163
touch.c legOS program, 162–163
TOUCH1.TXT pbForth program, 130–132
TOUCHCOUNT.TXT pbForth program, 132–133
trailer for Trailerbot (legOS)
    attaching to main body, 196
    constructing, 194–195

determining position of, 196
learning capabilities of, 197–198
Trailerbot
building, 190–197
controlling actions of, 200–202
learning from experiments with, 212–213
moving, 204–208
rewarding, 210–211
running, 211–212
"seeing" capabilities of, 198–200
trailerbot.c legOS program, 198
transcendental numbers, managing, 100–101
triangles beneath sensor ports for Seeker robot, 40
tubing for waterproof temperature sensors, 232
turtle-like robots created with stick—in-ring
    switches, 224
two-drop (2DROP) and two-dupe (2DUP) Forth
    words, 103
type sizes, managing in legOS, 187

U

u notation in Forth glossaries, 106–107
U. (u-dot) Forth word, 90, 99, 130
U< (u-less-than) operator in Forth, 106
U1 Pin1 LM324N bumper part placement, 260
Ultimate Accessory Pack for MINDSTORMS, 186
unlock firmware failed firmdl3 error message,
    diagnosing, 154
unsigned int type, managing in legOS, 187
upper limit parameter, using with range events in
    RCX 2.0 Firmware, 71–72
Upward Tones sound in RCX, 26
user display mode in RCX 2.0 Firmware, 57–58

V

values, rational approximations for, 100–101
variables
    consequences of displaying in RCX, 58–59
    in Forth, 142
    returning addresses of (Forth), 91, 93
    storing in standard firmware, 28
vectored execution, 125–126, 140
vectors, playing for sounds in legOS, 183
View button
    in legOS, 164–165
    in RCX, 111–112

View mode of RCX, determining threshold value
    for Seeker robot with, 43–44
viewing sensor 2 for Seeker robot, 44
Villa, Luis, 5
Visual Basic
    AA battery tester program in, 243–244
    biofeedback training program in, 240–241
    correcting temperature for passive sensors
        with, 229
    humidity sensor program in, 233
volatile firmware on RCX, 83
voltage input passive sensors, 242–244
voltage on + input, determining for differential
    light powered sensors, 265
voltmeters, using to test power sensor circuits, 254

W

wait.c legOS program, 168–169
wait_event legOS function, 167–169
wakeup_t legOS function, 167–168
Walter, W. Grey, 224
watch system clock in standard firmware, 28
waterproof temperature sensor, 231–232
weighted averages, 134–136
wet bulb temperature sensor, 232–233
wheels for Trailerbot (legOS), selecting size of, 195
wire strippers for making passive sensors, 223
wires
    acquiring for cut wire connectors, 223
    adding to Seeker robot, 32–33
    stripping insulation from when making
        passive sensors, 223
wiring, adding to Trailerbot (legOS), 193
WORD_TIME Forth word, 140
words in Forth dictionary. *See* Forth words

X

XOR operator in Forth, 107

Z

zero equal (0=) operator in Forth, 106
zero-less-than (0<) operator in Forth, 107

The Story Behind Apress

APRESS IS AN INNOVATIVE PUBLISHING COMPANY devoted to meeting the needs of existing and potential programming professionals. Simply put, the "A" in Apress stands for the "author's press™." Our unique author-centric approach to publishing grew from conversations between Dan Appleman and Gary Cornell, authors of best-selling, highly regarded computer books. They wanted to create a publishing company that emphasized quality above all—a company whose books would be considered the best in their market.

To accomplish this goal, they knew it was necessary to attract the very best authors—established authors whose work is already highly regarded, and new authors who have real-world practical experience that professional software developers want in the books they buy. Dan and Gary's vision of an author-centric press has already attracted many leading software professionals—just look at the list of Apress titles on the following pages.

Would You Like to Write for Apress?

APRESS IS RAPIDLY EXPANDING its publishing program. If you can write and refuse to compromise on the quality of your work, if you believe in doing more then rehashing existing documentation, and if you are looking for opportunities and rewards that go far beyond those offered by traditional publishing houses, we want to hear from you!

Consider these innovations that we offer every one of our authors:

- Top royalties with *no* hidden switch statements. For example, authors typically only receive half of their normal royalty rate on foreign sales. In contrast, Apress' royalty rate remains the same for both foreign and domestic sales.

- A mechanism for authors to obtain equity in Apress. Unlike the software industry, where stock options are essential to motivate and retain software professionals, the publishing industry has stuck to an outdated compensation model based on royalties alone. In the spirit of most software companies, Apress reserves a significant portion of its equity for authors.

- Serious treatment of the technical review process. Each Apress book has a technical reviewing team whose remuneration depends in part on the success of the book since they, too, receive a royalty.

Moreover, through a partnership with Springer-Verlag, one of the world's major publishing houses, Apress has significant venture capital behind it. Thus, Apress has the resources both to produce the highest quality books *and* to market them aggressively.

If you fit the model of the Apress author who can write a book that gives the "professional what he or she needs to know™," then please contact any one of our editorial directors, Gary Cornell (gary_cornell@apress.com), Dan Appleman (dan_appleman@apress.com), or Karen Watterson (karen_watterson@apress.com), for more information on how to become an Apress author.

Apress Titles

ISBN	LIST PRICE	AVAILABLE	AUTHOR	TITLE
1-893115-01-1	$39.95	Now	Appleman	Dan Appleman's Win32 API Puzzle Book and Tutorial for Visual Basic Programmers
1-893115-23-2	$29.95	Now	Appleman	How Computer Programming Works
1-893115-09-7	$24.95	Now	Baum	Dave Baum's Definitive Guide to LEGO MINDSTORMS
1-893115-84-4	$29.95	Fall 2000	Baum, Gasperi, Hempel, Villa	Extreme MINDSTORMS
1-893115-82-8	$59.95	Fall 2000	Ben-Gan/Moreau	Advanced Transact-SQL for SQL Server 2000
1-893115-14-3	$39.95	Winter 2000	Cornell/Jezak	Visual Basic Add-Ins and Wizards: Increasing Software Productivity
1-893115-85-2	$34.95	Winter 2000	Gilmore	A Programmer's Introduction to PHP 4.0
1-893115-17-8	$59.95	Now	Gross	A Programmer's Introduction to Windows DNA
1-893115-86-0	$34.95	Now	Gunnerson	A Programmer's Introduction to C#
1-893115-10-0	$34.95	Now	Holub	Taming Java Threads
1-893115-04-6	$34.95	Now	Hyman/Vaddadi	Mike and Phani's Essential C++ Techniques
1-893115-79-8	$49.95	Fall 2000	Kofler	Definitive Guide to Excel VBA
1-893115-75-5	$44.95	Now	Kurniawan	Internet Programming with VB
1-893115-19-4	$49.95	Now	Macdonald	Serious ADO: Universal Data Access with Visual Basic
1-893115-06-2	$39.95	Now	Marquis/Smith	A Visual Basic 6.0 Programmer's Toolkit
1-893115-22-4	$27.95	Now	McCarter	David McCarter's VB Tips and Techniques
1-893115-76-3	$49.95	Now	Morrison	C++ For VB Programmers
1-893115-80-1	$39.95	Fall 2000	Newmarch	A Programmer's Guide to Jini Technology
1-893115-81-X	$39.95	Fall 2000	Pike	SQL Server: Common Problems, Tested Solutions
1-893115-20-8	$34.95	Now	Rischpater	Wireless Web Development
1-893115-24-0	$49.95	Now	Sinclair	From Access to SQL Server
1-893115-16-X	$49.95	Now	Vaughn	ADO Examples and Best Practices

ISBN	LIST PRICE	AVAILABLE	AUTHOR	TITLE
1-893115-83-6	$44.95	Fall 2000	Wells	Code Centric: T-SQL Programming with Stored Procedures and Triggers
1-893115-05-4	$39.95	Fall 2000	Williamson	Writing Cross-Browser Dynamic HTML
1-893115-02-X	$49.95	Now	Zukowski	John Zukowski's Definitive Guide to Swing for Java 2
1-893115-78-X	$49.95	Fall 2000	Zukowski	Definitive Guide to Swing for Java 2, Second Edition

To order, call (800) 777-4643 or email sales@apress.com.